For
Professor Kenneth Binmore

Jung Soon Paik
NOV. 1, 2001
at Institute for Advanced Study
Princeton, USA

Contractarian Liberal Ethics
and the Theory
of Rational Choice

American University Studies

Series V
Philosophy
Vol. 122

PETER LANG
New York • San Francisco • Bern
Frankfurt am Main • Berlin • Wien • Paris

Jung Soon Park

Contractarian Liberal Ethics and the Theory of Rational Choice

PETER LANG
New York • San Francisco • Bern
Frankfurt am Main • Berlin • Wien • Paris

Library of Congress Cataloging-in-Publication Data

Park, Jung Soon
    Contractarian liberal ethics and the theory of
rational choice / Jung Soon Park.
        p. cm. — (American university studies. Series V,
    Philosophy ; vol. 122)
        Includes bibliographical references.
        1. Decision-making (Ethics).   2. Liberalism.
    3. Social contract.   I. Title.   II. Title: Rational choice.
    III. Series.
    BJ1419.P37   1992   171—dc20   91-18282
    ISBN 0-8204-1566-9   CIP
    ISSN 0739-6392

The paper in this book meets the guidelines for permanence and
durability of the Committee on Production Guidelines for
Book Longevity of the Council on Library Resources.

© Peter Lang Publishing, Inc., New York 1992

Printed in the United States of America.

Table of Contents

List of Tables

List of Abbreviations

AST   Nozick, Robert. *Anarchy, State, And Utopia*. New York: Basic Books, 1974.

LE   Hobbes, Thomas. *Leviathan*. ed. with Introduction. C.B. Macpherson. Harmondsworth: Penguin Books, 1968.

MA   Gauthier, David. *Morals By Agreement*. Oxford: Clarendon Press, 1986.

SC   Rousseau, Jean-Jacques. *Of The Social Contract*. Trans. Charles M. Sherover. New York: Harper & Row, 1984.

ST   Locke, John. *The Second Treatise Of Government* in *Two Treatises Of Government*. ed. Peter Laslett. New York: A Mentor Book, 1963.

TJ   Rawls, John. *A Theory of Justice*. Cambridge: The Belknap Press of Harvard University Press, 1971.

- - - - - - - - - - - - - - - - - - - -

C   Collective Rationality

CM   Constrained Maximization or -er

FR   Free-rider Problem or Free rider.

D   Non-Dictatorship

I   Independence of Irrelevant Alternatives

MRB   The Principle of Maximin Relative Benefit

MRC   The Principle Minimax Relative Concession

NPD   N- or Multi-Person PD

P   Pareto Principle

PD   Prisoner's Dilemma

SM   Straightforward Maximization or -er.

Acknowledgments

This work is the published version of my Ph.D. dissertation, "Contractarian Liberal Ethics and the Theory of Rational Choice" (Emory University, Department of Philosophy, 1990: copyright by Jung Soon Park) with minor changes. First and foremost I would like to thank Nicholas Fotion. Without his philosophic advice and personal encouragement this work could never have been brought to fruition. Both James Gouinlock and Donald Livingston have been of invaluable assistance to me in the completion of this work. Robert McCauley and Donald Rutherford are to be thanked for reading and offering comments on the manuscript. In addition, Gerard Elfstrom and Janice Fotion helped me at various stages of the development of the manuscript. I would also like to thank all the faculty, student, and staff members of the Philosophy Department of Emory University for giving me their unforgettable instruction, friendship, and support. I am proud that I served my philosophic apprenticeship in that department.

Grateful acknowledgment is made to the following publishers of quoted material for permission to reprint from their sources.

Table 3 is reprinted from T.C. Schelling, "Some Thoughts on the Relevance of Game Theory to the Analysis of Ethical Systems," in *Game Theory in the Behavioral Sciences*. Ira R. Buchler and Hugo G. Nutini, editors (Pittsburgh: University of Pittsburgh Press, 1969), p.50 by permission of the University of Pittsburgh Press. Copyright © 1969 by University of Pittsburgh Press.

Table 4 is reprinted from Allen Buchanan, "Revolutionary Motivation and Rationality," in *Philosophy & Public Affairs*, vol.9 (1979), p.64 by permission of Princeton University Press. Copyright © 1979 by Princeton University Press.

Tables 6 and 7 are reprinted from David Gauthier, *The Logic of Leviathan: The Moral and Political Theory of Thomas Hobbes* (Oxford: Clarendon Press, 1969), pp.79, 85 by permission of Oxford University Press. Copyright © 1969 by David Gauthier.

Table 8 is reprinted from R. Duncan Luce and Howard Raiffa, *Games and Decisions* (New York: John Wiley & Sons, Inc., 1957), p. 285 by permission of John Wiley & Sons, Inc. Copyright © 1957 by John Wiley & Sons, Inc. Copyright of *Games and Decisions* has been transferred to Dover Publications, Inc., 31 East 2nd Street, Mineola, NY 11501, which recently reissued the book in paperback. I want to thank Professor R. Duncun Luce and Dover Publications, Inc. for permission to reprint.

Table 9 is reprinted from Michael D. Resnik, *Choices: An Introduction to Decision Theory* (Minneapolis: University of Minnesota Press, 1987), Table 2-29, p.38 by permission of the University of Minnesota Press.   Copyright © 1987 by the University of Minnesota.

Table 13 is reprinted from Roberto Mangabeira Unger, *Knowledge and Politics* (New York: The Free Press, 1975), Figure 2, p.289 by permission of The Free Press, A Division of Macmillan, Inc. Copyright © 1975 by Roberto Mangabeira Unger.

Special acknowledgment is made to Oxford University Press for allowing me to use extensive quotes from David Gauthier, *Morals By Agreement* (Oxford: Clarendon Press, 1986). Copyright © 1986 by David Gauthier. Reprinted by permission of Oxford University Press. And also to Harvard University Press for allowing me to quote numerous portions of John Rawls, *A Theory of Justice* (Cambridge, Massachusetts: The Belknap Press of Harvard University Press, 1971). Copyright © 1971 by the President and Fellows of Harvard College. Reprinted by permision of Harvard Unviersity Press.

To my parents

In the Différend

The algebra I enlist for this purpose is the new mathematical Theory of Games; and I hope, by showing how it can yield results, to encourage others as well as myself to pursue and apply it further. . . . Perhaps in another three hundred years' time economic and political and other branches of moral philosophy will bask in radiation from a source — theory of games of strategy — whose prototype was kindled round the poker tables of Princeton.

R.B. Braithwaite, *Theory of Games as a Tool For the Moral Philosopher*, pp.54-5.

With a stiff seriousness that inspires laughter, all our philosophers demanded something far more exalted, presumptuous, and solemn from themselves as soon as they approached the study of morality: they wanted to supply a *rational foundation* for morality — and every philosopher so far has believed that he has provided such a foundation. Morality itself, however, was accepted as "given." How remote from their clumsy pride was that task which they considered insignificant and left in dust and must — the task of description — although the subtlest fingers and senses can scarcely be subtle enough for it.

Friedrich Nietzsche, *Beyond Good And Evil*, p.97.

Chapter I

Introduction:
Why Contractarian Ethics?

A. The Philosophical Significance of the Emergence of Contractarian Ethics

In recent decades, one of the most conspicuous phenomena in the domain of moral and political philosophy has been the revival of the theory of social contract. The contemporary revival has been mainly initiated by John Rawls' magnum opus, *A Theory of Justice*.[1] This book has attracted wide interest in part because many believe that the contractarianism put forward in this book "constitutes the most appropriate moral basis for a democratic society" (TJ,p.vii).

In the view of the tradition of social contract theory, Hobbes, Locke, Rousseau and Kant are all regarded as contractarians in the following sense. Each gives a secularistic, voluntaristic, individualistic, and rationalistic variation on a historical or hypothetical political theory of consent as the foundation of government, civil society, and political obligation in general.[2] Thus, until Rawls, contractarianism, except for the Kantian formulation, was not widely considered as a moral philosophy. In contrast, Rawls' aim in *A Theory of Justice* was "to present a [moral] conception of justice which generalizes and carries to a higher level of abstraction the familiar theory of the social contract" (TJ,p.11).[3] By abstraction Rawls means that "we are not to think of the original contract as one to enter a particular society or to set up a particular form of government" (TJ,p.11). Furthermore, Rawls' contractarian ethics is a rationalistic and systematic endeavor to meet the normative vacuity of meta-ethical theory — the dominant form of theorizing in ethics in English-speaking world for most of the twentieth century.

To try to find a relationship between morality and rationality is not in itself a novel enterprise. Since Socrates, moral philosophers have sought the rational foundation of ethics in various ways. They often asked questions such as, Is justice profitable? Is the virtuous person the happy person? What motives are there for doing what is right? What are the reasons for being moral? Why should I be moral?[4]

It is possible to read each of these questions as viewing the basic structure of morality as something that can be meaningfully appraised by reference to the criterion of rationality—and in this sense as an object of deliberated and reasoned choice by participating individuals. Broadly speaking, the Enlightenment project and the traditional social contract theory can be classified as versions of this rationalistic tradition of ethics.

However, in the nineteenth and twentieth centuries, there was a retreat from this ideal. First, the historicist view severely attacked the rationalist ideal on the ground that the prevailing moral and political institutional structures lie beyond any process of rational evaluation and choice.[5] Accordingly, the meaning and value of the moral and political institutions should be grasped by understanding their positions in the inexorable historical process. Hegel's cunning of historical reason and Marx's dialectical materialism are typical cases of the historicist view. Second, the retreat was to a deeply pessimistic, cynical and nihilistic obscurantist view.[6] According to this view, the moral and political institutional arrangements are to be understood as nothing more than the Nietzschean expression of prevailing de facto power relations, the Freudian repression of the human psyche, or the outgrowth of blind accidental custom and tradition.[7] Third, in the first half of this century, normative moral and political philosophy was finally excommunicated from the domain of meaningful philosophical inquiries at least in the English-speaking world. This excommunication was one of the far-reaching consequences issuing from the concept of scientific rationality largely propounded by the logical positivists. They attempted to deny any rational content to normative moral discourse at all.[8] Under the devastating influence of logical positivism, ethical inquiry had to confine itself to so-called "meta-ethics" which is mainly concerned with the meaning and logical relationships of ethical terms. At the time, it appeared that the only available ethical position open to logical positivism was emotivism.

The emotivists and later the prescriptivists criticized the naturalists and intuitionists for making unfounded claims to moral knowledge and ignoring the noncognitive character of moral judgments. In turn, the noncognitivists were condemned for ignoring the role of reasons in morality and for their single-minded focus on meta-ethics to the exclusion of normative ethics.[9]

After the demise of logical positivism, ordinary language analysis of morality provided the impetus for a new movement in ethics which came to be known as "the good reasons approach."[10] The main argument of this approach was that people give reasons for their moral beliefs and actions, and that some of these reasons are considered good or sufficient. In other words, in accordance with ordinary language analysis, certain principles are certified as morally right in that they state what constitutes good reasons in ethics. According to Toulmin, "the reason" for a moral judgment consists in "the fact that it is used to harmonize people's actions."[11] Baier maintains that moral reasons "must be for the good of everyone alike."[12] Since, according to them, it is appropriate to ask for or give reasons in ethics, moral evaluation is not simply a matter of intuition, emotion, or pure individual [existential] choice.

As a consequence of this "good reasons approach," the positivist distinction between facts and values began to be called into question because it seemed that actions could be justified by social practices or by social facts. However, the debate continued as to whether or not, on the basis of promises or contracts, values can be derived from fact.[13] And several philosophers demanded a more rigid rational justification than the "good reasons approach."[14] Toulmin and Baier's way to undertake establishing the relationship between morality and reason was to take it as a given that moral behavior is rational, and then seek a way of bringing moral reasoning and moral judgments within the nature and scope of that rationality. However, the idea of accommodating rationality to morality by these means did not appeal to those philosophers who stressed the importance of finding what reason or justification there is for being moral in a more rigorous fashion.

Thus, to them, the good reasons approach could not be better than ethical intuitionism. Just as the latter tried to solve normative moral issues by appeal to the dogmatic intuitive pronouncements, so the good reasons approach tried to settle such issues by "linguistic fiat."[15] But a more serious criticism emerged with the following point.[16]

> This approach ignores the existence of rival moral principles and 'reasons', and it offers no arguments in support of its own principles. In particular, it does not even try to show how its 'moral reasons' have themselves been ascertained by reason, i.e. by reasoning.

Under these circumstances, many philosophers looked for the theory of rational choice as a way to solve the problems of the ordinary language approach. They hoped that the rationalist trend in contemporary ethics would become more rigorous once it became associated with the theory of rational choice.

The theory of rational choice is actually an assemblage of several subtheories such as value-utility theory, game theory, and collective decision theory.[17] In the last three decades, the theory of rational choice as a new inter-discipline of social sciences has emerged from various attempts to apply models of rational choice to individual consumer action, group activities, and to public policy issues. Paradigmatic examples of these models are suggested by Von Neuman and Morgenstern, Luce and Raiffa, and Arrow.[18] These models reflect the ideal of the rational economic man, i.e., *homo economicus*: "Act so as to get the most value you can for the least value expended."[19]

Braithwaite's *Theory of Games as a Tool for the Moral Philosopher*, for example, tried to solve a problem of distributive justice through the help of game theory.[20] Indeed, John Rawls started his career as a moral philosopher by characterizing morality as a rational decision procedure for solving the conflicts of interest between people in his early article, "Outline of a Decision Procedure for Ethics."[21] Later he applied this idea more systematically to the ethical foundation of social contract theory in his paper, "Justice as Fairness."[22] In this paper, Rawls flatly maintains the following:[23]

> Having the element of morality is not a matter of [pure individual] choice, or of intuiting moral qualities, or a matter of the expression of feelings or attitudes (the three interpretations between which philosophical opinion frequently oscillates).

Eventually in his culminating work, *A Theory of Justice*, Rawls constructed a full-blown contractarian ethics according to which principles of justice are based upon fair consent among rational self-interested contractors behind a veil of ignorance.

B. Contractarian Ethics, the Adoption of the Theory of Rational Choice, and Its Liberal Ideological Implication

The importance and practical consequences of Rawls' theory of justice can be summarized as follows. First, in view of the dominance of meta-ethical inquiries before the publication of his book, his theory of justice represents a substantial or normative construction of an ethical system. Second, his theory evokes a systematic revival of contractarian liberalism, which can compete with and possibly be "superior" to liberal versions of utilitarian theory (TJ,p.viii). Third, his theory, as a moderate egalitarian liberalism, can be seen "as a way of resolving a major political schism of our time, one which separates the libertarian right from the egalitarian left."[24] In other words, the major political schism between liberty and equality may find a reconciliation in Rawls' two principles of justice. His famous difference principle for equal distribution, compatible with the condition of greatest possible liberty principle, can be regarded as an attempt at such a reconciliation.

A primal thrust of this book gains its focus from the first point above, that is, Rawls' theory of justice as the contractarian construction of a substantial or normative ethical system. I am especially interested in an interpretation of Rawls' contractarian ethics as a project which allegedly deduces morality from rationality. In view of the problem of the relationship between morality and rationality in contemporary ethics, the concept of rationality is obviously a very crucial one in Rawls' contractarian ethics. After all, for Rawls, it provides a deduction of principles of justice from the ground of agreement between rational self-interested contractors.

The basic aim of this book, then, is a critical appraisal of the nature and limits of contractarian ethics, which has been propounded in John Rawls' *A Theory of Justice* and also David Gauthier's *Morals By Agreement*.[25] Gauthier's *Morals By Agreement* has also attracted a wide readership and stirred much critical response even in the short period of time after its publication. In part this is because he asserts that the bargaining theory of justice put forward in his book constitutes the most appropriate rational project for contractarian ethics. According to Gauthier, under his contractarian rational formulation, "morality is thus given a sure grounding in a weak and widely accepted conception of practical rationality. No alternative account of morality accomplishes this" (MA,p.17).

More specifically, this study will devote attention to Rawls and Gauthier's contractarian project in so far as they seek to deduce morality from the theory of rational choice. The significance of this topic on the contractarian project derives from the fact that Rawls and Gauthier make explicit documented pronouncements of a relationship between contractarian ethics and the theory of rational choice.

When Rawls introduces the main idea of his theory, he clearly points out that "the theory of justice is a part, perhaps the most significant part of the theory of rational choice" (TJ,p.16). Similarly, in the general overview of his theory, Gauthier proposes that "we shall develop a theory of morals as part of the theory of rational choice" (MA,pp.2-3). Understandably, then, in order to comprehend these two contractarian characterizations of morality as part of the theory of rational choice, we have to begin with their concepts of rationality. According to Rawls, "the concept of rationality must be interpreted as far as possible in the narrow sense, standard in economic theory, of taking the most effective means to given ends" (TJ,p.14). Correspondingly, for Gauthier, "the maximization concept of rationality is almost universally accepted and employed in the social sciences. ... [I]t lies at the core of economic theory, and is generalized in decision and game theory" (MA,p.8). In view of this, we can infer that Rawls and Gauthier basically share the standard concept of rationality, the value-neutral instrumental maximization concept of rationality, found in the theory of rational choice, especially microeconomics and decision theory.

The reasons for adopting such a concept of rationality can be summarized as follows. First, Rawls and Gauthier want morality to be grounded in a notion of rationality that is itself independent of moral notions. For them, this is a basic requirement for the justification of contractarian moral principles (TJ,p.17; MA,p.2).

Second, the value-neutral maximization concept of rationality is compatible with the general motivations of contracting parties in the circumstances of justice as characterized by Hume.[26] In these circumstances, conflicts of interest among people are prevalent, and so rational contracting parties are mutually disinterested, not altruistic (TJ,p.127; MA,p.113). Third, the value-neutral concept of rationality as "all-purpose means"[27] provides a condition for the possibility of a consensus in the contractarian liberal society, in which there is no absolute conception of *summum bonum*. This derives from the fact that value-neutral rationality is not a criterion for ends or substantial content of individual values. Thus individual autonomy on any one person's own conception of the good is possible and a plurality of individual goods is tolerantly guaranteed (TJ,p.447f; MA,p.339). Fourth, through the value-neutral concept of rationality, Rawls and Gauthier try to find an Archimedean neutral conception of justice. According to them, the derivation of such a conception must not be influenced by any particular substantial values that may, in turn, have been influenced by a particular social system (TJ,p.260f; MA,p.233).

In view of these reasons, the value-neutral concept of rationality seems to provide contractarian ethics with four grand methodological foundations. They are the justification for contractarian consensus, non-altruistic clear choice motivation, the possibility of contractarian consensus in the circumstances of pluralism or relativism of individual autonomous values, and a neutral criterion for a just society. This means that the theory of rational choice is fundamentally connected with the basic structures of contractarian ethics since it characterizes the procedure, chooser, circumstances, and object of contractarian choice. Thus it follows that this book will deal with the issue of rationality in contractarian ethics, not as a partial problem, but as an essential foundational problem. With the help of reliable criticisms of contractarian ethics, I will show that the theory of rational choice is no guarantee of these four foundations in view of four corresponding predicaments. These predicaments are the dilemma of circularity or immorality held between morality and rationality, indeterminacy between various rational choice models, incompetent assessment of the contents of individual values as well as insufficient political sensibility of prevalent conflicts of individual goods, and non-neutrality resulting from the futility of the flight from liberal historical cultures.

However, my arguments are not purely negative. In agreement with an observation that predicaments of contractarian ethics come from its rational foundationalistic and liberal individualistic premises, I will suggest a viable non- or anti-foundational reconstruction of contractarian liberal ethics which can survive fundamental criticisms of individualistic liberalism.[28] Thus, in dealing with the relationship between contractarian ethics and the theory of rational choice, this book shall cover the two important aspects of contractarian ethics, i.e., the methodological aspect of foundationalism and the substantial aspect of liberalism.

C. The Current Impasse in Contractarian Ethics

First of all, adopting the value-neutral instrumental maximization concept of rationality invites recalcitrant difficulties for the proposed justificatory deduction of morality. It precludes any proper assessment of the content of individual values since instrumental rationality regards individual values as given. Even though Rawls mentions deliberative rationality under full information, he does so only for the purpose of bringing about the formal consistency of value, and not for the purpose of finding a fully evaluative criterion (TJ,p.416. cf. counting blades of grass as someone's subjectively unique good or pleasure. TJ,pp.432-3). Furthermore, unconstrained rational maximization of individual interest is clearly immoral in the sense that an individual can increase his or her self-interest at the expense of others. Thus, morality and rationality seem to be incompatible. This incompatibility engenders a difficult problem for contractarianism as "the most promising vehicle for the deducing project" of morality from a non-moral rational basis.[29]

Rawls' original solution to this incompatibility problem is a so-called "rationality *cum* fairness" solution.[30] Rawls' argument is that rational contractors can strike an agreement issued from the maximin strategy in the fair original position, i.e., an initial condition behind of the veil of ignorance and with formal constraints. The maximin strategy — maximization of minimum interests — "tells us to rank alternatives by their worst possible outcomes: we are to adopt the alternative the worst outcome of which is superior to the worst outcomes of the others" (TJ,pp.152-3). In effect, this means that the contracting parties in the original position choose the alternative which benefits the least advantaged. Thus Rawls' argument produces restrictions that are fair in the sense necessary for the rational contract agreement to constitute a morality (TJ,pp.130-42).

However, one of the most common objections against Rawls' theory of justice is that his characterization of the original position is not morally neutral.[31] Objection against neutrality is deployed not only against the introduction of fairness in the formal sense, but also against the introduction of fairness as a substantial sense of morality. It has been pointed out that "the motivation, beliefs and indeed the very rationality of Rawls' 'individuals' are recognizably those of some modern, Western, liberal, individualistic men."[32] This means that value-neutral instrumental rationality does not guarantee the supposed neutral Archimedean criterion. In connection with foundationalism, this also means that "foundational theory does not, indeed could not, purify political reflection of all culture or context specific influences."[33] Consequently, Rawls' original position covertly employs a substantial theory of the good, i.e., a liberal theory of the good.[34] This position, then, appears to be basically against his avowal of the "thin theory of the good" as a proper ground for the possibility of contractarian consensus in face of value pluralism in the circumstances of justice (TJ,p.397).

Concerning the neutrality debate in the formal sense, the crucial issue is whether Rawls' introduction of fairness commits a fallacy of circularity in view of the contractarian deduction project of morality from rationality. In this regard, I think that, as we have already seen through his "rationality *cum* fairness" solution, Rawls chose to pursue a less radical deduction project in his *A Theory of Justice*. Rawls elaborates this less radical deduction project in his recent article, "Kantian Constructivism in Moral Theory."[35] His second thoughts on the deduction project rely on the distinction between "the Reasonable and the Rational." According to Rawls, the Reasonable is the contractor's capacity for a sense of justice to honor the fair terms of social cooperation represented by the prior restrictions imposed on their rational agreement.[36] Thus, Rawls has to painfully admit his serious mistake in the contractarian deduction project as follows.[37]

> The Reasonable, then, is prior to the Rational, and this gives the priority of right. *Thus it was an error in Theory (and a very misleading one) to describe a theory of justice as part of the theory of rational choice.* ... There is no thought of trying to derive the content of justice within a framework that uses an idea of the rational as the sole normative idea. That thought is incompatible with any kind of Kantian view.

Now Rawls' task is "to survey how the basic intuitive ideas drawn upon in justice as fairness are combined into a political conception of justice for a constitutional democracy."[38]   This possibility of combination is heavily dependent upon the viability of the so-called reflective equilibrium between intuitive ideas and a general conception of justice as a non-foundational coherentist moral methodology (TJ,p.20f). Thus, for Rawls, the original position is not a deductive basis from which justice principles are to be derived. This is a direct repudiation of the "fully deductive moral geometry" seeking for an Archimedean point which Rawls held out as his ideal in his *A Theory of Justice* (TJ,p.121). If this is so, can Rawls' later position still be called a contractarian ethics? According to Rawls' own criterion, "in a contract theory all arguments, strictly speaking, are to be made in terms of what would be rational to choose in the original position" (TJ,p.75).

At this juncture, David Gauthier's *Morals By Agreement* gives us a valuable opportunity to assess the capacity of the contractarian tradition to provide a rational foundation for ethics. Gauthier's principal philosophical interest has been in the development of contractarian moral theory within the context of the theory of rational choice since his first book, *Practical Reasoning*.[39] As his second book, *The Logic of Leviathan* suggests, he has been known as a critical proponent of Hobbesian contractarianism.[40] Since his well-acknowledged article in the forum of Rawls commentators, "Justice and Natural Endowment: Toward A Critique of Rawls' Ideological Framework,"[41] he has tried to provide an alternative contractarian ethics to Rawls' Kantian contractarian ethics. In view of the general task of contemporary ethics and his consistent endeavor for the viability of the contractarian rational project, his book, *Morals By Agreement*, as a final version of his contractarianism deserves to be fully investigated.

D. The Modus Operandi of the Study

Here I would like to introduce a *modus operandi* of this study as a critical appraisal of Rawls' retreat from the contractarian rational deduction project and Gauthier's rehabilitation of the project. The *modus operandi* is the two versions of contractarianism and their dilemma. Since the contractarian agreement is hypothetical, the first requirement is to characterize the initial situation of the rational agreement. Either this initial situation is fair or it is not. If it is not, then the rational agreement hinges on strategic rational bargaining power. Thus the outcome of the resulting bargaining cannot be morally fair. Furthermore, in this situation, sheer self-interested individual rationality leads to collective self-defeating irrationality.[42] But if we idealize the initial situation with a prior requirement of fairness, then it is question-begging. In the former case, the outcome of contractarian agreement is required by rationality alone, but it is not thereby justified as moral. In the latter case, the outcome is morally fair, but it is rationally optional. "Thus as a means of providing a rational foundation for morals the contractarian methodology is either irrelevant or circular."[43]

Furthermore, choosing between various choice models cannot be easily determined in the domain of the theory of rational choice.[44] In view of the fact that Rawls chooses maximin strategy—maximization of minimum interests, whereas Gauthier chooses the minimax concession bargaining strategy—minimization of maximum relative concession (TJ,p.153; MA,p.145), we witness an indeterminacy that comports poorly with axiomatic rational choice in the initial position. Thus Fishkin points out that "even slightly different accounts of impartiality and slightly different notions of relevant claims or interests in these imaginary situations yield drastically different results."[45] This means that the concept of value-neutral rationality cannot provide a clear choice motivation, which, as I have mentioned, is among the four methodological foundations of contractarian ethics. In later chapters, I will develop these considerations more fully into a contractarian trilemma between irrelevancy, circularity, and indeterminacy.[46]

In recent years, the most frequently compared versions of contractarianism are those of Hobbes and Rawls. These two versions compose the two horns of the dilemma.[47] We have already seen why Rawls' "rationality *cum* fairness" deduction project becomes prey to the second horn of circularity. Hobbes' typical description of the state of nature in *Leviathan* reveals well the first horn of moral irrelevancy in the mere maximization of individual rational self-interest.

Then, how does Gauthier try to solve the contractarian dilemma? Gauthier's contractarian deduction project starts from the apparent conflict between morality as a constraint of rationality and rationality as an unconstrained maximization of self-interest. Thus Gauthier's primary task is to show in a contractarian scheme that morality as constraint of rationality is an outcome of the very concept of rationality as maximization. As Gauthier admits, this task is a "seeming paradox" (MA,p.2). Yet, without solving this seeming paradox, he cannot achieve a contractarian rational deduction project.

First, Gauthier aims to find a way of escaping the second horn (circularity via a prior moral assumption) of the dilemma: "our concern ... is to do this [contractarian rational deduction project] without incorporating into the premises of our argument any of the moral conceptions that emerge in our conclusions" (MA,p.6). In other words, he has to show that if an individual utility maximizer "makes a choice about how to make further choices, he chooses, on utility-maximizing grounds, not to make further choices on those grounds" (MA,p.158). Second, he endeavors to escape the first horn (moral irrelevancy of rational bargaining agreement) of the dilemma by an introduction of a fair initial bargaining position, viz., the Lockean proviso for property acquisitions or rights. It "prohibits worsening the situation of others except where this is necessary to avoid worsening one's own position" (MA,p.203). Gauthier rejects the Hobbesian framework proposed by James Buchanan in which the initial endowments of the agents are defined by a state of anarchistic equilibrium that includes predation in the state of nature (MA,pp.193-99).[48] Thus Gauthier maintains that "fair procedures yield an impartial outcome only from an impartial initial position" (MA,p.191). In order to avoid the first horn of the dilemma (moral irrelevancy of rational bargaining agreement), Gauthier has to show that the introduction of the Lockean proviso is a fair impartial initial situation to the extent that the results of bargaining agreement are fair.

And also the introduction of the proviso must not be a victim of the first horn of the dilemma (circularity via prior moral assumptions).

Gauthier's strategy hinges heavily on rational compliance theory of the resultant principle from the fair initial bargaining position. However, the resultant principle of relative minimax concession turns out to be a principle for strict meritocracy. And whether its normative practicality appeals to all rational contractors is controversial. Furthermore the Lockean proviso does not seem to vindicate the avowed rational compliance from all contracting parties. On the one hand, for the least advantaged persons, the proviso is too weak since it concerns only the most advantaged persons' property rights. On the other hand, for the most advantaged persons, the proviso is too strong since it is irrational for them to follow the proviso in the natural interaction with the former. Therefore the appeal to the rational compliance theory does not guarantee the Lockean proviso. Then, should I conclude that Gauthier's contractarian rational deduction project "fails, but it is a heroic failure" as one commentator says?[49] I would like to reserve this conclusion for further inquiry.

This book will be composed of five chapters including introduction and conclusion. Chapter II will survey the scope and nature of the theory of rational choice. In that chapter, I will especially make reference to the concept of instrumental rationality and the paradoxes of rationality, that is, the Prisoner's dilemma, the Free-rider problem, and Arrow's impossibility theorem. However, I will avoid becoming overly involved in the problems of rational choice theory *per se*. I will treat them to the extent that the introduction of the theory of rational choice is sufficient for understanding the rational choice framework of morality in which the debate concerning the possibility of a contractarian deduction project takes place. In view of this limited concern, I will keep in mind the three kinds of contributions of rational choice theory to ethics, which Thomas C. Shelling classified in his helpful article, "Some Thoughts on the Relevance of Game Theory to the Analysis of Ethical Systems."[50]

Chapter III will critically investigate the aforementioned two strikingly contraposed versions of contractarianism, that of Hobbes and Rawls. First, I will show how a rational choice theoretic interpretation of traditional social contract theory represents a viable ethical system, and what problems remain to be solved especially in the case of Hobbes. In this chapter, even though I will briefly mention the basic differences between Hobbes, Locke, Rousseau and Kant, I will not attempt a full historical survey of the traditional theory of social contract. The first section of this chapter is a kind of foil against which we can understand how Rawls tries to revise Hobbes' contractarianism (which will be discussed in the second section) in connection with the two versions of contractarianism and their dilemma.

Chapter IV will explore and assess Gauthier's rational choice theoretic construction of contractarian ethics and his avowed endeavor to overcome the dilemma which holds between Hobbes and Rawls. In these two chapters, the basic intention is to investigate the success and failure of contractarian ethics to generate an adequate moral theory on its own terms, i.e., by its own standards. This means that I will not apply an independent moral standard to judge the adequacy of the contractarian model. Rather, in connection with the dilemma as a predicament of foundationalism, I will confine my inquiries to the internal problems of contractarian ethics.

Focusing my attention on the internal problems, however, does not mean that external criticisms of contractarian ethics will be ignored. Generally speaking, contemporary systematic rivals of contractarian ethics can be classified into libertarianism, utilitarianism, communitarianism, and Marxism. Throughout the history of social contract theory, it has had to face many formidable critics. Starting from Hume, we can list utilitarians like Bentham and Mill as well as others, like Hegel and Marx, as major critics of social contract theory.[51]

Even though I will briefly introduce classical critics as a point of departure for the discussion of the related issues in proper places, my primary concern is to treat systematic criticisms of contractarian ethics through contemporary proponents of the above mentioned rivals. Thus since Nozick's libertarian and Harsanyi's utilitarian criticisms of contractarian ethics represent a kind of in-house debate in the domain of liberal rationality, I will in due course (in Chapters III and IV) pay special attention to their criticisms.

With respect to libertarianism, I will follow Nozick's libertarian criticism of Rawls' difference principle on the ground that this principle disturbs the natural rights to basic endowments of the advantaged people in the Lockean proviso.[52]   As I have mentioned, Gauthier is in agreement with Nozick that the Lockean proviso is a basis of distributive justice.   However, Gauthier's proviso is different from Nozick's formulation, and Gauthier criticizes Nozick in various ways.

With respect to the utilitarian criticism, Harsanyi's rational reconstruction of utilitarianism will receive much attention, since he, like Rawls, claims that the utilitarian principle can be derived from rational agreement under uncertainty.[53] Harsanyi resorts to the equiprobability model, whereas Rawls uses the maximin strategy for his two principles of justice. Not surprisingly, Harsanyi's approach leads to average-utilitarianism since if everybody has equal probability of turning out to hold any position of society, he or she will choose a society which promotes the average utility of society. As we have seen, Gauthier objects to these two models and proposes his option of minimax rational bargaining. In face of this plurality of rational decision modelling, it is important to ask seriously whether we can find a meta-rationality to assess these different choice models or not in order to avoid the indeterminacy between various choice models.

Detailed treatment of non-liberal communitarian and Marxist criticisms of contractarian ethics is beyond the scope of this book. Rather, in view of the result of the inquiry concerning the liberal rationality debate, I will show how non-liberal criticisms are related to the internal problems of contractarian ethics and liberal rationality. In this connection I will briefly discuss whether communitarian or Marxist ethics can be viable alternatives to liberal ethics, especially contractarian ethics, as an agenda for the future of ethics.

Sandel and MacIntyre's communitarian criticisms of the contractarian liberalism, to anticipate things, are among the most widely discussed in the literature.[54]   Because of its heavy reliance on methodological individualism, liberalism has been subjected to three related criticisms: "incompleteness, insufficiency, and incoherence."[55]   Furthermore, the "abstractness" of contractarian liberal ethics can be added to this list of criticisms.[56] Beyond these criticisms, Sandel and MacIntyre go on to propose their own communitarian ethics. For them, we are what we are in terms of our membership in a community of shared meanings and values of intrinsic ends and virtues, not merely of instrumental values. Rawls provides a rejoinder to this kind of criticism in his recent articles.[57] In contrast, Gauthier maintains that his contractarian liberal ethics can accommodate communitarian ideals of affective morality and sociability (MA,pp.338-9).

As to the Marxists, even Marx severely scolded social contract bourgeois liberalism in much of his writing. In the *Grundrisse*, Marx pointed out that "Rousseau's *contrat social* ... makes naturally independent individuals come in contact and have mutual intercourse by contract."[58] This is "the fiction and only the aesthetic fiction of the small and great adventure stories [of Robinson Crusoe]."[59] In contemporary times, Macpherson charges that social contract theory is the market ideology of possessive individualism.[60] Rawls gives his rejoinder to Marx that his final communist society is an utopian society beyond justice (TJ,p.281). Gauthier, in turn, has many interesting things to say about Macpherson's charge in his paper, "The Social Contract as Ideology"[61], and "Liberal Individuals" in *Morals By Agreement* (Chap. XI). In connection with Gauthier's adoption of the Lockean proviso for exclusive property rights, I will critically compare Gauthier's contractarian liberal ethics with Marx's cynical view on the primitive accumulation of capital, and Macpherson's attack on the Lockean proviso in Chapter IV.

In the conclusion, Chapter V, I will first assess the success and failure of Rawls and Gauthier's rational foundationalistic deduction projects in view of the contractarian internal trilemma of circularity, irrelevancy, and indeterminacy. As a part of this process, I will have to determine whether this trilemma is real or not. Second, I will endeavor to discover what kinds of contributions the theory of rational choice can make to ethics. Third, I will make an overall appraisal of the possibility or impossibility of a defense of contractarian liberal rational ethics against its external criticisms. Here, the most crucial issue is whether contractarian rationality is the general ground of human nature or the rationality of a particular historical tradition.

Through these inquiries, I will derive instructive lessons from contractarian liberal ethics for the agenda of contemporary ethics: "After Contractarian Liberal Ethics: End or Transformation?"[62]

Notes

1 John Rawls, *A Theory of Justice* (Cambridge, Massachusetts: The Belknap Press of Harvard University, 1971). Subsequent references to this book will be TJ.

2 Michael Lessnoff, *Social Contract* (Atlantic Highlands, New Jersey: Humanities Press International Inc., 1986), pp.6f.

3 Here, I am not maintaining that moral and political philosophies should be separated. Since Plato and Aristotle, the two have been interwoven closely. The separation is essentially a modern phenomenon. See Robert Gordis, *Politics and Ethics* (Santa Barbara, California: Center for the Study of Democratic Institutions, 1961). However, in view of the fact that Rawls has recently tried to confine his theory of justice to a political conception of justice, the relation between the two must be reconsidered. Cf. Rawls, "Justice as Fairness: Political not Metaphysical," *Philosophy & Public Affairs*, 14 (1985), pp.223-53. For a general discussion of this problem, see David Schaefer, "'Moral Theory' Versus Political Philosophy: Two Approaches to Justice," *Review of Politics*, 39 (1977), pp.192-219.

4 William K. Frankena, "Rational Action in the History of Ethics," *Social Theory and Practice*, 9 (1983), pp.165f.

5 Edward F. McClennen, "Rational Choice and Public Policy: A Critical Survey,' *Social Theory and Practice*, 9 (1983), p.335. Besides the historicism, the evolutionist paradigm (the long process of cultural evolution of moral and political institutions beyond individual rational choices), the Hayekian spontaneous order (moral and political arrangements are "the result of human action but not of human design"), and Rorty's conception of contingency (human societies as historical contingencies rather than as expression of underlying, ahistorical human nature, or as realizations of suprahistorical goals) can be grouped in the same vein. For a good explanation of the evolution theory, see James M. Buchanan, *Explorations into Constitutional Economics* (Austin: Texas A & M University Press,1989), pp.44-5; Greta Jones, *Social Darwinism and English Thought* (Sussex: The Harvester Press,1980), ch.vii. "Rationality and Irrationality." For the Hayekian perspective, see Friedrich Hayek, *Law, Legislation and Liberty*. 3 vols. (Chicago: University of Chicago Press, 1973,1976,1979) and *The Fatal Conceit: The Errors of Socialism* (Chicago: University of Chicago Press,1989). We can find very helpful comments on Hayek in the symposium on "F.A. Hayek's Liberalism," *Critical Review*, 3 (1989). For Richard Rorty's

view, see mainly his *Contingency, Irony, and Solidarity* (Cambridge: Cambridge University Press,1989).

6   McClennen, p.336.

7   For a more detailed discussion, see Geoffrey Hawthorn, *Enlightenment and Despair*, 2nd ed. (Cambridge: Cambridge University Press, 1976); Peter Sloterdijk, *Critique of Cynical Reason*, trans. Michael Eldred (Minneapolis: University of Minnesota Press, 1987; original German ed. 1983); Donald A. Crosby, *The Specter of the Absurd: Sources & Criticisms of Modern Nihilism* (Albany: State University of New York Press, 1988).

8   John Rajchman and Cornell West, eds., *Post-Analytic Philosophy* (New York: Columbia University Press, 1985), "Introduction: Philosophy in America," p.xxii.

9   See Roger N. Hancook, *Twentieth Century Ethics* (New York: Columbia University Press, 1974); George C. Kerner, *The Revolution in Ethical Theory* (Oxford: Oxford University Press, 1966); and W.D. Hudson, *Modern Moral Philosophy*, 2nd ed. (New York: St. Martin's Press, 1970).

10 Joseph P. DeMarco and Richard M. Fox, eds., *New Directions in Ethics* (London: Routledge & Kegan Paul, 1986), p.11.

11 Stephen Toulmin, *An Examination of the Place of Reason in Ethics*, 2nd ed. (Chicago: The University of Chicago Press, 1986; lst. ed. 1950), p.145.

12 Kurt Baier, *The Moral Point of View* (Ithaca: Cornell University Press, 1958), p.200.

13 J. R. Searle, "How to derive 'ought' from 'is'," *The Philosophical Review*, 73 (1964) and James Thomson and Judith Thomson, "How not to Derive 'ought' from 'is'," *The Philosophical Review*, 73 (1964). Both articles are reprinted in Wilfrid Sellars and John Hospers, eds., *Readings in Ethical Theory*, 2nd ed. (Englewoood Cliffs: Prentice-Hall, 1970), pp.63-72, pp.73-85 respectively. For a more comprehensive treatment, see W.D. Hudson, ed., *The Is/Ought Question* (London: Macmillan, 1969).

14 John Rawls, "Review of Stephen Toulmin's *An Examination of the Place of Reason in Ethics*," *The Philosophical Review*, 60 (1951), pp.572-80. John Hospers, "Baier and Media on Ethical Egoism," *Philosophical Studies*, 12 (1961), pp.10-6.

15 Alan Gewirth, "The Future of Ethics," *Nôus*, 15 (1981), p.19

16 Ibid.

17 Michael D. Resnik, *Choices: An Introduction to Decision Theory* (Minneapolis: University of Minnesota Press, 1987).

18 J. Von Neuman and O. Morgenstern, *Theory of Games and Economic Behavior* (Princeton: Princeton University Press, 1944); R.D. Luce and H.

Raiffa, *Games and Decisions* (New York: Wiley, 1957); Kenneth J. Arrow, *Social Choice and Individual Values* (New York: John Wiley & Sons, 1951).

19 C. Dyke, *Philosophy of Economics* (Englewood Cliffs, New Jersey: Prentice-Hall, 1981), p.29. And also see Martin Hollis and Edward J. Nell, *Rational Economic Man: A Philosophical Critique of Neo-Classical Economics* (London: Cambridge University Press, 1975).

20 R.B. Braithwaite, *Theory of Games as a Tool for the Moral Philosopher* (Cambridge: Cambridge University Press, 1955).

21 Rawls, "Outline of Decision Procedure for Ethics," *The Philosophical Review*, 60 (1951), pp.177-97.

22 Rawls, "Justice as Fairness," *The Philosophical Review*, 67 (1958), pp.164-99. Rpt. in Sellars and Hospers, *Readings in Ethical Theory*, pp.578-95. See n.13.

23 Ibid., p.589.

24 H. Gene Blocker and Elizabeth H. Smith, eds., *John Rawls' Theory of Social Justice* (Athens: Ohio University Press, 1980), "Editors' Introduction," p.xiii.

25 David Gauthier, *Morals By Agreement* (Oxford: Clarendon Press, 1986). Hereafter abbreviated as MA in the text for citation. My basic aim does not mean that Rawls and Gauthier exhaust the list of contractarian ethicists. However, various contractarian ethical formulations in the works of G.R. Grice, James Buchanan, David Richards, T.M. Scanlon, and Jan Narveson remain too underdeveloped to be fully considered as definite ethical alternatives.

26 David Hume, *A Treatise of Human Nature*, ed. L.A. Selby-Bigge, 2nd ed. (Oxford: The Clarendon Press, 1978), bk.III, pt.II, sec.ii, and *An Enquiry Concerning the Principles of Morals*, ed. L.A. Selby-Bigge, 3rd ed. (Oxford: Clarendon Press, 1975), sec.iii, pt.i. The condition of moderate scarcity is the objective circumstances, and that of mutual disinterest is the subjective circumstances. For a detailed discussion of this matter, see TJ, sec.22, "the Circumstances of Justice."

27 Rawls, "The Priority of Right and Ideas of the Good," *Philosophy & Public Affairs*, 17 (1988), p.258. In view of this, it is natural that Rawls rejects perfectionism because of its ideal-regarding character (TJ,p.326). Thus Rawls make it clear that "systems of ends are not ranked in value" (TJ,p.19). Gauthier agrees with Rawls that "the theory of rational choice disclaims all concerns with the ends of action" (MA,p.26). Gauthier explicitly defends subjectivism and relativism of value (MA,p.55). However, Rawls' position is a kind of pluralism.

28 For contractarian ethics as foundationalism, see Evan Simpson, ed., *Anti-foundationalism and Practical Reasoning* (Edmonton: Academic Printing and Publishing,1987); Arthur Ripstein, "Foundationalism in Political Theory," *Philosophy & Public Affairs*, 16 (1987), pp.116-137, and Don Herzog,

Without Foundations: Justification in Political Theory (Ithaca: Cornell University Press, 1985). For contractarian ethics as liberalism, see Michael Sandel, ed., *Liberalism and Its Critics* (New York: New York University Press, 1984); Alfonso Damico, ed., *Liberals on Liberalism* (Totowa, New Jersey: Rowman & Littlefield, 1986), and Andrzej Rapaczynski, *Nature and Politics: Liberalism in the Philosophies of Hobbes, Locke, and Rousseau* (Ithaca: Cornell University Press, 1987).

29 David Braybrooke, "Social Contract Theory's Fanciest Flight," *Ethics*, 97 (1987), p.751.

30 Jody S. Kraus and Jules L. Coleman, "Morality and the Theory of Rational Choice," *Ethics*, 97 (1987), p.720.

31 The Objections against neutrality come from Mary Gibson, "Rationality," *Philosophy & Public Affairs*, 6 (1977), pp.193-225. Adina Schwartz, "Moral Neutrality and Primary Goods," *Ethics*, 83 (1983), pp.294-397. For a more detailed discussion, see Norman Daniels, ed., *Reading Rawls* (Oxford: Basil Blackwell, 1975; 2nd ed. with "New Preface" Stanford: Stanford University Press, 1989), "Introduction."

32 Steven Lukes, *Essays in Social Theory* (New York: Columbia University Press, 1977), p.189.

33 Alfonso J. Damico, "The Politics After Deconstruction: Rorty, Dewey, and Marx," in William J. Gavin, ed., *Context Over Foundation* (Dordrecht: D.Reidel Publishing Co., 1988), p.177.

34 William Galston, "Defending Liberalism," *The American Political Science Review*, 76 (1982), p.625, and see Patrick Neal, "A Liberal Theory of the Good?" *Canadian Journal of Philosophy*, 17 (1987), pp. 567-82.

35 Rawls, "Kantian Constructivism in Moral Theory," *The Journal of Philosophy*, 77 (1980), pp.515-72.

36 Ibid., pp.528-30.

37 Rawls, "Justice as Fairness: Political not Metaphysical," p.237. n.20. Emphasis mine.

38 Ibid., p.223.

39 David Gauthier, *Practical Reasoning* (Oxford: Clarendon Press, 1963).

40 Gauthier, *The Logic of Leviathan* (Oxford: Clarendon Press, 1969).

41 Gauthier, "Justice and Natural Endowment: Toward A Critique of Rawls' Ideological Framework," *Social Theory and Practice*, 3 (1974), pp.3-26.

42 This problem is the so-called paradoxes of rationality. The paradoxes of rationality are mainly discussed under the issue of "the Prisoner's Dilemma" and "the Free-rider Problem." We find a general survey of the paradoxes of

rationality in Richmond Campbell and Lanning Sowden, eds., *Paradoxes of Rationality and Cooperation* (Vancouver: The University of British Columbia Press, 1985). I will deal with this problem in Chapter II.

43 L.W. Sumner, "Justice Contracted," *Dialogue*, 16 (1987), p.524. This dilemma can be posed in terms of the absence or the presence of the veil of ignorance. See Michael Lessnoff, *Social Contract*, p.148, p.154. In connection with a dilemma of foundationalism, see Richard Dien Winfield, *Reason and Justice* (New York: State University of New York Press, 1988), p.11. For a more detailed discussion of it in view of rational choice theory, see C.A. Hooker, J.J. Leach, and E.F. McClennen, eds., *Foundations and Applications of Decision Theory*, vol.II: *Epistemic and Social Applications* (Dordrecht: D. Reidel Publishing Co., 1978), pp.xi-ii.

44 See Stephen W. Ball, "Choosing Between Choice Models of Ethics," *Theory and Decision*, 22 (1987), pp.209-24. And also Mark J. Machina, "'Rational' Decision Making Versus 'Rational' Decision Modelling?" *Journal of the Mathematical Psychology*, 24 (1981), pp.163-175.

45 James Fishkin, "Liberal Theory: Strategies of Reconstruction," in Damico, ed., *Liberals On Liberalism*, p.57.

46 Cf. Hans Albert's Münchhausen Trilemma of foundationalism, i.e., that all attempts to discover ultimate foundations result in either logical circularity, infinite regress, or an arbitrary end to the process of justification, in his *Treatise on Critical Reason*. trans. Marry Varney Rorty. (Princeton: Princeton University Press, 1985; original German ed., 1975), p.18.

47 Sumner, p.524. Cf. James M. Buchanan and Loren E. Lomasky, "The Matrix of Contractarian Justice," in Ellen Frankel Paul, Fred D. Miller, Jr., and Jefferey Paul, eds., *Liberty and Equality* (Oxford: Basil Blackwell, 1985), p.12f.

48 James Buchanan elaborates the anarchistic equilibrium in his *The Limits of Liberty: Between Anarchy and Leviathan* (Chicago: The University of Chicago Press, 1975). In connection with the contractarian dilemma, see Sumner, p.535 and Kraus and Coleman, p.725. See n.43, n.30.

49 Alan Nelson, "Economic Rationality and Morality," *Philosophy & Public Affairs*, 17 (1988), p.166.

50 Thomas C. Schelling, "Some Thoughts On the Relevance of Game Theory to the Analysis of Ethical Systems," in Ira R. Buchler and Hugo G. Nutini, eds., *Game Theory in the Behavioral Sciences* (Pittsburgh: University of Pittsburgh Press, 1969), pp.53-60. First, there are the ethical problems to which rational choice theory has already addressed itself, and about which some results are ready at hand. Second, there is the possible use of the theory of rational choice or some of its conceptual apparatus by those whose main concern is moral philosophy. Third, there are some ethical issues that tend to be raised by the general methodological assumptions of the theory of rational choice.

51 See J.W. Gough, *The Social Contract* (Oxford: Clarendon Press, 1936), and also Lessnoff, *Social Contract*.

52 Robert Nozick, *Anarchy, State, and Utopia* (New York: Basic Books, 1974), pp.183-228. Abbreviated as AST.

53 John C. Harsanyi, *Essays on Ethics, Social Behavior, and Scientific Explanation* (Dordrecht: D. Reidel Publishing Co., 1976).

54 Michael J. Sandel, *Liberalism and the Limits of Justice* (Cambridge: Cambridge University Press, 1982). Alasdair MacIntyre, *After Virtue*, 2nd ed. (Notre Dame: University of Notre Dame Press, 1984; 1st ed., 1981); *Whose Justice? Which Rationality?* (Notre Dame: University of Notre Dame Press, 1988).

55 Alfonso J. Damico, *Liberals On Liberalism*, "Introduction," p.1. The accusation of incompleteness argues that liberalism neglects the social formation of individual interests and how these formative processes impact upon individuals' public and private lives. The theory is said to be insufficient because it cannot sustain the praise or importance that liberals often accord such things as the public interest and political participation. And, finally, critics have often said that the theory is incoherent in that it cannot account for such things as subjects' obligations without drawing upon concepts alien to the individual model (Ibid., pp.1-2).

56 John Dunn, *Rethinking Modern Political Theory* (Cambridge: Cambridge University Press, 1985), p.163. Modern contractarianism offers an abstract and philosophically debilitated reverie on how ethical and political value should be conceived - not a relatively powerful account of how human beings have a good reason to *act* in the political settings in which they happen to find themselves (Ibid.).

57 Rawls, "The Idea of an Overlapping Consensus," *Oxford Journal of Legal Studies*, 7 (1987), pp.1-25, and also "The Priority of Right and Ideas of the Good."

58 *Grundrisse* (*Foundations of the Critique of Political Economy*) in *Karl Marx: Selected Writings*, ed. David McLellan (Oxford: Oxford University Press, 1977), p.346.

59 Ibid. In the communitarian vein, Marx found fault with contractarian liberalism that "None of the supposed rights of man ... goes beyond the egoistic man, man as he is, as a member of civil society; that is, an individual separated from the community, withdrawn into himself, wholly preoccupied with his private interest and acting with his private caprice."; "It has become the spirit of civil society, of the sphere of egoism and of the *bellum ominum contra omnes* (war of all against all)."; *On the Jewish Question* in *Karl Marx: Early Writings*, trans. and ed. T.B. Bottomore (New York: McGraw-Hill Book Company, 1963), pp.26, 15.

60 C.B. Macpherson, *The Political Theory of Possessive Individualism* (Oxford: Oxford University Press, 1962). Also see his *Democratic Theory: Essays on Retrieval* (Oxford: Clarendon Press, 1973); *The Rise and Fall of Economic Justice and Other Essays* (Oxford: Oxford University Press, 1985).

61 Gauthier, "Social Contract as Ideology," *Philosophy & Public Affairs*, 6 (1977), pp.130-64.

62 I have adopted this title of the agenda both from MacIntyre's *After Virtue* and Kenneth Baynes, James Bohman, and Thomas McCarthy, eds., *After Philosophy: End or Transformation?* (Cambridge: The MIT Press, 1987).

Chapter II

The Nature and Limits of the Theory of Rational Choice

A. The Basic Structure of the Theory of Rational Choice

1. *Homo Economicus* and Rational Choice Theory

As we have already seen in the previous chapter, Rawls and Gauthier agree that contractarian ethics can be a part of the theory of rational choice. However, despite the singular title that is commonly used to refer to it, rational choice theory is not a single coherent theory. Different disciplines deal with different problems, and thus we have a rather heterogeneous field of research here. There are many theories, each depending on its own assumptions concerning rationality. But this does not mean that there is no "common theoretical core."[1] Rawls and Gauthier, for example, both are basically committed to the concept of instrumental consistent maximization (TJ,p.143; MA,p.26). Beyond this basic agreement, Rawls and Gauthier differ with respect to the appropriate model of rational choice of which contractarian ethics is a part. In order to understand the similarity and difference between Rawls' and Gauthier's views, I will survey (a) the basic structure of rational choice theory, (b) the paradoxes of rationality which it engenders, and (c) some of the limitations of that theory.

Hahn and Hollis in their *Philosophy And Economic Theory* start from the following general observation.[2]

> When English-speaking philosophers think of economics, they usually have a particular kind of pure theory in mind. This is the class of theories predominantly taught in western universities and often called neo-Classical. Purity here is a matter of conceiving *homo economicus* in abstraction from his social setting.

Rational choice theory basically reflects the instrumental consistent maximization concept of rationality embedded in neo-classical *homo economicus*, i.e., the rational economic man.[3] The most essential aspect of neo-classical economics is as follows. It reduces various market phenomena to considerations of individual choice and, in this way, suggests that the sciences of economics can be grounded on the basic structure of individual act of subjectively maximizing choice among alternatives.[4] Thus neo-classical microeconomics adopts the concept of methodological individualism in its attempt to explain human choice and behavior.[5] Admittedly, social contract theory has been interpreted as a major proponent of methodological individualism.   Here we find a "structural isomorphism" between neo-classical rational choice theory and social contract theory.[6] In view of this, it is not surprising that rational choice theory resurrects a contractarian notion of polity and society to understand and explain how and why groups of individuals arrive at an aggregate social equilibrium.[7]

Here, we can raise an important question. Why must a human being make a choice? According to Robbins, economics is defined as "the science which studies human behavior as a relationship between ends and scarce means which have alternative uses."[8] To a very real extent, rational choice theorists have seen human behavior from the viewpoint of scarcity.[9] Thus when the supply of goods is not limitless, human beings are forced to make a choice of forgoing the pursuit of some goals in order to achieve more important ones. It is not surprising, then, that Rawls and Gauthier regard the condition of moderate scarcity of natural and social resources as a primary condition in the circumstance of justice (TJ,p.128; MA,p.112).[10]

Concerning the nature of *homo economicus* and rational choice theory, probably the most controversial issue is whether economic rationality is primarily a description of how men act or a normative standard of how they ought to act.[11] This descriptive/normative distinction on the nature of rational choice theory is an economic version of the so-called is/ought distinction. In detail, this twofold distinction can be developed into a fourfold distinction between description, prediction, explanation, and/or normativity. This issue is also involved in "the battle for human nature,"[12] which is really two battles. One is between the selection of specific traits for any partial man (*homo partialis*) and the preservation of undissected whole man (*homo totus*),[13] and the other is between different models of partial men (e.g., *homo economicus, homo faber, homo sociologicus*, etc.).[14]

These issues will be treated in Section C. In the present context, I am concerned with these issues insofar as they impinge on Rawls' and Gauthier's views on the nature of rational choice theory. Rawls thinks that in adopting the theory of rational choice, conceptions of justice can be "explained and [normatively] justified" (TJ,p.16). "It is another question how well human beings can assume the role [of rationality] in regulating their practical reasoning" (TJ,p.147). Gauthier regards rational choice theory primarily as "a justificatory framework" of a "normative theory." (MA,p.2). Derivatively, rational choice theory has "an explanatory role in so far as persons actually act rationally" (MA,p.3).

2. Basic Concepts of Rationality: Consistency and Maximization.
How is rationality characterized in rational choice theory? Usually, in neo-classical economics, it is referred to simply as utility-maximization.[15]   However, this characterization is insufficient and confusing, since utility-maximization is used in two distinct senses which relate to two different interpretations of rationality, that is, "internal consistency" and "self-interest maximization."[16]   The instrumental consistent maximization concept of rationality, which I have regarded as the common theoretic core of rational choice theory, is actually an unrefined mingled expression of those two interpretations.

The first interpretation, internal consistency of rationality, applies to the agent's system of preferences. Internal consistency requires that the relation of preferences in the set of available alternatives must have the features of connectedness and transitivity.[17] Connectedness means that for any two possible alternatives, the rational chooser must either prefer one to the other or be indifferent between them.   Transitivity means that if the first alternative is preferred or indifferent to the second, and the second is preferred or indifferent to the third, then the first must be either preferred or indifferent to the third.   A relation of preferences satisfying both conditions of the connectedness and transitivity is termed a "weak ordering" because the two conditions do not exclude indifference.[18] Rawls and Gauthier both adopt these two conditions as the formal conditions for ordering or ranking conflict claims in their contractarian rational choice systems (TJ,p.134; MA,pp.39f).

However, rationality as internal consistency is criticized in the following way. If an individual chooses exactly the opposite of what he or she would want to achieve, and does this with flawless internal consistency, he or she can hardly be seen as rational (although he or she is still rational according to the internal criterion).[19] This means that internal consistency cannot itself be an adequate condition of rationality.

Thus, in order to avoid this absurdity, some sort of correspondence between desires/beliefs, on the one hand, and the process of choice, on the other hand, must be added to what is meant by rationality.[20] When this is done, rationality is said to have the characteristic of "efficiency" in achieving given desires in the context of given beliefs.[21] Normally, rationality as consistency *cum* efficiency is called instrumental rationality. Utility-maximization in this sense is a purely formal specification of individual motivation having no substantive implications for the content of individual preference or desires. It is well-known fact that Hume and Weber were major proponents of instrumental rationality.[22]

Instrumental rationality as consistency *cum* efficiency is most famously demonstrated in "the theory of revealed preference."[23] Here, an individual's actually observed consistent choice is considered to be rational regardless of the content of his choice. As we have already seen in Chapter I, both Rawls and Gauthier accept instrumental rationality. However, both Rawls and Gauthier do not adopt the theory of revealed preference. For Rawls, "it only records the outcome" of choice (TJ,p.558). According to Gauthier, it cannot be "sufficient for rationality" (MA,p.27).

Admittedly, "compulsive consumption," that is, the problem of "addiction and back-sliding" is fatal to the theory of revealed preference.[24] According to the theory, value is identified with whatever an individual maximizes. This is the pure spirit of the maxim, "*de gustibus non est disputandum* (there is no disputing about tastes)." And the theory presupposes that an individual behaves irrationally, or fails to maximize values, if and only if his behavior cannot be given a consistent and efficient maximization interpretation. This means that even addictive behavior can satisfy the rationality condition since the theory deals only with a behavioral dimension of preference revealed in actual observable choice.

Even though Rawls and Gauthier do not resort to an absolutistic ideal for the content of rational desires, both provide minimum criteria for it through "deliberative rationality" (TJ,p.416) and "considered preference" (MA,p.26) respectively. However, in view of a persistent objection that instrumental rationality "precludes any assessment of the content of persons' desires, ends, or beliefs,"[25] I will have to treat this objection more fully in the chapters on Rawls and Gauthier.

I now move to the second interpretation of rationality: viz., self-interest maximization. Rationality as self-interest maximization gives us the second meaning of utility-maximization within neoclassical economics. This interpretation is, in fact, based on demanding an "external correspondence" between the choices that an individual makes and the self-interest of the individual.[26] Thus rationality as self-interest maximization avoids the criticism made against the internal consistency view of rationality.

Furthermore, self-interest maximization rationality determines the content of rational desires, whereas instrumental rationality (especially in the sense of efficiency) merely admits given desires. In this regard, self-interest maximization is not merely instrumental rationality but rationality of ends or ends-rationality.[27] Here, as well, utility-maximization takes on a substantive form and becomes the definite aim of individuals rather than a mere characterization of consistent and efficient behavior.

In terms of historical lineage, the self-interest interpretation of rationality goes back to the beginning of modern capitalism. Self-interest is "the soul of modern economic man."[28] The traditional theory of utility provides a firm basis for the rationality of pursuing one's utility— defined either by Benthamite felicific calculus, or by various formulations of desire-fulfillment; pleasure, happiness, satisfaction, benefit, advantage, etc.[29]

Utility-maximization in the form of self-interest must assume that all "interests" are commensurable into a single dimension— utility— so that an individual chooses the alternative which gives maximal utility in view of his or her comparable utility content of alternatives.[30]

However, the attempt at tying rational choice firmly to the pursuit of self-interest has to face many problems. First, there are ambiguities in the various concepts of utility and preference. The various formulations differently or selectively characterize interest, desire, happiness, pleasure, welfare, well-being, satisfaction, prudence, etc. Second, there are difficulties in measuring individual utility and interpersonal comparison of utility. Utility measurement and comparison is frustrated in the face of multidimensional criteria (Bentham himself suggested seven criteria!).[31] The detailed history of various attempts to deal with these problems in the domain of economics and rational choice theory is beyond the scope of present discussion.[32]

Rawls and Gauthier seem to follow the basic idea of the second, that is, the self-interest maximization interpretation of rationality since the motivational assumption in the circumstances of justice — especially the subjective circumstances of mutual disinterestedness or unconcern (TJ,p.146; MA,p.87) — corresponds well with it. According to Rawls, rational contracting parties are "conceived as not taking an interest in one another's interests" (TJ,p.13). They are "concerned to further their own interests" (TJ,p.11). Similarly, for Gauthier, "the rational person ... seeks the greatest satisfaction of her own interests" (MA,p.7).

However, both Rawls and Gauthier do not think that self-interest maximization is a rationality of ends or ends-rationality in the substantive sense. For Rawls, "the details of particular ends and interests" are not accessible to the rational parties in the original position because of the veil of ignorance (TJ,p.142). For Gauthier, "on the maximization conception it is not interests in the self, that takes as object, but interests of the self, held by as subject" (MA,p.7). In plain words, this means that the specific content of self-interest maximization is determined by a subjective individual.

Another important related issue concerning the rationality as self-interest maximization is whether this concept of rationality leads to a purely selfish or egoistic position.[33] Rawls and Gauthier both flatly claim that even though contracting parties are pursuing their own interests, they are not selfish or egoistic (TJ,p.147; MA,p.87. n.6).

3. Formal Models of Rational Choice Theory

We have investigated the concept of rationality as instrumental self-interest maximization in rational choice theory. However, it is not possible to move directly from this concept of rationality to an ethical position because specifications of the choice situation and a justificatory device to derive certain moral principles from the situation are required.   In contractarian ethics, these additional requirements are concerned with how to characterize the state of nature in which rational contract parties are supposed to make a decision. For Rawls, this task of characterization consists of two parts: "(1) an interpretation of the initial situation and of the problem of choice posed there, and (2) a set of principles which, it is argued, would be agreed to" (TJ,p.15). For Gauthier, the characterization consists of (1) an "*ex ante*" characterization of the agreement in the initial position, and (2) an "*ex post*" rational motivation for compliance of the agreed moral principles (MA,p.14). In addition, Rawls and Gauthier resort to different formal models of rational choice theory respectively in order to deal with the above requirements.

Following Luce and Raiffa, the formal models of rational choice theory can be classified into the now classical fourfold distinction as follows.[34]

Table 1. Classification of the Formal Models of Rational Choice Theory

(1)   Individual decision making under certainty
(2)   Individual decision making under risk or uncertainty
(3)   Game theory
(4)   Social choice theory

(1), (2), and (3) together are often called utility theory while (2) and (3) together are called decision theory.[35]

(1) Individual decision making under certainty is held in the condition that each individual action is known with certainty to lead invariably to a specific outcome. Here all an individual needs to do is determine which outcome he or she likes best, since he or

she has perfect information about the outcomes that will follow from the alternative courses of action. A typical case is when an individual chooses among different makes of car after having had access to accurate or complete consumer-report documents. An important assumption about *homo economicus* which I have not mentioned is that economic man is assumed to know not only what all the courses of action open to him or her are, but also what the outcomes of any action will be. This is the so-called "complete information" assumption of rational economic man.[36] However, this assumption must be relaxed in the incomplete information situation under risk or uncertainty.

(2) Individual decision making under risk or uncertainty is held in a situation of incomplete information. Risk is defined as a situation in which numerical probabilities can be assigned to the various possible outcomes of each course of action. Uncertainty is defined as a situation in which the probabilities of the outcomes are completely unknown or are not even meaningful. Choices between bets on roulette wheels, fair coins, or dice are typical cases under risk, whereas drawing from two urns each containing a different ratio of black to red balls without information (probability unknown) and the date when one will become a great grand parent (probability meaningless) are typical cases under uncertainty. Under risk or uncertainty, rationality is defined more specifically as "expected-utility maximization".[37]

(3) Game theory concerns interdependent decision making under either noncooperative conditions (the theory of noncooperative games) or cooperative conditions (negotiation or bargaining games) between two or more individuals. As I will show in the next section, the Prisoner's Dilemma game is a typical example of noncooperative game. In the noncooperative game the players choose their strategies independently. Communication and bargaining are not allowed and coalition formation is therefore usually assumed to be impossible. In the cooperative game, binding agreements and coalition formation are allowed, as they are in many everyday interactions, e.g., in case of a bargaining between labor union and employer.[38]

(4) Social choice theory is often called collective decision making. Here the problem is how to aggregate different choices of individuals with different preferences into social preferences and

choices. Political democratic theorists employ social choice theory in order to settle upon a voting procedure. In the domain of economics, the theory of social welfare functions is a paradigmatic case.

Given these models, our primary concern is to show which ones are used in Rawls' and Gauthier's contractarian ethics and additionally in Harsanyi's utilitarian ethics. Rawls and Harsanyi agree that (2), individual choice under uncertainty, is the proper model. In detail, however, Rawls and Harsanyi employ different operational principles under uncertainty respectively, i.e., the maximin principle and the equiprobability principle. Gauthier resorts to (3), the bargaining game theory and uses the minimax relative concession as the operational principle.[39]

B. The Paradoxes of Rationality

1. The Prisoner's Dilemma

In the previous section, we surveyed the basic structure of individual rational choice. Traditionally, in economics, individual rationality is applied in the perfectly competitive market where demands and supplies dovetail well into an optimal equilibrium. This is the basic assumption of laissez-faire economics. Under this assumption, Adam Smith claimed that each individual, pursuing own self-interest, was led as if by an invisible hand to general harmony.[40] However, in certain situations, individual rationality may not produce such supposed general harmony. These situations are called "market failures."[41] These failures are revealed by several paradoxes of rationality, which entrench themselves in various discrepancies between individual rationality and collective rationality. Under these paradoxes, perfect rational *homo economicus* dramatically degenerates into "rational fool."[42]

The most famous problem used by rational choice theory to demonstrate the self-defeating aspects of rationality (as self-interest maximization) is the Prisoner's Dilemma.[43] In this dilemma two prisoners are alleged to have committed a crime. They are brought before the district attorney and interrogated separately. The attorney tells them the following. If neither one confesses, each will spend a year in prison. But if one prisoner confesses, but the other does not, the latter will receive a heavy term of ten years while the former will be released. If they both confess, each will get five years. In this situation, acting according to their self-interest maximization, both prisoners confess and both receive five-year sentences. This means that isolated individual rationality does not lead to collective optimality. The following table depicts the situation of the possible combinations of their actions in terms of years in prison.

Table 2. The Prisoner's Dilemma

	prisoner b	
	not confess	confess
prisoner a not confess	1,1	10,0
confess	0,10	5,5

Table 2 reveals how the dominant strategy of each prisoner (i.e., confession) is in equilibrium. (1) Either the other prisoner will confess or he or she will not. (2) If he or she will confess, then confession is better than no confession (five years is better than ten years). (3) If he or she will not, then again confession is better than no confession (no years in prison is better than one year).[44]

As Rawls points out, the Prisoner's Dilemma arises

> whenever the outcome of the many individuals' decisions made in isolation is worse for everyone than some other course of action, even though, taking the conduct of the others as given, each person's decision is perfectly rational (TJ,p.269).

The Dilemma thus can be characterized as a problem of isolation. In this connection, many rational choice theorists emphasize that the Dilemma is not an unique problem of egoism. In order to show this, they construct the "Altruist's Dilemma" in which each person in the choice situation is very altruistic as follows.

Table 3. The Altruist's Dilemma

	altruist b sitting	standing
altruist a sitting	0,0	1,-2
standing	-2,1	-1,-1

In Table 3, the pay-off matrix is held between two altruistic passengers.[45] They both refrain from taking the single unoccupied seat on the bus, which can seat them both, although not too comfortably, with the altruistic motivation of leaving it free for the other to occupy. If the motive of each is to increase the pay-off of the other, then the dominant choice is standing. The outcome of this choice is clearly worse for both when compared to the outcome of egoistic or selfish choice, viz., sitting.[46] In view of the Altruist's Dilemma, rational choice theorists flatly claim that "the Prisoner's Dilemma presupposes a *divergence in preferences* but not selfishness or indifference towards others."[47]

2. The Free-rider Problem
Free riders are those who enjoy the benefits of cooperation without sharing the burdens. The Free-rider Problem in economics and rational choice theory is more rigorously defined in terms of public goods. There are basically two types of economic goods, i.e., private goods and public goods. A private good has the property that an individual's consumption of it (e.g., eating an apple) totally precludes others from consuming it. However, in case of public goods, the situation is quite different. First, an individual's

consumption of a pure public good does not diminish other people's consumption. In addition, once the good is produced, no one can be excluded from its benefits. National defense is a typical example of such a public good.[48]

Rawls explains how the Free-rider Problem arises:

> Where the public is large and includes many individuals, there is a temptation for each person to try to avoid doing his share. This is because whatever one man does his action will not significantly affect the amount produced. He regards the collective action of others as already given one way or the other. If the public good is produced his enjoyment of it is not decreased by his not making a contribution. If it is not produced his action would not have changed the situation anyway (TJ,p.267).

This situation of the Problem can be illustrated by the following table.

Table 4. The Free-rider Problem

G: public good
C: contribute
Numbers: preference ordering

	others	
	C	not C
individual C	benefits of G 2 costs of C	no benefits of G 4 costs of C
not C	benefits of G 1 no costs of C	no benefits of G 3 no costs of C

According to Table 4[49], for a free-rider, the lower left cell is most preferred, the upper right is least preferred. If everybody follows this preference ordering, public goods cannot be provided. In this regard, it has been pointed out that the Free-rider Problem is the "multi- or n-person, or large scale" Prisoner's Dilemma.[50]

Thus the Problem can be interpreted as a game of the Dilemma not between two individuals, but between a single individual and all the other individuals. It also has been pointed out that the Problem can happen to an altruist. Since his or her contribution is not significantly perceptible, he or she still does not rationally contribute towards the provision of any public or collective good.[51]

However, altruism can be considered exceptional and self-interested behavior is usually thought to be dominant especially when economic or distributive issues are at stake. Thus the *locus classicus* of the Problem in Olson's *The Logic of Collective Action* reads:[52]

> Indeed, unless the number of individuals in a group is quite small, or unless there is coercion or some other special device to make individuals act in their common interest, *rational, self-interested individuals will not act to achieve their common or group interests.*

On the one hand, the Prisoner's Dilemma and the Free-rider Problem seem to give a challenge to Rawls' and Gauthier's contractarian attempt to derive morality from rationality as instrumental self-interest maximization. In a sense, these two paradoxes of rationality can be interpreted as descriptive phenomena of market failure. Thus, it seems to be natural that they can be easily rejected in the domain of normative theory. However, even though Rawls and Gauthier both adopt rational choice as normative theory, both have to solve the two paradoxes. Since Kant, the maxim that 'ought' implies 'can' has been considered as a necessary condition for construction of ethics. As we have already seen in Chapter I Section B, Rawls and Gauthier regard the instrumental self-interest maximization concept of rationality as an essential motivational foundation. This means that if contractarian normative ethics has no motivational foundation in the descriptive sense, contractarian ethics cannot have practical applicability.

On the other hand, from the two paradoxes of individual rationality as phenomena of market failure, contractarianism can find its own ground. In the situation of market failure, it may be possible to improve the situation through non-market solutions. Contractarianism can be seen as a typical non-market solution for market failure. Even though the concept of individual rationality becomes very difficult to define, contractarian attempt to escape from the paradoxes through the use of the notion of collective rationality would involve ideas that relate to the concept of morality. Here contractarian ethics can find its starting point.

As it has been mentioned, for Rawls, the Dilemma is the isolation problem. Rawls thus tries to show that his contractarian "principles of justice ... are collectively rational from the perspective of the original position" (TJ, p.577). In other words, it is rational for isolated individuals to become involved in contractarian mutual cooperation. The Problem is interpreted as an assurance or compliance problem. "Here the aim is to assure the cooperating parties that the common agreement is being carried out" (TJ,p.270). Thus for Rawls "it remains to be shown that this disposition to take up and to be guided by the standpoint of justice accords with the individual's good" (TJ,p.567). But Rawls ends up presupposing "the strict compliance" in his just society since "principles are to be chosen in view of the consequences of everyone's complying with them" (TJ,p.132).

At this juncture, Gauthier attempts to solve the two paradoxes more rigorously. The two paradoxes are unique phenomena of market failure and "morality arises from market failure" (MA,p.84). The Dilemma can be solved by his contractarian moral principle which is derived from the *ex ante* agreement underlying a fair and rational "cooperative venture" for "mutual advantage" (MA,pp.14f). Gauthier devotes special attention to the Problem. Even though a contract might yield a better result than the market, still each individual "fails to adhere in the hope of benefiting from her own defection" (MA, p.12). Contractarian *ex post* argument is to provide rational motivation for compliance of the agreed moral principle. Here Gauthier's significant modification of the standard concept of rationality into "rationality of constrained maximization as a disposition" appears (MA, p.183).

3. Arrow's Impossibility Theorem

The two previous paradoxes of rationality arise in the domain of individual rational choice in game situations. In contrast, Arrow's Impossibility Theorem appears in the domain of social choice theory, especially in welfare economics and the theory of democracy. As Gauthier's expression, "the dread specter" indicates,

Arrow's Theorem has had far-reaching negative instructive influences on normative social disciplines, including ethics.[53]

As we have already mentioned in the formal models of rational choice theory in the first section, social choice theory deals with the problem of how to bring about collective preference ordering from the given individual orderings.   Accordingly the primary task of social choice theory is to construct an aggregation device for collective choice which makes the preference ordering of society a function of individual preference orderings.   In democratic political theory, the various possible voting schemes are simply all aggregation devices.   These devices in welfare economics are known as "social welfare functions."[54]   Arrow's Impossibility Theorem consists of imposing certain apparently reasonable conditions on a social welfare function and demonstrating that there can be no consistent social welfare function (as a rational aggregation device) since these conditions are mutually inconsistent.[55]

The conditions for Arrow's social welfare function are as follows.[56]

(C) Collective rationality: For any possible set of individual preference orderings, there should be defined a social preference ordering (connected and transitive) which governs social choices.

(P) Pareto principle: If everybody prefers alternative A to alternative B, then society must have the same preference.

(I) Independence of irrelevant alternatives: The social choice made from any set of available alternatives should depend only on the orderings of individuals with respect to those alternatives.

(D) Non-dictatorship: The social decision procedure should not be dictatorial, in the sense that there is one whose preferences prevail regardless of the preferences of all others.

Condition C imposes on the social ordering the same requirement of rationality, viz., internal consistency of connectedness and transitivity, assumed on individual ordering, which has already been discussed in the previous section A.2. Conditions P and D for citizens' sovereignty are widely considered as basic requirements for democracy. The only condition that requires elaboration is I. First, condition I rejects an alternative which is logically possible but in fact not available. For example, in case of choosing alternative methods of city transportation (rapid transit, automobile, bus, etc.), "transportation by dissolving the individual into molecules in a ray gun and reforming him elsewhere in the city" has no bearing on the choice to be made.[57] Second, condition I in effect restricts social decision procedures to generalized forms of voting; only preferences among the available candidates are used in deciding an election.[58]

Arrow's Theorem is related to the most commonly used collective decision rule in democratic societies, namely that of majority voting. Majority rule basically seems to satisfy all of the four conditions. However, the Theorem demonstrates that the inconsistency of these four conditions, C, P, I, and D is in fact a generalized form of the paradox of majority voting.

Imagine three voters (1, 2, and 3) trying to choose between three alternatives (A, B, and C). Collective decision is to be made by majority rule. The paradox of voting can be shown in the following table.

Table 5. The Paradox of Voting

	Voters		
	1	2	3
Preference	A	B	C
Ordering	B	C	A
	C	A	B

Two of the three voters (1 and 3) prefer A to B, two (1 and 2) prefer B to C, but two (2 and 3) prefer C to A. This means that a set of transitive individual preferences has generated an intransitive collective preference called a "cyclic majority."[59] Consequently, majority rule violates Arrow's condition C. The Theorem then means that there is no way of removing this paradox of majority voting without violating one of the other of the Arrow conditions.[60]

The evaluation of the Theorem has led to considerable controversy, still persisting. And there have been various suggestions for evading it. Assuming the proof of the Theorem valid, which of the four conditions on rationality should we give up? Are these conditions a set of apparently reasonable and widely accepted conditions? Detailed discussion of these issues is outside the scope of present concern.[61]

If the preference ordering of all individuals were always identical for all states, Arrow's Theorem would not arise since the unanimous consensual decision can cut the cyclic majorities. However, Arrow thinks that the unanimous consensus is too ideal to be applied generally in the real-world situation, where conflict between individual preference orderings is common and where the presupposition of an unanimous and homogeneous society is not consonant with the pluralistic individual democratic society. Thus Arrow critically points out that "the assumption of unanimity is the idealist view of political philosophy" and that "the doctrine of consensus" is "a foundation for social ethics."[62]

As we have already seen in Chapter I Section B, both Rawls and Gauthier acknowledge that contractarian ethics presupposes an individualistic pluralistic society. Thus they cannot agree with the following communitarian rejoinder to Arrow that "in any particular society there is a considerable degree of commonness of ends, so Arrow's theorem is of interest mainly to the academic theorist."[63] Even though Rawls and Gauthier believe that contractarian unanimous consensus or agreement is possible, they claim that the consensus can be derived from instrumental rationality of self-interest in the hypothetical fair initial situation, not from actual voting, or from idealistic perfectionist concept of ends, and or from communitarian commonness of ends.

However, Rawls and Gauthier have to answer the following persistent objection to the contractarian unanimous consensus. "In politics the public interest is always a matter of debate and a final agreement can never be reached; to imagine such a situation is to dream of a society without politics."[64]

C. The Limitations of The Theory of Rational Choice

1. Psychological and Sociological Criticisms of Rational Choice Theory

The neo-classical concept of rationality as instrumental self-interest maximization has been subject to a broad range of criticisms.

Even the paradoxes of rationality can be regarded as a kind of "immanent criticism."[65] To be sure, the paradoxes do not challenge the rationality assumptions. But they do show that these assumptions are either inconsistent or lead to undesirable results. Yet over and above immanent criticism, the rationality assumptions themselves may be suspect and, if not correct, may place rational choice theory on a shaky foundation. In the literature, we can find various critical labellings of rational choice theory: "unrealistic, unproductive, and amoral"; "on the one hand too demanding, on the other hand too restrictive"; "too permissive or too restrictive"; "pure fictions"; even "puppet" and "chimera."[66] In view of the structural isomorphism between neo-classical rational choice theory and social contract theory (which I have mentioned in Section A.1.) it is not surprising that, generally speaking, the same labellings have been attached to social contract theory.

In the domain of social sciences, psychology and sociology send formidable challenges to the so-called "unrealistic" assumptions of rationality. The psychological challenge starts from the observed irrationality of individual behavior. "They [People] brush their teeth but do not fasten their seat belts; they continue to smoke twenty years after the Surgeon General's report; they purchase costly, unsuitable life insurance and pay stock brokers for useless advice, and so on."[67] Almost every psychological approach claims that something other than rationality determines human behavior.[68]

> For learning theorists, it is schedules of reinforcement; for Freudians, unconscious motivations; for developmentalists, the individual's stage of cognitive developments; for social psychologists, the current social context and the way the individual represents it; even cognitive psychologists argue that the individual's particular information processing machinery will constrain his or her performance.

No rational choice theorist maintains that human behavior is always rational. Furthermore advocates of rational choice theory seem to recognize that human behavior frequently departs from the canons of rationality, so that rational choice models are not realistic.[69] The claim of rational choice approach is not so much that the assumption of rationality is descriptively accurate, but rather it performs an important "heuristic function": It is a useful simplification and it provides the means of identifying the place of non-rational elements in human behavior.[70]

This kind of rejoinder was initiated by Friedman. Friedman's argument was that models should be constructed so as to abstract "the common and crucial elements from the mass of complex and detailed circumstances surrounding the phenomena to be explained."[71] The claim here is that unrealistic assumptions can nevertheless yield realistic predictions in so far as they are aimed at excluding what is inessential. In virtue of this, many economists have been willing to concede the psychologist's objections to the rational choice axioms, but argue that they are irrelevant. This is the so-called "pragmatic defense of rationality."[72] There are serious methodological problems with such a defense of rationality, which need not detain us here.[73] At this moment, it is more important that we take seriously the following question.[74]

> Why ... cannot economic psychology devote itself to using psychological methods for classifying and studying these irrationalities or to producing a more realistic description of human choice on which a more realistic economics could be based?

In fact, there has been a systematic endeavor to carry out this task.[75] Whether it can be done is not my direct concern. Here I simply point out that Rawls' discussion of developmental moral psychology (of mainly Piaget's and Kohlberg's) can be considered as a compromise between rationality and psychology (TJ,pp.460ff).

Sociological challenge to rational choice theory starts from the claim that realistic *homo sociologicus* must be considered to be an advance over unrealistic *homo economicus*. Since the concept of *homo sociologicus* was introduced by Dahrendorf, there has been a relative degree of consensus among sociologists concerning the fundamental properties that must be accorded to the social agent in order to conduct a sociological analysis.[76] First, confronted with a choice, *homo sociologicus* acts according not to what he or she rationally prefers but to what habit, tradition, custom, role, internalized values, and social norms force him or her to do. Second, social agent's preferences and the feasible set of alternatives to be chosen are in general treated by the sociologist as a function of the environment.

Concerning the first point, the most relevant topic is that human action must be understood in terms of social norms rather than individual rationality. This means that social norms are prior to individuals in the explanatory order, and that they cannot simply be reduced to individual preferences. The second point implies social determinism with respect to the content of individual preferences in view of the fact that in rational choice theory the content of individual preferences is supposed to be given.

Against the first claim, rational choice theorists point out that there are innumerable cases of traditional norms being discarded when new opportunities become available. The cases can be found because individuals find that discarding them serves their goals better. This means that there is no well confirmed theory specifying the conditions under which norms override rationality. It is especially not clear what conditions determine when norms remain stable and when they yield to the individual rationality in the social norm explanation. Against the second claim, rational choice theorists acknowledge that even though the feasible set of alternatives is determined by the environment (actually this is the condition I of Arrow's welfare function), this does not mean that nothing is left to choice.[77] In this connection, rational choice theorists resort to a protest against "the oversocialized conception of man" and try to find a rational theoretic case for "bringing men back in."[78]

I am not making here a final assessment of the debate between rational choice theory and sociology.[79] Along with the issue of methodological individualism, the debate is closely related with Marxist and communitarian criticisms of contractarian ethics, which I will treat in Chapters IV and V.

2. The Two Suggested Alternatives to the Standard Rational Choice Theory: Imperfect and Extended Schools of Rationality

In the first section of this chapter, we surveyed the two senses of utility-maximization, that of consistent/ efficient choice, and of self-interest maximization. In connection with these two senses, there have been systematic endeavors to propose viable alternatives in the domain of rational choice theory. These endeavors are partially related to the psychological and sociological criticisms of the standard rational choice theory.

The double-barreled critical labelling of rational choice theory, which I mentioned in the previous subsection (i.e., "on the one hand too demanding, on the other hand too restrictive") is directly connected with these endeavors.[80] It is too demanding in the sense that individuals are required to perceive, evaluate and calculate with absolute precision, and too restrictive in limiting attention to narrow self-interest as the sole motivation of individual action. In terms of the two senses of utility-maximization, the former labelling is against the instrumental rationality as consistency *cum* efficiency and suggests that some degree of practical inefficiency in the pursuit of given ends must be accepted. The latter is against the substantive rationality as self-interest maximization and suggests that a broader class of possible individual motivators should be recognized.

At the heart of an alternative to instrumental rationality is the notion of satisficing or bounded rationality, first developed by Simon.[81] It asserts that individuals are inherently inefficient and so may be inconsistent in their actions, but that they may come to recognize their own limitations and undertake action which is good enough or satisfactory. This means that satisficing or bounded rationality is more realistic than the perfect calculation of maximization. For example, when people try to buy a house, they usually choose the first or second house they look at since they think that that house is satisfactory.

This consideration of boundedness exemplifies the more general notion of imperfect rationality and the possibility of individuals' adopting behavioral strategies of a second-best, rationality-improving kind in order to offset, but not completely eliminate, their own irrationality. In this connection, the issues of self-control, precommitments, and weakness of will (akrasia), and of time-discounting present utility versus time-considering future orientated prudential utility have been widely discussed by Schelling, Elster, Parfit, and others.[82] For instance, Elster interprets time-discounting instantaneous short-sightedness as a symptom of imperfect rationality so that weakness of will is regarded as the source of the strictly irrational tendency to discount future utility.[83] Interestingly enough, his discussion of Ulysses' instruction to have himself tied to the mast so as to avoid the temptation of the Sirens points to "the need for a theory of *imperfect rationality* that has been all but neglected by philosophers and social scientists."[84] Ulysses' instruction is a kind of self-control or precommitment in anticipation of his weakness of will in the near future. Whether standard rational choice theory solely relies on time-counting or -discounting utility is controversial. Thus it is not surprising that Rawls and Gauthier take different views on this matter. Gauthier claims that "practical reason takes its standpoint in the present" (MA,p.38), whereas Rawls maintains that "future aims may not be discounted solely in virtue of being future" (TJ,p.420).

Traditionally the above issues of imperfect rationality are expressed by the maxim, "*video meliora proboque deteriora sequor*" (I see the good and I approve of it but I still take the wrong path). Generally speaking, the imperfect school of rationality tries to supersede revealed preference theory (the limits of which I have already dealt with Section A.2). The school deals with the issues of the formation and endogenous or exogenous changes of the content of individual preferences, which are ignored in revealed preference theory.

Imperfect rationality forms a major critical alternative to instrumental rationality, whereas extended rationality occupies a similar position with respect to the substantive rationality of self-interest maximization. The fundamental points in the extended rationality are that self-interest maximization is not the sole motivation of individual action, and that there exists an internal tension between self-interest and other motivational goals.[85] The extended rationality school of thought has been developed by Sen, Arrow and others in terms of a range of commitments going beyond self-interest.[86] The range of commitments is so wide that it involves "duty, loyalty and goodwill," "extended sympathy," and "reciprocal altruism."[87]

In recent years, a method of incorporating altruism into rational egoism has been made in terms of a more indirect, strategic or evolutionary appeal to self-interest.[88] The general idea of this approach is that while altruism may appear to be not self-interested in the short-run, its long term benefits — including the benefit of living in a society of altruists — may compensate these short-run costs even in the egoist's private calculus. Gauthier's contractarian ethics strongly reflects this approach since, as I have emphasized repeatedly in Chapter I and the previous section, his transformation of rationality as maximization into rationality as constrained maximization strategically appeals to the very conception of rationality as maximization.

Generally speaking, extended rationality can be defined in terms of the rejection of narrow self-interest as the sole motivator in favor of a view of rationality which recognizes a number of distinct motivators or commitments (where self-interest may, of course, be included in that number). Such a view naturally leads to an interpretation of the relevance of a conception of morality to rationality as a form of ranking over multiple alternative motivations.[89] One more time, Gauthier's distinction between straightforward and constrained maximizations (as alternative motivations) and his conception of morality as rational constraint are basically on the side of this interpretation (MA,p.167).

In order to properly assess the viability of the imperfect and extended schools of rationality, three major issues must be solved. First, can these two alternatives be subsumed in the neo-classical conception of rationality? Second, can these two alternatives solve the paradoxes of rationality? As we have already seen in the previous section, the paradoxes apply to altruist as well as non-altruistic positions. Third, are these alternatives substitutes for rational choice theory as normative or descriptive theory? Given the purpose of this study, I cannot answer these questions in detail. Rather I am raising them primarily in connection with Rawls' and Gauthier's adoption of the neo-classical rationality of instrumental self-interest maximization.

As we have seen in Section A. 1., Rawls and Gauthier regard rational choice theory as normative. "There is no alternative to rational-choice theory as a set of normative prescriptions."[90] It just tells us to do what will best promote our given ends, whatever they are. Thus bounded and imperfect rationality can be seen as the basis for a descriptive or explanatory theory of imperfect behavior while retaining full, unbounded instrumental rationality as the appropriate normative ideal. However, extended rationality cannot be seen simply as a descriptive theory since it attacks the substantive and normative theory of rationality as self-interest maximization. The only part of the theory that is somewhat controversial from the normative point of view is that which deals with the object of normative maximization or the content of rational desires.

These two alternatives would seem to provide a basis of criticisms of Rawls' and Gauthier's contractarian rational ethics since the two alternatives challenge the two senses of rationality respectively. However, Rawls' and Gauthier's contractarian ethics might be defended against them, or interpreted as already considering their major points. On the imperfect rationality argument one might continue to support the assumption of perfect instrumental rationality in the original or initial contractarian position, since the imperfect, real individual striving for rationality could be held as a normative ideal for contractarian agreement. But Rawls and Gauthier share the imperfect school's emphasis on the content of rational desires since both try to avoid the problems of revealed preference theory. In a sense, Rawls reflects the basic point of bounded rationality since the veil of ignorance eliminates "the complication caused by so much information" (TJ,p.148).

The extended rationality school carries strong implication for ethical theory. Basically Rawls and Gauthier, and this school share the limits of narrow self-interest maximization as exemplified in the paradoxes of rationality. However, Rawls and Gauthier do not accept the altruistic motivation from the beginning since, in the circumstances of justice, mutual disinterested self-interest rationality prevails because of scarcity of natural and social resources. Rather, both Rawls and Gauthier claim that their rationality models will eventually mitigate narrow self-interest maximization. Their practical results (not premises) can be consonant with the extended school:

> Now the combination of mutual disinterest and the veil of ignorance achieves the same purpose as benevolence. For this combination of conditions forces each person in the original position to take the good of others into account. In justice as fairness, then, the effects of good will are brought about by several conditions working jointly. The feeling that this concept of justice is egoistic is an illusion fostered by looking at but one of the elements of the original position (TJ,p.148).

> [L]et us note an interesting parallel to our theory of constrained maximization - Robert Trivers' evolutionary theory of reciprocal altruism. We have claimed that a population of constrained maximizers would be rationally stable; no one would have reason to dispose herself to straightforward maximization. Similarly, . . . a population of reciprocal altruists would be geneti-

cally stable; a mutant egoist would be at an evolutionary disadvantage (MA,p.187).

In view of these passages, in one sense, Rawls and Gauthier believe that the extended rationality can be subsumed in the neo-classical rationality. Gauthier especially tries to demonstrate the subsumption through a very rigorous bargaining game approach. In contrast, Rawls does not make a clear case for the subsumption.[91] As we have already seen in Chapter I. Section C, Rawls eventually denies that the theory of justice is part of the theory of rational choice, which he claimed in *A Theory Justice*. This means that the extended rationality cannot be subsumed in neo-classical rationality. Rawls then directly appeals to the extended rationality as an explicit deontological meta-ranking of individual preferences: "A capacity for a sense of justice" is "higher-order interests."[92]

3. Rational Choice Theory, Morality, and Ideological Implication. The general purpose of this chapter is to give some background for understanding the basic scheme of contractarian ethics as part of the theory of rational choice. As the results of the discussions on Rawls' and Gauthier's views on the paradoxes of rationality and on their relation to the two alternative schools, I can infer that they are not merely passive advocates but rather critical revisionists of the standard choice theory.

Thus far I have argued that rational choice theory is a very helpful heuristic device, conceptual apparatus, or analytic tool for elucidating various moral problems in conflict situations. But I still hesitate to conclude that rational choice theory can give a final justificatory solution to contractarian ethics and broadly to moral philosophy. In Chapter I, I expressed this hesitation in terms of the four predicaments of contractarian ethics, especially in terms of the contractarian dilemma between irrelevancy and circularity. I interpreted the dilemma as an immanent criticism since the dilemma is composed of the very assumption of rationality in contractarian ethics. This interpretation will be further explored in subsequent chapters. With the help of our discussions of rational choice theory in the present chapter, I will critically investigate how Hobbes' and Rawls' contractarianisms comprise the two horns of the dilemma in Chapter III, and whether Gauthier's contractarianism can avoid the dilemma in Chapter IV.

Since I have indicated the liberal ideological implication of contractarian adoption of rational choice theory in Chapter I. A.2., I have to inquire into it in detail now. This issue is primarily related to the avowed neutrality of contractarian use of rational choice theory. More specifically, the issue is whether rational theoretic approach is ideologically favored with capitalistic liberalism in regard to its market orientation and the very criterion of rationality. One the one hand, I have shown in the present chapter that rationality as self-interest maximization is the soul of the modern capitalistic economic man.[93] On the other hand, rational theoretic approach is suspect from the liberal or libertarian ideology of the market in view of the paradoxes of rationality, especially the Free-rider Problem and the Arrow's Impossibility Theorem — as phenomena of market failure by its own market rationality and the liberal democratic citizen or "consumer sovereignty".[94] It is interesting to note here that in recent years there has appeared a number of works employing rational choice theoretic approach to Marxism, so-called analytical Marxism.[95] In this regard, rational choice theoretic approach might be regarded as a neutral foundation independent from the perspective of these ideological issues.[96] However, whether rational choice theoretic interpretation of Marxism is plausible and whether rational choice theory is a viable foundation for ethics and political economy or philosophy in general are still problematic.[97]

At the beginning of the present section, I have discussed the psychological and sociological criticisms of the rational choice theory. In view of the ideal and abstract construction of rational choice theory, it might be the case that "it is ... a foundation that many critics have claimed to be built on sand."[98] Even though there have been two major alternatives, that of the imperfect and extended schools of rationality, still "we do not yet know what we mean by rationality."[99] I have shown in the present chapter, there are basically four models and various operational principles under each models. In Chapter I, I have pointed out that this plurality eventually falls into the indeterminacy between different models and even between different operational principles under the same model. Furthermore, the substantive normative ethical conclusions are heavily influenced by the initial characterization of basic model and rationality assumptions. Rawls later admits that "there seems to be no one best interpretation of rationality."[100] In this regard, we have to raise a serious question whether methodological pluralism of rational choice models can be compatible with the rational foundationalism.

Another related issue is to choose among the various methods of measurements and interpersonal comparisons of utility and preference. As we have seen, ethical conclusions might be heavily influenced by the methods since they limit the scope of whose and which utility and preference are considered. Much more space is needed to elaborate this problem. However, since I have discussed this problem briefly in Section A. 2. of this chapter, I am here merely pointing out that, as I will show in the next two chapters, Rawls and Gauthier try to solve it in terms of the primary social goods, and more refined conceptions of utility, value, and preference, respectively.

Notes

1 Peter Gärdenfors and Nils-Eric Sahlin, eds., *Decision, Probability, and Utility* (Cambridge: Cambridge University Press, 1988), p.ix.

2 Frank Hahn and Martin Hollis, eds., *Philosophy and Economic Theory* (Oxford: Oxford University Press, 1979), "Introduction," p.1.

3 Martin Hollis and Edward J. Nell, *Rational Economic Man: A Philosophical Critique of Neo-Classical Economics*, p.54. The role of rational economic man is "the rational *primum mobile* of neo-Classical economics" (Ibid.). However, Dyke thinks that the concept of rational economic man is found throughout economic theory from its beginnings. Thus rational economic man is either assumed or insisted upon by all classical and neo-classical economics. Cf. C. Dyke, *Philosophy of Economics*, p.29. n.6.

4 Douglas Greenwald, ed., *Encyclopedia of Economics* (New York: McGraw-Hill Book, 1982), "Neoclassical economics," by Laurence S. Moss, p.699.

5 Hollis and Nell, *Rational Economic Man*, p.1.

6 Hans Van Den Doel, *Democracy and Welfare Economics*, trans. Brigid Biggins (Cambridge: Cambridge University Press, 1979), p.6. For a more detailed treatment, see Timothy W. Luke, "Methodological Individualism: The Essential Ellipsis of Rational Choice Theory," *Philosophy of the Social Sciences*, 17 (1987), pp.341-55; and Steven Lukes, *Individualism* (Oxford: Basil Blackwell, 1973).

7 Timothy W. Luke, "Reason and Rationality in Rational Choice Theory," *Social Research*, 52 (1985), p.72.

8 Lionel Robbins, *An Essay on the Nature and Significance of Economic Science*, 2nd ed. (London: Macmillan and Co., 1935), p.16. Cf. Daniel M. Hausman, ed., *The Philosophy of Economics* (Cambridge: Cambridge University Press, 1984).

9 For instance, see Harsanyi, "Basic Moral Decisions and Alternative Concepts of Rationality," *Social Theory and Practice*, 9 (1983), p.232. According to economic terminology, the goals an individual gives up are his "opportunity costs" of pursuing the remaining goals.

10 In connection with Hume's characterization of the circumstances of justice, see Chapter I. n.26.

11 Paul Diesing, "The Nature and Limitations of Economic Rationality," *Ethics*, 61 (1950), p.12. For a helpful discussion, see K. R. MacCrimmon, "Descriptive and Normative Implications of Decision Theory Postulates," in K. Borch and J. Mossin, eds., *Risk and Uncertainty* (London: Macmillan, 1968); Clem Tisdell, "Concepts of Rationality in Economics," *Philosophy of the Social Sciences*, 5 (1975), pp.259-73; John Broome, "Choice and Value in Economics," *Oxford Economic Papers*, 3 (1978), pp.313-333.

12 Barry Schwartz, *The Battle for Human Nature* (New York: W. W. Norton & Co., 1986).

13 Fritz Machlup, *Methodology of Economics and Other Social Sciences* (New York: Academic Press, 1978), p.267.

14 See Leslie Stevenson, *Seven Theories of Human Nature*, 2nd. ed. (Oxford: Oxford University Press, 1974).

15 Thomas Schwartz, "Rationality and the Myth of the Maximum," *Nôus*, 6 (1972), p.97.

16 Amartya Sen, *On Ethics and Economics* (Oxford: Basil Blackwell, 1987), p.12, p.15.

17 Arrow, *Social Choice and Individual Values*, p.13. Often the expression "connected" is substituted by "complete." Cf. Sen, *Collective Choice and Social Welfare* (San Francisco: Holden-Day, Inc., 1970), p.3. "Consistent" is also interchangeable to "coherent" (TJ,p.143; MA,p.38).

18 Arrow, Ibid. A strong ordering is "a ranking in which no ties are possible." Ibid., pp.13-4.

19 Sen, *On Ethics and Economics*, p.13. Sen elaborates upon this point elsewhere as follows. Take a choice function C, assumed to be rational, and let R be the internal consistent relation representing it. Construct the relation R' from R by 'reversing' every preference, and let C' be the exact opposite choice function generated by R'. If an individual with unchanged characteristics (i.e., the same values, tastes, beliefs) is to end up choosing in exactly the 'opposite' way in each case, according to C' rather than C, "it would be hard to claim that his or her choices have remained just as 'rational'. But the 'opposite' choices are exactly as consistent!" Sen, "Rationality and Uncertainty," *Theory and Decision*, 18 (1985), p.110.

20 Sen, *On Ethics and Economics*, p.13.

21 Alan P. Hamlin, *Ethics, Economics and the State* (New York: St. Martin's Press, 1986), p.13.

22 Hume, *A Treatise of Human Nature*, bk.II, pt.II, sec.iii., pp.415f. Weber made a distinction between Wertrationalität and Zweckrationalität (value-rationality and purpose-rationality). The former is usually called intrinsic or substantive rationality and the latter instrumental or formal rationality. See

M. Rheinstein, ed., *Max Weber on Law in Economy and Society* (Cambridge, Massachusetts: Harvard University Press, 1954), p.1.   For a detailed comment on Weber, see Rogers Brubaker, *The Limits of Rationality: An Assay on the Social and Moral Thought of Max Weber* (London: Allen and Unwin, 1984).

23 Hamlin, p.15. The theory of revealed preference was initiated by P.A. Samuelson's *Foundations of Economic Analysis* (Cambridge: Harvard University Press, 1947).

24 G.C. Winston, "Addiction and Back-Sliding: A Theory of Compulsive Consumption," *Journal of Economic Behavior and Organization*, 1 (1980), pp.259-324. The principle of diminishing marginal utility does not work in this case.

25 Mary Gibson, "Rationality," *Philosophy & Public Affairs*, 6 (1977), pp.193-225.

26 Sen, *On Ethics and Economics*, p.15.

27 Hamlin, p.16.

28 Milton L. Myers, *The Soul of Modern Economic Man: Ideas of Self-Interest; Thomas Hobbes to Adam Smith* (Chicago: The University of Chicago Press, 1983), p.11.

29 Utilitarian principle of utility is a special case of the more general self-interest theory. For Bentham and Mill, the principle of utility is not for a mere instrumental value, but takes a form of intrinsic value. According to Bentham, the principle of utility is a *"principle* which states the greatest happiness of all those whose interest is in question, as being the right and proper, and only right and proper and universally desirable, end of human action." *An Introduction to the Principles of Morals and Legislation* in *The Utilitarians* (Garden city, New York: Anchor Books: 1973), pp.290f. n.1. Similarly, for Mill, "the utilitarian doctrine is, that happiness is desirable, and the only thing desirable, as an end; all other things being only desirable as means to that end." *Utilitarianism* in *The Utilitarians*, p.438.

30 Hamlin, p.17.

31 They are intensity, duration, certainty or uncertainty, propinquity or remoteness, fecundity, purity, and extent. Bentham, *An Introduction to the Principles* ..., p.38.

32 See Arrow, "Current Developments in the Theory of Social Choice," *Social Research*, 44 (1977), pp.607-22. Rpt. in Brian Barry and Russell Hardin, eds., *Rational Man and Irrational Society?*, (Beverly Hills: Sage Publications, 1982), pp.252-63.

33 See Richard L. Lippke, "The Rationality of the Egoist's Half-Way House," *The Southern Journal of Philosophy*, 25 (1987), pp.515-528.

34 Luce and Raiffa, *Games and Decision*, "2.1. A Classification of Decision Theory," pp.12-4.

35 Harsanyi, "Morality and the Theory of Rational Behavior," in A. Sen and B. Williams, eds., *Utilitarianism And Beyond* (Cambridge: The University Press, 1982), p.43.

36 W. Edwards, "The Theory of Decision Making," in Ward Edwards and Amos Tversky, eds., *Decision Making* (Baltimore: Penguin Books, 1967), p.14.

37 Harsanyi, "Morality and the Theory ...," p.44. In case of risk, expected-utility maximization is possible according to objective probabilities of possible outcomes, whereas under uncertainty probabilities are determined by individual's subjective estimations. Various operational principles including maximin principle for subjective estimations are not my present concern. See, Luce and Raiffa, pp.278-86. There, Luce and Raiffa mention four different operational principles: the maximin criterion, the minimax risk criterion, the pessimism-optimism index criterion of Hurwicz, the criterion based on the principle of insufficient reason. See Chapter III, n.58.

38 Andrew M. Colman, *Game Theory And Experimental Games: The Study of Strategic Interaction* (Oxford: Pergamon Press, 1982), p.143.

39 For the meanings of terms, see Chapter I. D. and Chapter IV. B.1.

40 Adam Smith, *An Enquiry into the Nature and Causes of the Wealth of Nations*, ed. Edwin Cannan (Chicago: The University of Chicago,1976), two vols. in one, vol.II, p.477.

41 See Andrew Schotter, *Free Market Economics: A Critical Appraisal.* (New York: St. Martin's Press, 1985), ch.ix. "Rationality and Market Failure."

42 A. Sen, "Rational Fools: A Critique of the Behavioral Foundations of Economic Theory," *Philosophy & Public Affairs*, 6 (1976-7), pp.317-44.

43 Luce and Raiffa, pp.94ff. Luce and Raiffa characterize the Prisoner's Dilemma as an example of a two-person non-zero-sum noncooperative game; non-zero-sum because the game is not strictly competitive, i.e., it is not the case that what one person gains the other loses and vice versa, and noncooperative because no preplay communication is permitted between players and agreement between them is not binding.

44 Campbell and Sowden, p.5. See Chapter I, n.42.

45 Schelling, p.50. See Chapter I, n.50. Cf. Edna Ullmann-Margalit, *The Emergence of Norms* (Oxford: Clarendon Press, 1977), p.48. n.7. Passenger model is Ullmann-Margalit's interpretation of the dilemma.

46 Ullmann-Margalit, Ibid.

47 Campbell and Sowden, p.10.

48 Doel, p.29. Table 2.1. A typology of pure and impure social goods (economic and non-economic goods). See n.6.

49 Allen Buchanan, "Revolutionary Motivation and Rationality," *Philosophy & Public Affairs*, 9 (1979), p.64.

50 Colman, p.156. The preference ordering of the free- rider is exactly the same matrix as the preference ordering of the prisoners in Table 2, i.e., release is preferred to one year to five years to ten years.

51 Richard Tuck, "Is there a free-rider problem, and if so, what is it?" in Ross Harrison, ed., *Rational Action* (Cambridge: Cambridge University Press, 1979), p.148. In this regard, the Problem is related to the ancient paradox of the Sorites (the paradox of the heap). There can never be a heap of stones since addition of one stone to something that is not a heap can never transform it into a heap. Alternatively there can never be anything but a heap of stones since if you take away one stone from a heap of stones, what remains is still a heap. See Tuck, p.152.

52 Mancur Olson, *The Logic of Collective Action* (Cambridge: Harvard University Press, 1965), p.2.

53 Gauthier, "Justice as Social Choice," in David Copp and David Zimmerman, eds., *Morality, Reason and Truth* (Totowa, New Jersey: Rowan & Allanheld, 1984), p.253.

54 Arrow, *Social Choice and Individual Values*, p.23.

55 Ibid., pp.22-33. The classical statement of the Theorem is in the first edition (1951) of the book. In the second edition (1963) and in other publications, Arrow provided several versions of the Theorem.

56 I follow Arrow's more succinct presentation in "Values and Collective Decision-Making," in P. Laslett and W.G. Runciman, eds., *Philosophy, Politics, and Society*, 3rd. ser. (Oxford: Basil Blackwell, 1967), pp.215-232, and "Formal Theories of Social Welfare," in P. Wiener, ed., *Dictionary of the History of Ideas* (New York: Charles Scribner's Sons, 1973), pp.276-84.

57 Arrow, "Values and Collective ...," p.226.

58 Ibid. If, for instance, several candidates are running for an office and the voter's preferences for these candidates are known, then the withdrawal of one candidate will not affect the relative preferences for the other candidates.

59 Ibid., p.227. The paradox is often called Condorcet's paradox.

60 For example, vote-trading (log-rolling) infringes P and I. Similar problem arises if resort is made to casting vote, pressure, and propaganda as a counter-intransitivity device. See C. Rowley and A. Peacock, *Welfare Economics: A Liberal Restatement* (London: Martin Robertson, 1975), pp.40f.

61 See Alfred F. Mackay, *Arrow's Theorem: The Paradox of Choice; A Case Study in the Philosophy of Economics* (New Haven: Yale University Press, 1980); and also J.S. Kelly, *Arrow's Impossibility Theorem* (New York: Academic Press, 1978); Paul Seabright, "Social Choice and Social Theories," *Philosophy & Public Affairs*, 18 (1984), pp.365-387; Charles R. Ploit, "Axiomatic Social Choice Theory: An Overview and Interpretation," *American Journal of Political Sciences*, 20 (1976), pp.511-96.

62 Arrow, *Social Choice and Individual Values*, p.74, p.84.

63 Scott Gordon, *Welfare, Justice, and Freedom* (New York: Columbia University Press, 1980), p.13.

64 Chantal Mouffe, "Rawls: Political Philosophy without Politics," *Philosophy and Social Criticism*, 13 (1987), p.114. And also see Douglas W. Rae, "The Limits of Consensual Decision," *The American Political Science Review*, 69 (1975), pp.1270-98.

65 Schotter, pp.36, 134. See n.41.

66 Amitai Etzioni, *The Moral Dimension: Toward a New Economics* (New York: The Free Press, 1988), p.2; Hamlin, p.21; Sen, "Rationality and Uncertainty," *Theory and Decision*, 18 (1985), p.110; Max Weber, "The Meaning of 'Ethical Neutrality' in Sociology and Economics," in *The Methodology of Social Sciences*, ed. and trans. E.A. Shils and H.A. Finch (Glencoe, Illinois: The Free Press, 1949), p.44; Alfred Schutz, "The Problems of Rationality in the Social World," *Econometrica*, 10 (1943), rpt. in Dorothy Emmet and Alasdair MacIntyre, eds., *Sociological Theory and Philosophical Analysis* (New York: The MacMillan Co., 1970), p.106; Russell Hardin, "Difficulties in the Notion of Economic Rationality," *Social Science Information*, 23 (1984), p.454.

67 Etzioni, p.xi.

68 Stephene Lea, Roger Tarpy, and Paul Webley, *The Individual in the Economy: A Survey of Economic Psychology* (Cambridge: The University Press, 1987), p.103.

69 For example, A. Downs claims that his models "should be tested primarily by the accuracy of their predictions rather than by the reality of their assumptions." in his *An Economic Theory of Democracy* (New York: Harper, 1957), p.21.

70 Barry Hindess, *Choice, Rationality, and Social Theory* (London: Unwin Hyman, 1988), p.2.

71 Milton Friedman, "The Methodology of Positive Economics," in *Essays in Positive Economics* (Chicago: University of Chicago Press, 1953), p.14.

72 Lea et al., p.128.

73 Ibid. "The analogy with the ideal gas laws of elementary physics is much overworked in this context: Just as physicists make assumptions about molecules that are known to be absurd (even novice physicists know that molecules are not smooth, perfectly elastic spheres) but are good enough to predict the behavior of real gases, so economists may make assumptions about individuals that are known to be false but are good enough to predict the behavior of the economy as a whole." However, the analogy is not so convincing since the economist's predictions do not approach to the level of the physicist's predictions.

74 Ibid., p.531.

75 Robin M. Hogarth and Melvin W. Reder, eds., *Rational Choice: The Contrast between Economics and Psychology* (Chicago: University of Chicago Press, 1986).

76 Ralf Dahrendorf, *"Homo Sociologicus,"* in *Essays on the Theory of Society* (London: Routledge & Kegan Paul,1968). I generally follow Boudon's explanation of the concept in the text. Raymond Boudon, *The Logic of Social Action: An Introduction to Sociological Analysis*, trans. David Silverman (London, Routledge & Kegan Paul, 1979), pp.155-62. For another helpful treatment of sociological challenge to rational choice theory, see Jon Elster, eds., *Rational Choice* (Oxford: Basil Blackwell, 1986), "Introduction," pp.22-5.

77 These rejoinders are from Elster, *Rational Choice*, pp.22f.

78 Denis H. Wrong, "The Oversocialized Conception of Man in Modern Sociology," *American Sociological Review*, 26 (1961), pp.183-93; G.E. Homans, "Bringing Men Back In," *American Sociological Review*, 29 (1964), pp.809-18.

79 Several attempts for a reconciliation between the two have been made. See Frederic Schick, *Having Reasons: An Essay on Rationality and Sociality* (Princeton: Princeton University Press, 1984); L. Levy-Garboua, ed., *Sociological Economics* (London: Sage Publishing, 1979).

80 Hamlin, *Ethics, Economics and the State*, p.21.

81 Hebert A. Simon, "A Behavioral Theory of Rational Choice," *Quarterly Journal of Economics*, 69 (1954), pp.99-118; *Reason in Human Affairs* (Stanford: Stanford University Press, 1983); *Models of Bounded Rationality*: vol.I, *Economic Analysis and Public Policy*; vol.II, *Behavioral Economics and Business Organization* (Cambridge: Cambridge University Press, 1982). Michael Slote has adopted this idea and philosophically developed it in *Beyond Optimizing: A Study of Rational Choice* (Cambridge: Harvard University Press, 1989).

82 T.C. Schelling,"Self-Command in Practice, in Policy, and in a Theory of Rational Choice," *American Economic Review*, 74 (1984), pp.1-11; J. Elster, *Ulysses and the Sirens: Studies in Rationality and Irrationality* (Cambridge:

Cambridge University Press, 1979); Derek Parfit, *Reasons and Persons* (Oxford: Oxford University Press, 1986); Edward F. McClennen, *Rationality and Dynamic Choice: Foundational Explorations* (Cambridge: The University Press, 1990). He uses his dynamic or resolute choice to criticize Gauthier: "Constrained Maximization and Resolute Choice," in Ellen Paul et al. eds., *The New Social Contract: Essays on Gauthier* (Oxford: Basil Blackwell, 1988), pp.95-118; Brian Skyrms, *The Dynamics of Rational Deliberation* (Cambridge: Harvard University Press, 1990).

83 Elster, pp.67-8. Alternatively, Parfit proposes that the observation of discounting is an argumentation for the extended concept of rationality (we shall see shortly), which holds not only that utility is whenever it occurs, but also that utility is utility whoever it occurs to (pp.117-94). Thus Parfit skillfully combines the present-aim theory with no-self theory for utilitarianism. There are many problems in Parfit's proposition, see "Symposium on Derek Parfit's *Reasons and Persons*," *Ethics*, 96 (1986).

84 Elster, p.36. Emphasis original. I do not think that imperfect rationality has been totally neglected through the history of philosophy. Plato, Aristotle, Aquinas, Kant, Hume discussed weakness of will. In contemporary times, Hare dealt with the problem of weakness of will as a crucial challenge to his prescriptivism: "it is maintained (in Hume's words), 'tis is one thing to know virtue, and another to conform the will to it'; people are constantly doing what they think they ought not to be doing; therefore prescriptivism must be wrong." R.M. Hare, *Freedom and Reason* (Oxford: Oxford University Press, 1963), p.67. Recently Donald Davidson and Alan Donagan and others take the imperfect rationality seriously in connection with philosophy of action, mind, or psychology theory. For a general instructive discussion and bibliography, see Myles Brand, *Intending And Acting* (Cambridge: MIT Press, 1984). For material more directly related to our topic, see David Pears, *Motivated Irrationality* (New York: Oxford University Press, 1984); Alfred R. Mele, *Irrationality: An Essay on Akrasia, Self-Deception and Self-Control* (New York: Oxford University Press, 1987); Chirstopher Cherniak, *Minimal Rationality* (Cambridge: MIT Press, 1986).

85 Hamlin, p.22.

86 Sen, "Choice, Ordering and Morality," in Stephen Körner, ed., *Practical Reason* (New Haven: Yale University Press, 1974), pp.54-82, and his "Rational Fools," and *On Ethics and Economics*; Arrow, *Social Choice and Individual Values* (1963); Rogger Trigg, *Reason and Commitment* (Cambridge: Cambridge University Press, 1973).

87 Sen, *On Ethics and Economics*, p.18; Arrow, "Extended Sympathy and the Possibility of Social Choice," *Philosophia*, 7 (1978), pp.223-37; R.L. Trivers, "The Evolution of Reciprocal Altruism," *Quarterly Review of Biology*, 46 (1971), pp.35-57.

88 See H. Margolis, *Selfishness, Altruism and Rationality* (Cambridge: Cambridge University Press, 1982); J. Philippe Ruston, *Altruism, Socialization, and Society* (Englewood Cliffs: Prentice Hall, 1980); David

Collard, *Altruism and Economy: A Study in Non-Selfish Economics* (New York: Oxford University Press, 1978); Edmund S. Phelps, *Altruism, Morality, and Economic Theory* (New York: Russell Sage Foundation, 1975); C.R. Badcock, *The Problem of Altruism: Freudian-Darwinian Solutions* (Oxford: Basil Blackwell, 1986); Robert Axelroad, *The Evolution of Cooperation* (New York: Basic Books, 1984); Richard Dawkins, *The Selfish Gene* (Oxford: Oxford University Press, 1976; new ed. 1989). For an informative as well as critical discussion, see Bernard Linsky and Mohan Matthen, eds., *Philosophy and Biology, Canadian Journal of Philosophy*, 14, suppl. (1988); Michael Ruse, *Philosophy of Biology Today* (Albany: State University of New York Press, 1988).

89   Hamlin, p.42. Also see Jon Elster, ed., *The Multiple Self* (Cambridge: Cambridge University Press, 1986). Plato's charioteer might be the first successful controller of the multiple motivations. However, there still remains the possible conflict or schizophrenia. See Peter Barham, *Schizophrenia and Human Values* (Oxford: Basil Blackwell, 1984); Gilles Deleuze and Félix Gauttari, *Anti-Oedipus: Capitalism and Schizophrenia*, trans. Robert Hurley et al. (Minneapolis: University of Minnesota Press, 1983). The ancient metaphor of a battle between virtue and temptation or reason and passion explain the possibility well. At this juncture, the extended school can have a relation with the imperfect school. What Davidson says about "the underlying paradox of irrationality," from which he thinks no theory can entirely escape is very instructive: "if we explain it too well, we turn it into a concealed form of rationality; while if we assign incoherence too glibly, we merely compromise our ability to diagnose irrationality by withdrawing the back ground of rationality needed to justify any diagnosis at all." "Paradoxes of Irrationality," in Richard Wollheim and James Hopkins, eds., *Philosophical Essays on Freud* (Cambridge: Cambridge University Press, 1982), p.303. Richard Rorty comments on this: "Davidson urges that the only way to resolve the paradox is, in the case of an individual person whose behavior is 'irrational', to 'partition' the mind in the manner of Freud - - so that the person contains two distinct, mutually inconsistent but internally (more or less) consistent systems of belief and desire, with elements of the one acting as cause of (but not as reason for) alterations in the other." I think that Rorty interprets Davidson not in terms of the extended school but in terms of the causal decision theory (even though Rorty does not use these terms). See Rorty, "Beyond Realism and Anti-Realism," in Ludwig Nagl and Richard Heinrich, eds., *Wo Steht Die Analytische Philosophie heute?* (MÜchen: R. Oldenbourg, 1986), pp.114-5. The causal decision theory is discussed in detail in Campbell and Sowden, and in Gädenfors and Sahlin (see n.42 of Chapter I and n.1 of this Chapter).

90   Elster, *Rational Choice*, p.22.

91   I have interpreted Rawls' rational deduction project of morality, i.e., rationality *cum* fairness, as a less radical deduction project in comparison with Gauthier's radical deduction project. See Chapter I. Section A.

92 Rawls, "Justice as Fairness: Political not Metaphysical," p.233; p.224. n.2. Cf. MA,pp.5-7; 184-187 for Gauthier's mentioning of the two schools.

93 See Myers' *The Soul of Modern Economic Man*, n.28. For other comments, see Fred M. Frohock, *Rational Association* (Syracuse: Syracuse University, 1987), ch.3. Liberal Models in Collective Choice; Anthony Arblaster, *The Rise and Decline of Western Liberalism* (Oxford: Basil Blackwell, 1984), ch.19. Liberalism Today: The Revival of Liberal Political Economy.

94 Brian Burket, *Radical Political Economy: An Introduction to the Alternative Economics* (New York: New York University Press, 1984), p.145. Burket interprets the Theorem that the developments occurred "within the mainstream of neoclassical economics, whose ideology pushed to its logical conclusion destroys its own foundations." Ibid. Nozick's discussion of Sen's paradox (AST,pp.164ff) supports the suspicion, too. See Sen, *Collective Choice and Social Welfare*, pp.78-88; "The Impossibility of A Paretian Liberal," *The Journal of Political Economy*, 78 (1970), pp.152-7. Sen's paradox is a developed version of Arrow's Theorem. See John L. Wriglesworth, *Libertarian Conflicts in Social Choice* (Cambridge: The Cambridge University Press, 1985); Jon Elster and Aanund Hylland, eds., *Foundations of Social Choice Theory* (Cambridge: The University Press,1986). Arrow's Theorem and Sen's Paradox are problematic to utilitarianism, too. See Jonathan Riley, *Liberal Utilitarianism* (Cambridge: Cambridge University Press, 1988).

95 J. Elster, "Marxism, Functionalism and Game Theory," *Theory and Society*, 11 (1982), pp.453-82; John Roemer, "Rational Choice Marxism: Some Issues of Method and Substance," in Roemer, ed., *Analytical Marxism* (Cambridge: Cambridge University Press,1986), pp.191-201. For a general introduction, see Allen E. Buchanan, "Marx, Morality, and History: An Assessment of Recent Analytical Work on Marx," *Ethics*, 98 (1987), pp.104-36.

96 McClennen, "Rational Choice and Public Policy," p.372.

97 See Paul Gomberg, "Marxism and Rationality," *American Philosophical Quarterly*, 26 (1989), pp.53-62; Andrew Levine, Elliott Sober, and Erik Olin Wright, "Marxism and Methodological Individualism, *New Left Review*, 162 (1987), pp.67-84; Alan Carling, "Rational Choice Marxism," *New Left Review*," 160 (1986), pp.24-62; Scott Lash and John Urry, "The New Marxism of Collective Action," *Sociology*, 18 (1984), pp.33-50.

98 Anthony Heath, *Rational Choice and Social Exchange* (Cambridge: Cambridge University Press, 1976), p.75.

99 Patrick Suppes, "Decision Theory," in Paul Edwards, ed., *The Encyclopedia of Philosophy*, p.310.

100 Rawls, "Kantian Constructivism in Moral Theory," p.529.

Chapter III

Hobbes, Rawls, and the Contractarian Dilemma

A. Hobbes' Contractarian Ethics

1. Rational Foundation of Hobbes' Ethics

The *modus operandi* of this study (i.e., two versions of contractarianism and its dilemma) starts from Rawls' exclusion of Hobbes' contractarianism: "My aim is to present a conception of justice which generalizes and carries to a higher level of abstraction the familiar theory of the social contract theory as found, say, in Locke, Rousseau, and Kant" — to which Rawls appends that "For all of its greatness, Hobbes' *Leviathan* raises special problems" (TJ,p.11;p.11. n.4). The primary task of this chapter is to show (a) what Hobbes' problems are and (b) how Rawls revises Hobbes so it will become clear how Hobbes' and Rawls' systems of contractarian ethics comprise the two horns of the contractarian dilemma.[1] As elaborated in Chapter I, the horns are either moral irrelevancy of rationality or circularity of moral assumptions prior to rationality. Derivatively, I will mention Rawls' second thoughts on the rational deduction project of contractarian ethics, which he developed after *A Theory of Justice*.

Hobbes' ethics has been generally neglected or rejected through the history of moral philosophy since Hobbes has been regarded basically as a political philosopher or an advocate of relentless egoism. In his major work, *Leviathan*, which is my main concern, Hobbes definitely points out that it is "the Doctrine of the POLITIQUES" whose major subject is "a Political Common-wealth" (LE,47,p.715;18,p.228).[2] But he appends that "the true and only Moral Philosophy" or "the Science of Natural Justice is the onely Science necessary for Soveraigns, and their principal Ministers"

(LE,15,p.215f; 31,p.407). Furthermore, he was considering "how much depth of Moral Philosophy is required [to] have the Administration of the Soveraign Power" (LE,31, p.407). In view of these passages it is clear that for Hobbes moral and political philosophies are complementary of each other.[3]   And also we have to see whether his alleged true moral philosophy is merely an implausible egoism. Our rational choice theoretic interpretation of Hobbes' ethics as the first horn of the dilemma is, in the end, congenial to the traditional rejection of it. However, I will analyze the failure of Hobbes' ethics into specific problems under the refined setting of rational choice theory.

Hobbes' contractarian ethics is composed of the following three stages: a characterization of the state of nature; the laws of nature as moral principles to overcome such a state; and the establishment of absolute sovereign power for compliance to laws of nature. I will elaborate the rational choice theoretic interpretation of these stages in the next subsection. The first task is to investigate the rational foundation of Hobbes' ethics, which is in support of this kind of interpretation in view of his general philosophical position.[4]

In *Leviathan*, Hobbes starts from his philosophical empiricism, which stresses sense-experience as the source of knowledge. Accordingly, his philosophical method for ethics starts from what he takes to be empirical premises (i.e., factual truths about human nature) and arrives at his conclusions by deductive arguments based upon these premises: "I ground the Civill Right of Soveraigns, and both the Duty and Liberty of Subjects, upon the Known naturall Inclinations of Mankind" (LE,A Review and Conclusion, p.725).[5]

Hobbes' philosophical empiricism holds both an ontological individualism/nominalism and a mechanistic concept of movement. Hobbes' view on human nature thus derives from these two sources. Every real thing in nature is "Individuall and Singular" (LE,4,p.102) and is in a perpetual motion: "When a Body is once in motion, it moveth (unless something els hinders it) eternally" (LE,2,p.88). For Hobbes, man, like other natural beings and objects, is an entity whose natural condition is not rest but motion. The types of motion which animate human behavior are classified into the two headings of 'appetite or desire' and 'aversion' and these forms of movement, either towards or away from things, are the springs of all human behavior (LE,6,p.119).

Thus the "general inclination of all mankind" is "a perpetual and restlesse desire of Power after Power, that ceaseth onely with death." (LE,11,p.161). Power is defined as the "present means to attain some future apparent Good" or "means and Instruments to acquire more" (LE,10,p.150). Good is in turn defined: "whatsoever is the object of any mans Appetite or Desire; that is it, which he for his part calleth *Good*: And the object of his Hate, and Aversion, *Evill*" (LE,6,p.120). In other words, "*Good* and *Evill*, are names that signifie our Appetites, and Aversions; which in different tempers, customes, doctrines of men, are different" (LE,15,p.216). And "of all voluntary Acts, the Object is to every man his own Good" and "every man is presumed to do all things in order to his own benefit" (LE,15, p.209; p.213). Accordingly, "Moral Philosophy is nothing else but the Science of what is *Good*, and *Evill*." (LE,15,p.216).

In this regard, Hobbes explicitly rejects the Aristotelian view that men, as a political animal (zoon politikon), are naturally social creatures. And he contrasts human beings with "certain living creatures, as Bees, and Ants, who live sociably one with other" (LE, 17,p.225).[6] From his ontological individualism — the natural world is composed of unique and discrete individual bodies — Hobbes derives an individualistic conception of human beings: "We do not therefore by nature seek Society for its own sake, but that we may receive some Honor or Profit from it; these we desire primarily, that secondarily."[7] This idea is manifested by the idea of Hobbes' social contract as a methodological individualism — civil society as "Artificial Body" is solely founded on an agreement between self-interested individuals (LE,A Review and Conclusion,p.728).[8]

To sum up, this discussion on the methodological foundations of Hobbes' ethics in view of his general philosophical position seems to be quite favorable to a rational theoretic interpretation. First, Hobbes' ethics as methodological individualism shares a structural isomorphism with rational choice theory. Second, generally speaking, power can be broadly regarded to be a practical capacity for utility-maximization (as desire-fulfillment), and good and evil are measured by a subjective and relativistic utility of self-interest maximization (basic concept of neo-classical rationality).

However, appetite and aversion as a measure of individual self-interest maximization are the faculties of passions (LE,6, p.122).[9] This means that rational theoretic interpretation is still incomplete. Our remaining task is how to explain passions in connection with the neo-classical concept of rationality.

In contrast to his emphasis on passions, Hobbes repeatedly points out that the laws of nature (moral principles) are derived from "dictates of Reason" and that "Reason ... dictateth to every man his own good" (LE,15,p.216;p.203). Therefore "the true doctrine of the Lawes of Nature, is the true Morall Philosophie" (LE,15,p.216). And also he points out that "The Lawes of Nature are Immutable and Eternall" (LE,15,p.215). At this juncture, I think that the apparent discrepancy between reason and passion, and between subjectivity/relativity and eternality might be solved through a careful appreciation of Hobbes' conception of reason. The thrust is that, for Hobbes, reason is a purely instrumental rationality such that even though individual utility is subjective and relativistic, instrumental rationality can provide common inter-subjective instrumental goods (peace, self-preservation, comfortable living, etc.). Then, instrumental rationality and passion can be compatible, or can take divisions of labor such that they provide a justificatory and motivational foundation for the contractarian agreement in face of individualistic and relativistic concept of good.[10]

For Hobbes, reason as a faculty of mind is primarily characterized as a purely calculative ability.

> For Reason, in this sense [faculty of mind], is nothing but *Reckoning* (that is, Adding and Substracting) of the Consequences of general names agreed upon, for the *marking* and *signifying* of our thoughts (LE,5,p.111).

Then, how is reason as reckoning related to appetites or desires which animate and dominate our actions? At this point, Hobbes' concept of reason is dramatically defined as a purely instrumental (perhaps only less dramatic than Hume's)[11]: "the Thoughts, are to the Desires, as Scouts, and Spies, to range abroad, and find the way to the things Desired" (LE,8,p.139). In other words, Hobbes' reason is an instrumental rationality which maximizes individual's own good which is given by his own desire and appetite.[12]

This observation is confirmed by the fact that Hobbes explicitly rejects every form of the traditional intrinsic concept of rationality in his time. First, he rejects Platonic moral realism and Stoic natural law theory: "There being nothing simply and absolutely so [good or evil]; nor any common Rule of Good and Evill, to be taken from the nature of the objects themselves" (LE,6,p.120). Second, he rejects Aristotelian fixed hierarchic or perfectionistic concept of good: "there is no such *Finis ultimus*, (utmost ayme,) nor *Summum Bonum* (Greatest Good)" (LE,11,p.160). Third, he rejects Christian theological views - Augustinian and Thomistic divine command (will or law) theory of good (something is good because God wills it, or alternatively, God wills it because it is good): Individual will determines his or her own good and "will" is "the last Appetite in Deliberating" (LE,6,p.128). And then, "the Divines Lawes" are nothing but "Dictates of Naturall Reason" which follow natural inclinations of human beings. (LE,31,p.319). More explicitly, Hobbes wants to know "what Praecepts are dictated to men, by their Natural Reason onely, without other word of God" (LE,31,p.399).

From Hobbes' rejection of the above traditional moral philosophies, I infer that even though Hobbes uses the medieval terminology of natural right or laws of nature, these are grounded on a modern rational foundationalism of instrumental rationality.[13]

2. State of Nature, Laws of Nature, and Absolute Sovereign Power: Rational Choice Theoretic Interpretation

Hobbes' ethics is composed of the three stages as he succinctly summarizes:

> That the condition of meer Nature, that is to say, of absolute Liberty, such as is theirs, that neither are Soveraigns, nor Subjects, is Anarchy, and the condition of Warre: That the Praecepts, by which men are guided to avoyd that condition, are the Lawes of Nature: That a Common-wealth, without Soveraign Power, is but a word, without substance, and cannot stand (LE,31,p.395).

With the help of our previous discussions of rational choice theory, these stages can be classified into: (1) an initial choice situation as

PD (Prisoner's Dilemma) non-cooperative situation; (2) resultant agreement of moral principles as possibility of cooperation; (3) coerced compliance to the agreed principles as avoidance of NPD (N-person PD) or FR (Free-rider Problem).

The state of nature is typically characterized as "a condition of Warre of every one against every one [*bellum omnium contra omnes*]; in which case every one is governed by his own Reason" (LE,13,p.189). This means that the state of nature is a non-moral situation in which reason, as maximization of instrumental rationality, is fully employed without any moral constraint:

> To this warre of every man against every man, this is also consequent; that nothing can be Unjust. The notions of Right and Wrong, Justice and Injustice have there no place. Where there is no common power, there is no Law: where there is no Law, no Injustice. Force, and Fraud, are in warre the two Cardinal vertues (LE,13,p.188).

In this regard, Hobbes relates the right of nature, or natural right to the concept of liberty "as the absence of external Impediments" (LE,14,p.189). Liberty is to use an individual's own power for the preservation of his or her own life and to permit him or her to do anything, according to the "Reason, hee shall conceive to be the aptest means thereunto" (LE,14,p.189). Consequently, "every man has a right to everything; even to one anothers body" (LE,14, p.190).[14] Hobbes' concept of the linkage between natural right and liberty once again confirms the non-moral unlimited maximizational view of instrumental rationality.

It is straightforwardly clear that the state of nature, in which unlimited free right is exercised by all individuals, falls into the state of war in which there is "no security to any man, (how strong or wise soever he be,)" of preserving his or her own life (LE,14,p.190). Here, Hobbes' concept of equality is added to the main causes of conflict in the state of nature. "Nature hath made men so equall, in the faculties of body, and mind" (LE,13,p.183). From this initial equality, all men are considered to be equal in the state of nature firstly by virtue of the equality due to insecurity (even the weakest can kill the strongest), and secondly by virtue of the equality of their rational hopes in attaining the satisfaction of their desires. To sum up, Hobbes claims that "all men equally, are by Nature Free" (LE,21,p.268). Hobbes' pronouncement of free and equal (rational) human beings in the state of nature became a classical statement of the liberal, or possibly liberal democratic concept of liberty and equality. In the domain of contractarian liberalism, even though Locke, Rousseau, and Kant did not agree with Hobbes' non-liberal or non-democratic political absolutism, all of them admitted Hobbes' liberal or democratic premises (leaving aside the variation in the practical contents of liberty and equality, and its relation).[15] Even Rawls, who abandons Hobbes for Kant, starts from "a free and equal rational being" (TJ,p.252).

Another important thing is that Hobbes characterizes the major conflict in the state of nature as a problem of distributive justice. According to Hobbes, from the freedom and equality, "every man is contended with his share" and "therefore if any two men desire the same thing, which neverthelesse they cannot both enjoy, they become enemies" (LE,13,p.184).[16] This is the first among the principal causes of conflict in the state of nature, that is, "Competition" for gain. The other two causes are "Diffidence" and "Glory" which are required for safety and for reputation (LE,p.13,p.185).[17] Thus every individual in the state of nature suffers from the "incommodities of such a war" — the famous passage: "the life of men, solitary, poore, nasty, brutish, and short" (LE,13,p.186).

Under the "incommodities" of the state of war, every individual realizes that "Peace is good" and therefore also "the way or means of Peace, which ... are the Laws of Nature, are good" (LE,15,p.216). Along with the passions, the fear of death and desire for commodious living, "Reason suggesteth convenient Articles of Peace, upon which men may be drawn to agreement" (LE,13,p.188). Here, an important observation concerning Hobbes' rational deduction project of morality is that if reason brings human beings into the state of war, it can also lead them out of it. Laws of nature are precepts, "found out by Reason, by which man is forbidden to do, that, which is destructive of his life" (LE,15,p.189). Accordingly, the precept, or general rule of reason is "That every man, ought to endeavor Peace, as farre as he has hope of obtaining it; and when he cannot obtain it, that he may seek, and use, all helps, and advantage of Warre" (LE,14,p.190). The first part of this statement is called the first and fundamental law of nature. The second part is just the right of nature, which is conditionally added to the first. This means that Hobbes' concept of morality is a conditional morality, not like an absolute sense of the maxim: Let justice be done though the heaven falls [*Fiat justitia, ruat caelum*].

This concept of conditional morality immediately leads to the second law of nature, which is the cornerstone of Hobbes' account of contractarian morality:

> That a man be willing, when others are so too, as farre-forth, as for Peace, and defence of himselfe he shall think it necessary, to lay down this right to all things; and be contented with so much liberty against other men, as he would allow other men against himselfe" (LE,14, p.190).

Since the unlimited right of nature gives rise to war, the second law of nature requires a person to lay down his or her right to all things. He or she may do this through renunciation or transfer. Hobbes' view on obligation is grounded upon those activities of renouncing or transferring of right: An individual is "said to OBLIGED, or BOUND, not to hinder those, to whom such Right is granted, or abandoned, from the benefit from it" (LE,14,p.191). At this point morality as a constraint enters Hobbes' account since "such hindrance is INJUSTICE, and INJURY, as being SINE JURE [without right]" (LE,14,p.191).

This concept of morality however is strictly conditioned by the basic essentials of contract. A man will of course only transfer or renounce his right in exchange for "some GOOD to himselfe," in particular "for some RIGHT reciprocally transferred to himselfe" (LE,14,p.192). This mutual transferring of right is called 'contract' (pact or covenant) and "without mutall acceptation," there is no contract (LE,14,p.197).[18] Hobbes' emphasis on mutuality or reciprocity of contract is connected with another important aspect of contract, that is, voluntary act. For Hobbes, the object of a voluntary act is to gain some good to himself and there is "no Obligation on any man, which ariseth not from some Act of his own" (LE,21,p.268).

These basic essentials of contractual condition are explicitly employed in Hobbes' defense of the second law. It is plain that as long as every man holds his right of nature, every man falls into the state of war.

But if other men will not lay down their Right, as well as he; then there is no Reason for any one, to devest himselfe of his: For that were to expose himselfe to Prey, (which no man is bound to) rather than to dispose himselfe to Peace (LE,14,190).

Right after this, Hobbes points out that this strictness of mutuality reflects the golden rule: "Whatsoever you require that others should do to you, that do ye to them." Yet, Hobbes' thought is slightly misleading since the golden rule does not rely on strict mutuality in so far as it is concerned with loving or caring for others unilaterally.[19] In this regard, Kavka correctly interprets Hobbes' second law as 'the copper rule': "Do unto others as they do unto you" because "it glitters less brightly as an inspiring ideal of moral conduct than does the golden rule."[20] As I emphasized as the cornerstone of Hobbes' contractarian ethics, the second law has attracted wide interest: Rawls interprets it as *modus vivendi* of morality, Gauthier as rational bargain, Axelrod as tit-for-tat, Taylor as conditional cooperation, Braybrooke even as a no suckers rule.[21]

In view of the strict mutuality of the second law, a contract would not serve its purpose of securing peace if it was not kept. Thus Hobbes introduces the third law of nature: "men performe their Covenants made: without which, Covenants are in vain, and but Empty words" (LE,15,p.201). And Hobbes considers it as "the Fountain and Originall of Justice" (LE,15,p.202). The reason why Hobbes makes the second and third laws separate is that agreement and compliance are quite different things. Even though contracting parties agree on moral principles, still there is no security or assurance that the others will perform their duties. Here, Hobbes introduces a distinction between a void and non-void contract. Unilateral performance (making oneself a prey to others) is forbidden as we saw in Hobbes' defense of the second law. Thus, an individual should not do his or her part unless he or she is sure that the others will do theirs. A covenant of mutual trust in the state of nature is therefore void "upon any reasonable suspicion": "For he that peformeth first, has no assurance the other will performe after." And therefore he "does but betray himself to his enemy" (LE,14,p.196). But "if there be a common Power set over them both, with right and force sufficient to compell performance; it is not Voyd" (LE,14,p.196).

Thus Hobbes comes to the last stage of his contractarian ethics. The central point (leaving aside the details of contracting procedure between political sovereign and subjects and its resultant government formation) is that "the Validity of Covenants begins not but with the Constitution of a Civil Power, sufficient to compell men to keep them" (LE,15,p.203). The contract of transferring of rights to the civil power institutes "an Absolute and Arbitrary Legislative Power" which is itself not a party of the contract and thus guaranteed to do whatever is necessary to secure peace (LE,A Review and Conclusion,p.721). Thus Hobbes strongly proclaims that "Covenant, without the Sword, are but Words, and of no strength to secure a man at all" (LE,17, p.223).

We are now in a position to interpret the three stages according to PD situation.[22] The state of war resulted from the state of nature, in which nonmoral rationality employed, is a noncooperative situation.

In the state of nature, it is assumed that each individual has a choice between two strategies, P and W (strategies of peace and war). Even though the state of peace is preferred by every individual to the state of war, choosing P creates insecurity because in the state of nature those who unilaterally move from W to P will be preyed upon if, as is likely, the other parties choose W. This means that W is the rational strategy for each man in the sense that it is the dominant strategy regardless of the others' choice of P or W. Thus we can infer that Hobbes' state of nature is a PD situation.

Then how can the power of the absolute sovereign solve the PD problem? Hobbes' says: "there must be some coercive Power, to compell men equally to the performance of their Covenants, by the terrour of some punishment, greater than the benefit they expect by the breach of their Covenant" (LE,15,p.202). Actually coercive power changes individual preference ordering through punishment.[23] Thus the situation under coercive power is no longer PD structured.   In the terminology of rational choice, this is a transition from a PD game to an assurance game.[24] This means furthermore that the assurance game under absolute sovereignty can solve the problem of NPD or FR. "The Foole" challenges Hobbes on the score that under the security of the other parties' performance of their duties, a free-rider can stand with "that

Reason, which dictateth to every man his own good" (LE,15,p.203). According to Hobbes, "he that having sufficient Security, that others shall observe the same Lawes towards him, observes them not himselfe, seeketh not Peace but War" (LE,15,p.215). Hobbes' observation of this matches up perfectly with the interpretation of FR as a generalized PD or NPD, as was discussed in Chapter II. Free-rider's preference ordering is also changed by the fear of punishment.

In sum, Hobbes' absolute sovereign constitutes a solution to the binary problem of transition from the state of war to the state of peace and of stabilization of compliance to the contractarian moral principles.[25] Gauthier clearly shows how individual preference ordering is changed according to Hobbes' solution through the following two tables.[26]

Table 6. PD Game in the Hobbesian State of War

Numeration: Preference ordering
W,P: Strategies of War, Peace
Equilibrium: W,W (3,3)

		Individual B	
		P	W
Individual A	P	2,2	4,1
	W	1,4	3,3

Table 7. Assurance Game under the Hobbesian Sovereign

Equilibrium: P,P (1,1)

		Individual B	
		P	W
Individual A	P	1,1	4,2
	W	2,4	3,3

3. Hobbes' Ethics as the First Horn of the Contractarian Dilemma: Moral Irrelevance of Rationality

As I mentioned at the beginning of this chapter, I will uncover the failure of Hobbes' ethics through Rawls' criticism of it. First, concerning Hobbes' state of nature, the basic problem is whether it is an appropriate hypothetical initial choice situation.[27] According to rational choice interpretation, Hobbes' contractarian decision in the state of nature is a complex version of a problem in strategic bargaining, in which concepts such as the status quo, threat advantage and strategy play a key role. In this contracting process, individuals are assumed to possess full self-knowledge; they know who they are, what concept of the good they hold, and what their endowments and practical powers are. Thus ethical conclusions that emerge necessarily reflect this knowledge. This problem is directly connected with an essential issue of distributive justice: the issue of "locating the appropriate 'baseline' for rational choice or bargaining approaches to distributive justice."[28]   In plain words, what can contracting parties initially bring to the bargaining table from which distributive shares of cooperative surplus are determined?[29]

I interpreted the major conflict in Hobbes' state of nature as a conflict in the circumstances of justice in which everyone contends with everyone for his or her secure distributive shares. Hobbes' initial egalitarian assumption of free and equal rational being does not lead to an egalitarian view on distributive justice.[30] This means that, in the state of nature, unfair or unequal equilibrium between individuals as well as groups can prevail. Concerning individuals and groups, Hobbes explicitly points out this possibility respectively:

> The most frequent reason why men desire to hurt each other, ariseth hence, that many men at the same time have an Appetite to the same thing; which yet very often they can neither enjoy in common, nor divided it; whence it follows that the strongest must have it, and who is strongest must be decided by the Sword (*De Cive*, p.46)."

> Nor is it the joyning together of a small number of men, that gives them this security [under sovereign]; because in small numbers, small additions on the one side or the other, make the advantage of strength so great, as is sufficient to carry the Victory" (LE,17,p.224).

In view of these two passages, it is understandable why Rawls criticizes Hobbes' ethics as "a *modus vivendi*, the stability of which does depend on happenstance and a balance of relative forces."[31] Rawls relates this observation to "the Hobbesian strand in liberalism," that is, "liberalism as a *modus vivendi* secured by a convergence of self- and group-interest as coordinated and balanced by well-designed constitutional arrangements."[32]   In this regard, Rawls rejects the Schumpeter-Dahl model of liberal democracy (TJ,pp.361f).[33] Such liberals abandon the moral justification of liberalism. They consider democratic constitutionalism instead as merely a decision procedure which provides the framework for settling conflicts among competing interest groups for politically distributable goods.[34]

As mentioned in Chapter I, Rawls' rationality *cum* fairness model of the original position under the veil of ignorance is devised to correct the moral irrelevancy of Hobbes' rational deduction project. Rawls repeatedly emphasizes that, in the original position, the parties have no basis for "bargaining" or acting on the "ideal of a game" (TJ,pp.139,145) since no one knows his or her situation in society nor his or her natural assets, and therefore no one is in a position to tailor principles to his or her advantage. Even though Rawls still thinks that his theory of justice is a part of rational choice theory, he puts an important qualification on the use of rational choice theory as the foundation of morality: An unfair initial situation of the bargaining model cannot guarantee the fair resultant determination of distributive shares. In this same spirit, Rawls explicitly rejects Braithwaite's game theoretic model of distributive justice (TJ,p.134,n.10).[35] For Braithwaite's bargaining game solution necessarily generates the principle "to each according to his threat advantage" which "is hardly the principle of fairness."[36]

Now to move to the second problem with Hobbes' ethics. Concerning the institution of the absolute sovereign for compliance with contractarian agreement, the basic problem is whether coercion is a real solution to NPD or FR or whether coercion is compatible with voluntary moral motivation. Before dealing with this basic problem, I will treat another related issue: viz., the liberal agenda for the appropriateness of Hobbes' monarchic absolute state in which the arbitrary power of the State is "incommunicable and inseparable" (LE,18,p.236).

Admittedly, throughout the contractarian liberal tradition, various 'governmental contracts' (*pactum subjectionis*) have been suggested as revisions to Hobbes' non-liberal absolute state. And also, in the domain of social choice or democratic theory, it has been pointed out that Hobbes' absolute state breaches Arrow's condition D (non-dictatorship).[37] Further, Locke and Rousseau suggested their versions of limited government. Locke proposed a representative parliamentarianism, whereas Rousseau proposed a popular democratic republicanism (ST,11,140; SC,II,6,104).[38] But whatever their differences may be, the liberal rationale of Locke and Rousseau for establishing sovereignty is basically the same as Hobbes' to the extent that sovereignty provides the coercive power for contractarian compliance (recall Hobbes' distinction between void—vain, invalid— and non-void agreement in our discussion of his third law of nature). Locke explicitly points out that "the law of nature would ... be in vain, if there were no body that in the Sate of Nature, had a *Power to Execute* that Law, and thereby preserve the innocent and restrain offenders" (ST,2,7). Rousseau, by the same token, declares in his famous as well as controversial passage that:[39]

> In order, then, that the social pact may not be a vain formula, it tacitly includes this engagement, which can alone give force to the others—that whoever refuses to obey the general will shall be constrained to do so by the whole body; which means nothing else than that he shall be *forced to be free* (SC,I,7,54; emphasis mine).

From the above two passages, I infer that Locke and Rousseau regard sovereignty as the coercive solution to FR since they are talking about "the transgressor" (ST,2,7) and the person that "he would be willing to enjoy the rights of a citizen without being willing to fulfill the duties of a subject" (SC,I,7,53).

If this is the case, the issue of the limitation of government is a slightly different one. This issue comes down to the rationality of contracting parties. This means that even though the institution of sovereignty as a guarantee of compliance is basically rational to contracting parties, it is irrational to give absolute power. It follows that Hobbes' rational deduction project is not only morally irrelevant but also irrational. Rawls as an advocate of liberal democracy criticizes Hobbes' absolute state on the score of rationality, that is, cost-benefit analysis. Through this analysis, Rawls claims:

> The establishment of a coercive agency is rational only if these disadvantages [taxational burden and interference in individual freedom] is less than the loss of liberty from instability. Assuming this to be so, the best arrangement is one that minimizes these hazards" (TJ,p.241).

However, it is noteworthy that Hobbes recognizes this problem: "But a man may here object, that the Condition of Subjects is very miserable; as being obnoxious to the lusts, and other irregular passions of him, or them [sovereignty] that have so unlimited a Power in their hands" (LE,18,p.238). But Hobbes considers a willing acceptance of these burdens on the part of subjects as the cost of peace under the severe situation of NPD or FR.

The liberal agenda brings us around to the basic problem of compliance which was mentioned at the beginning of this subsection. That is, the problem is whether contractarian liberal ethics can provide compliance through a non-coercive voluntary solution to NPD or FR. In this connection, the important thing is whether Hobbes' coercive solution fails in view of the rational deduction project of morality.

In the domain of rational choice, it has been frequently pointed out that Hobbes' coercive solution fails in view of rational voluntary compliance. The standard argument against Hobbes is that he does not show 'the Foole' (free rider) that the fool's behavior does not "stand with that Reason, which dictateth to every man his own good" (LE,15,p.203). According to the fool's calculation, if free riding makes it reasonable (rational in the sense of maximization) to break a valid covenant, then the third law of nature, "That men perform their Covenants made" (LE,15,p.201), is not a rule of reason (i.e., reason cannot be equated with rationality as self-interest maximization). "The Hobbesian equation of morality with rational prudence then collapses."[40] In terms of voluntariness, Hobbes does not show that "rational *non tuistic* agents will voluntarily agree either to establish such a sovereign or to keep it in being." For "they keep it in being by acting rationally on their fear of coercion; not by anything like continued adherence to a voluntary continued contract."[41]

Rawls basically agrees with the standard argument against Hobbes' coercive solution to the contractarian compliance. And Rawls interprets Hobbes' failure as moral peril of psychological egoism.[42] As we saw in chapter II, Rawls explicitly indicates that even though his contractarian ethics hinges on the rational choice, it does not endorse egoism. Rawls thus regards general egoism — "everyone is permitted to advance his interests as he pleases" — as no agreement point in the original position (TJ,pp.124,147). In this respect, Rawls asserts that general egoism leads to "the general case of the prisoner's dilemma of which Hobbes' state of nature is the classical example" (TJ,p.269).

However, it is notable that Rawls does not belong to the following philosophers: "Everyone knows that coercion is necessary for ordinary men, yet many philosophers have believed that perfectly good and wise men could do without it, that perfect men left alone would inhabit utopias."[43] Rawls admits coercion as a necessary condition for compliance on many occasions: "a coercive sovereign is presumably always necessary, even though in a well-ordered society sanctions are not severe and may never need to be imposed" (TJ,p.240). However, Rawls claims that coercion is a necessary condition, but not a sufficient condition for compliance. Thus, for Rawls, "it remains to be shown that this disposition to take up and to be guided by the standpoint of justice accords with the individual's good" (TJ,p.567). The thrust of Rawls' view on voluntary compliance relies on the Platonic grand theory of 'congruence'; "in a well-ordered society, being a good man (and in particular having an effective sense of justice) is indeed a good for that person" (TJ,p.577). Against Hobbes, Rawls finally maintains that "the hazards of the generalized prisoner's dilemma are removed by the match between the right and the good" (TJ,p.577).

To recapitulate, Hobbes' contractarian ethics of rational foundationalism fails since it cannot guarantee a fair agreement in the non-moral rational initial choice situation. Nor can it guarantee voluntary rational compliance to the valid contractarian moral principles. This means that Hobbes' ethics fails both with respect to *ex ante* and *ex post* rational foundationalism. Therefore I conclude that Hobbes' contractarian ethics cannot escape the first horn, the moral irrelevancy of rationality.

Braybrooke pinpoints in his helpful paper, "The Insoluble Problem of the social contract," that "To be sure of arriving at a contract, and of having it kept up, one must change the problem [of Hobbes], either by assuming different circumstances or by assuming different motivations."[44]   Both Rawls and Gauthier change the circumstances as well as the motivations. As explained in the two previous chapters, Rawls pays attention to the circumstances (original position under the veil of ignorance), whereas Gauthier pays attention to the motivations (rationality as constrained maximization). Rawls eradicates the Hobbesian roots of contractarian bargaining from his original position, whereas Gauthier keeps the basic spirit of Hobbes with his way of taming Leviathan.

Our next task then is to elaborate and assess Rawls' contractarian ethics in his *A Theory of Justice*.

B. Rawls' Contractarian Ethics in A Theory of Justice

1. Fairness cum Rationality in the Original Position

Even though Rawls' book, *A Theory of Justice*, is composed of dense and complicated arguments, it can be interpreted as a system of three stages: (1) the initial or original choice situation; (2) a set of principles of justice derived from the situation; (3) the application of these principles and the compliance to them.[45]   In this section, I will show how these three stages are related to our very limited focus of the book, that is, to Rawls' contractarian rational deduction project of morality. First, I will elaborate on the characterization of the first stage, i.e., the original position. Next, I will explain Rawls' maximin derivation and his theory of compliance to his two principles of justice. Finally, I will show how Rawls' contractarian ethics falls victim of the second horn of the contractarian dilemma.

Rawls' book opens with the claim that "justice is the first virtue of social institutions" (TJ,p.3). The primary subject of justice is "the basic structure of society, or more exactly, the way in which the major social institutions distribute fundamental rights and

duties and determine the divisions of advantages from social cooperation" (TJ,p.7). According to Aristotle's terminology, this kind
of justice is called distributive justice.[46]

Thus, Rawls' contractarian ethics is a methodologicial framework for distributive justice. He appeals to a modified traditional
theory of social contract where the original contract is neither a
social contract proper of a historical civil society nor a governmental contract, but a hypothetical construct. His guiding idea is that:

> the principles of justice for the basic structure of society are the object of the
> original agreement. They are the principles that free and rational persons
> concerned to further their own interests would accept in an initial position of
> equality as defining the fundamental terms of their association (TJ,p.11).

This way of regarding the principles of justice Rawls calls 'justice as
fairness' (TJ,p.11). As Rawls admits, justice as fairness is
'individualistic' and as such society is defined as 'a cooperative
venture for mutual advantage' of individuals (TJ,pp.264,4).
However, the cooperative venture is not in a setting of perfect
harmony. Rawls says that "it is typically marked by a conflict as
well as by an identity of interests" (TJ,p.4). In terms of distributive
justice, this means that social cooperation can provide cooperative
surplus to individuals, but individuals strive for greater distributive
shares of cooperative surplus than others'. Rawls thus thinks that
if ethics is a guideline for social cooperation, "any reasonably
complete ethical theory must include principles for" distributive
justice (TJ,p.10).

In view of his guiding idea, Rawls is basically in line with the
basic assumptions of traditional contractarian liberalism concerned
as it is with free and equal rational human beings and the possibility
of contractarian agreement in the midst of a conflict of interests.[47]

However, this observation must not overshadow Rawls' persistent claim that justice as fairness is a remedy for traditional
contract theory, especially of Hobbes' (TJ,p.584, p.11). For Rawls'
justice as fairness, the original position corresponds to the state of
nature in the traditional theory. Rawls' task is foremost how to
characterize 'the original position', so that it will guarantee a fair
agreement. Even though Rawls admits that there are possibly
many interpretations of 'the initial situation,' he emphatically maintains that 'the original position' is 'philosophically most favored'

(TJ,p.121f).   If this is the case, individual rational choice is employed under the preinstalled fair conditions of the original position.   In other words, Rawls' rational deduction project represents a rationality *cum* fairness framework.   This means that "the original position ... unites in one conception a reasonably clear problem of choice [from individual rationality] with the conditions that are widely recognized as fitting to impose on the adoption of moral principles" (TJ,p.584).

What conditions does Rawls impose on the original position according to the above union of rationality *cum* fairness?   The conditions of the original position can be classified mainly into four categories.[48]   The first condition is the circumstances of justice in which "human cooperation is possible and necessary" (TJ,p.126). As mentioned several times before, these are the objective circumstances of 'moderate scarcity' of natural and social resources and the circumstances of the subject whose motivation is 'mutual disinterest' (TJ,p.128).   Rawls thinks that these circumstances represent general and perpetual conditions of mankind.   That is, he thinks that human beings are neither in a pure competitive 'zero-sum game society,' nor in one of abundance or affluence concerning natural and social resources.   Further, he says, they are not in the society of 'saints and heroes' (in the sense of self-interest sacrifice) concerning subjective motivations (TJ,pp.539,127,130).[49]   In other words, the circumstances as to the general facts of human society are not curtailed off by the veil of ignorance, as we will see shortly.

The second condition is 'the formal constraints of the concept of right.'   Rawls asserts that the following five formal requirements hold for the choice of all ethical principles, and not only for those of justice.   Parties in the original position must limit their choice of principles to those which satisfy the requirements of universality, generality, publicity, ordering and finality.   "a conception of right is a set of principles, general in form and universal in application, that is to be publicly recognized as final court of appeal for ordering the conflicting claims of moral persons" (TJ,p.135).   These constraints are in a relative degree considered as proper formal conditions for morality throughout the history of ethics (especially from Kant to Hare).   One constraint, which needs to be specified, is ordering. Rawls' concept of ordering refers to the internal consistency of rationality, i.e., connectedness and transitivity, as were discussed in Chapter II (TJ,p.134).   When Rawls sets forth this concept of ordering, he actually has in mind that his theory of justice can overcome Arrow's Impossibility Theorem (TJ,p.134. n.9).

The third condition is the (celebrated as well as controversial) veil of ignorance. For Rawls, this condition warrants the fairness of agreement. Rawls clearly summarizes his basic intention for the veil of ignorance:

> Among the essential features of this [original] situation is that no one knows his place in society, his class position or social status, nor does any one know his fortune in the distribution of natural assets and abilities, his intelligence, strength, and the like. I shall even assume that the parties do not know their conceptions of the good or their special psychological propensities. The principles of justice are chosen behind a veil of ignorance. This ensures that no one is advantaged or disadvantaged in the choice of principles by the outcome of natural chances or the contingency of social circumstances. Since all are similarly situated and no one is able to design principles to favor his particular condition, the principles of justice are the result of a fair agreement" (TJ,p.12).

The only kinds of information available to the parties pertains to the circumstances of justice and 'the general facts about human society': political affairs of social organization, economic development of society, and the laws of human [moral] psychology (TJ,p.137).

Why does Rawls impose this kind of a thick and wide veil of ignorance? Can fairness be secured uniquely and exclusively by this veil? Under this veil of ignorance, seemingly under amnesia or oblivion, is a meaningful and rational choice possible? What remains of the identity of the parties as contracting agents? "Why, if this agreement is never actually entered into, should we take any interest in these principles [from the veil of ignorance], moral or otherwise?" (TJ,p.21; transformed into an interrogative sentence). To these anticipated objections to the veil of ignorance, Rawls provides two rejoinders.   First, the various particular facts mentioned above are 'arbitrary contingencies' or 'arbitrary from a moral point of view' (TJ,pp.141,15). In order to guarantee fairness in the sense of a free, equal, unbiased, and impartial starting point, those facts must be nullified.

In this regard, Rawls relates his theory to 'the Kantian interpretation of justice as fairness' (TJ,p.251). And he adds that Kant's categorical imperative of moral will (as beyond empirical contingencies) gives a philosophical foundation to Rousseau's idea of the general will (TJ,p.264). Hence Rawls' veil of ignorance can be viewed as combining Kant and Rousseau to form a powerful vehicle to move from a corrupted heterogeneous and individual will to a morally secured autonomous general will.[50] Consequently, Rawls argues that only such a veil of ignorance can eradicate an individual bargaining or group coalition. As made clear in his criticism of Hobbes, bargaining or coalition relegates the criterion of justice to 'the relative balance of social forces' which is just a de facto solution (TJ,pp.140f, 120). Here Rawls abandons Hobbes for Rousseau, who flatly denies partial or group association in the state (SC,II,3,77). Secondly, a clear and simplified model of individual choice under uncertainty can be practically derived from the veil of ignorance: "we can view the choice in the original position from the standpoint of one person selected at random" since everyone is situated equally (TJ,p.139). Rawls thus maintains that an unanimous consensual agreement is reached through this way.

The last condition imposed in the original position is the determination of rationality and motivation of contracting parties. Since the veil of ignorance conceals the individual's concept of end-rationality (his or her particular concept of good), it seems that rational choice in the sense of instrumental self-interest maximization is impossible. In plain words, if given ends are unknown to individuals, how can they decide which conceptions of justice are most to their own interest and advantage?

Here Rawls introduces his 'thin theory of the good' and the concept of 'the primary social goods' (TJ,pp.397, 92). The thin theory of good means that whatever a person's ends or rational plan of life might be, there exists certain primary goods that are always instrumental to their attainment. The primary social goods, i.e., 'rights and liberties, opportunities, income and wealth, the bases of self-respect,' are derived from the theory (TJ,p.92). As we saw in Chapter II, Rawls holds to the neo-classical concept of rationality: self-interest consistent instrumental maximization. With the introduction of the primary social goods, the rationality of parties is specified that "they would prefer more primary goods rather than less" (TJ,p.142). These primary social goods are 'the basis of expectations' as well as the object to which distributive principles are applied (TJ,p.90).

Another point related to our previous discussion in Chapter II is that, in the situation under ignorance or uncertainty, rationality as utility-maximization is defined as expected-utility maximization. Rawls hopes that his theory of the primary social goods will help to yield a practical and reliable method of measurement and interpersonal comparison of utility-preference expectation, and that it will be a remedy for the operational difficulties involved in the traditional theory of utility, especially utilitarianism (TJ,p.90f).[51]

In line with his concept of rationality, Rawls determines the motivation of parties as 'mutual disinterestedness' that "the parties do not seek to confer benefits or to impose injuries on one another; they are not moved by affection or rancor. ... they are not envious or vain" (TJ,p.144). This determination of motivation reflects the subjective circumstances of justice. Here it is noteworthy that Rawls tries to steer a neutral, midway stance between two opposite extreme motivations. Basically Rawls' choice of this path is closely related to his grand ultra-motif, i.e., to find an Archimedean point for the neutral conception of justice. Rawls asserts that the original position 'sets up an Archimedean point for assessing the social system without invoking' any substantial values and motivations through the value-neutral instrumental primary social goods (TJ,p.261). Using Spinozistic terminology, Rawls notes that "to see our place in society from the perspective of this position is to see it *sub specie aeternitatis* [under the aspect of eternity]" (TJ,p.587).[52]

In view of the overall conditions of the original position, Rawls' rational deduction project of morality is in a sense very limited and encapsulated. However, Rawls thinks that, in the original position, he substitutes "for ethical judgment a judgment of rational prudence" "since on the contract view the theory of justice is part of the theory of rational choice" (TJ,pp.44,47). At this juncture, we have to ask what the exact meaning of Rawls' thought concerning rational choice is. Rawls says that "principles of justice may be conceived as principles that would be chosen by rational persons, and that in this way conceptions of justice may be explained and justified" (TJ,p.16). Additionally, "the procedure of contract theories provides a general analytical method for the comparative study of justice" (TJ,p.121).[53] In this regard, Rawls connects justice as fairness with "the idea of pure procedural justice" since "a fair procedure translates its fairness to the outcome" (TJ,pp.120,86).

I do not think that anybody seriously argues against the usefulness of the original position as an analytic or explanatory device except perhaps certain intuitionists.[54] And even though Rawls' connection of justice as fairness with pure procedural justice may also be polemical especially when it is compared with Nozick's market proceduralism (Nozick thinks Rawls' justice as fairness, as end-result proceduralism of redistribution not as pure proceduralism: AST,p.198), this is not our primary concern.[55] The most crucial issue concerns the original position as rational justificatory device. Rawls asserts:

> It is clear ... that one conception of justice [indeed his] is more reasonable than another [traditional theories of justice, especially utilitarian], or justifiable ... if rational persons in the initial situation would choose its principles over those of the other for the role of justice. ... This connects the theory of justice with the theory of rational choice (TJ,p.17).

However, concerning justification, Rawls mentions another device, 'reflective equilibrium' between considered judgments and principles, and between conditions of initial position and principles via considered judgments (TJ,p.20). As Lyons points out, the relation between rational justification and reflective equilibrium justification is very controversial.[56] There is textual evidence that reflective equilibrium justification is primary and that rational contract justification is a mere subsidiary affirmative device (TJ,pp.20,580f). However, on the score that Rawls mentions that "I shall not, of course, actually work through this process [of reflective equilibrium]," I consider the contractarian rational deduction project as independent and primary "since in a contract theory all arguments, strictly speaking, are to be made in terms of what it would be rational to choose in the original position" (TJ,pp.21,75). This consideration is affirmed by the fact that Rawls regards derivation of his two principles of justice from maximin criterion as 'a conclusive argument' to which we now move (TJ,p.153).

2. The Maximin Derivation of the Two Principles of Justice and Their Strict Compliance

In view of the choice situation of contracting parties in the original position under the veil of ignorance, Rawls' formal choice model becomes 'individual decision making under uncertainty,' as was defined in Chapter II. Basically, the problems of distributive justice are subsumed under social-collective or public-choice theory. As Daniels correctly indicates, Rawls' contractarianism "provides a concrete model for reducing a relatively complex problem, the social choice of principles of justice, to a more manageable problem, the rational individual choice of principles."[57]

There are many operational rules or criteria in the choice under uncertainty.[58] However, Rawls asserts that "it is rational for the parties to adopt the conservative attitude" expressed by "the maximin rule" (TJ,p.152f): The maximin rule tells us to rank alternatives by their worst outcomes: we are to adopt the alternative the worst outcome of which is superior to the worst outcomes of the others. As Rawls admits, "clearly the maximin rule is not, in general, a suitable guide for choices under uncertainty" (TJ,p.152) since it is too conservative. But Rawls thinks that "it is attractive in situations marked by certain special features" (TJ,p.153). He enumerates the following three (TJ,p.154). First, "the situation is one in which a knowledge of likelihoods is impossible, or at best extremely insecure." Second, "the person choosing has a conception of the good such that he cares very little, if anything, for what he might gain above the minimum." Third, "the rejected alternatives have outcomes that one can hardly accept." Rawls' task, then, is to show that the original position manifests these features (TJ,pp.155f). First, through the veil of ignorance, the knowledge of probability is excluded. Second, his two principles of justice guarantee a 'satisfactory minimum.' Third, other conceptions of justice may lead to institutions that the contracting parties would find intolerable. Here Rawls especially calls attention to the fact that utilitarianism (total or average) cannot secure a satisfactory minimum since the total or average sum of utility can be increased regardless of increasing the utility of the least advantaged (TJ,p.156).

Rawls' argument for the maximin rule in the original position means that, in the pursuit of the primary social goods, contracting parties estimate various alternatives from the standpoint of the least advantaged person. Through this argument, Rawls maintains that his two principles of justice are chosen over the other traditional principles of justice especially over the utilitarian principle, in the original position.[59] Rawls regards the argument from the maximin rule as 'a conclusive argument' (TJ,p.152).

It remains then to be elaborated how Rawls' description of the original position possessing the special features fit for the maximin rule is connected to his derivation of the two principles of justice. Rawls thinks that the contracting parties, as free and equal rational beings, in the first place, start with a strict egalitarian principle (TJ,p.151). However, Rawls immediately adds that a strict equal division of all primary goods is irrational in view of the possibility of bettering everyone's circumstances by accepting certain inequalities. This possibility has to do with the augmentation of cooperative surpluses. In other words, inequalities are permitted in return for contributions to cooperative surplus. These inequalities set up various "incentives which succeed in eliciting more productive efforts" (p.151). "The function of unequal distributive shares is to cover the cost of training and education, to attract individuals to places and associations where they are most needed from a social point of view" (TJ,p.315).

Rawls' claim that inequality for productive incentives or for cooperative surplus are not unjust is basically in line with the traditional concept of meritocratic society.[60] And also it accords with Pareto efficiency or optimality in the sense that a social configuration is efficient or optimal whenever it is impossible to make some persons (at least one) better off without at the same time making the others worse off.[61] But, as we will see, Rawls' two principles of justice impose a significant qualification in view of the basic needs of and attendant redistribution for the least advantaged person to the efficient meritocratic concept of justice.

Contracting parties following the maximin rule under the conditions of inequalities means that one must look at the system of unequal distribution "from the standpoint of the least advantaged representative man" (TJ,p.151). More exactly, "Inequalities are permissible when they maximize, or at least all contribute to, the long-term expectations of the least fortunate group in society"

(TJ,p.151).   From this inference, Rawls leads to 'the general conception of justice' (TJ,p.303).

General Conception of Justice

All social primary goods—liberty and opportunity, income and wealth, and the bases of self-respect—are to be distributed equally unless an unequal distribution of any or all of these goods is to the advantage of the least favored.

Rawls' two principles of justice are a special case of the general conception of justice.   In the general conception, there are no restrictions on what sorts of inequalities are permissible.   It is thus theoretically possible that a condition of slavery is allowed as long as this condition is to the advantage of the least favored.   A less drastic possibility is that a lesser liberty is traded for a greater economic and social gain (TJ,p.63).   In order to rule out this possibility of trade-off between primary social goods, Rawls pays special attention to the matter of priority among the goods.   Rawls' two principles of justice, as a special conception of justice, are hence a serial or lexical ordering of principles expressing such an underlying priority (TJ,p.302).

Special Conception of Justice

First Principle: Each person is to have an equal right to the most extensive total system of equal basic liberties compatible with a similar system of liberty for all.

Second Principle: Social and economic inequalities are to be arranged so that they are both; (a) to the greatest benefit of the least advantaged, consistent with the just savings principle, and (b) attached to offices and positions open to all under conditions of fair equality of opportunity.

Rawls' special conception of two principles of justice is actually composed of four principles.   The first principle is the principle of greatest equal liberty.   The second principle consists of the difference principle and the principle of fair equality of opportunity.   An additional principle attached to the difference principle is the just savings principle.[62]   These principles are lexically arranged according to two priority rules (TJ,p.302).   The first priority rule is 'the priority of liberty', i.e., the first principle of liberty is prior to the second principle.   The second priority rule is that the principle of fair opportunity is prior to the difference principle. And the second principle is prior to the principle of efficiency and to that of maximizing the sum of advantage, i.e., 'the priority of justice over efficiency and welfare.'

Concerning the principle of greatest equal liberty, a crucial issue is how to explain the priority of liberty over social and economic advantages according to the defined conception of rationality of contracting parties. Rawls' basic idea is that contracting parties in the original position will not exchange a lesser liberty for an improvement in their economic well-being, "at least not once a certain level of wealth has been attained" (TJ,p.542). In this regard, Rawls' principle of equal liberty reflects the historical circumstances of society:

> Now the basis for the priority of liberty is roughly as follows: as the conditions of civilization improve, the marginal significance for our good of further economic and social advantages diminishes relative to the interests of liberty, which become stronger as the conditions for the exercises of the equal freedoms are more fully realized. Beyond some point it becomes and then remains irrational from the standpoint of the original position to acknowledge a lesser liberty for the sake of greater material means and amenities of office (TJ, p.542).

Rawls here appeals to the principle of diminishing marginal utility: the values of liberty and economic advantages can be compared through the different degree of diminishing marginal utilities of them. More exactly, Rawls thinks that the marginal utility of liberty increases, whereas the marginal utility of social and economic advantages decreases beyond a certain level of economic development. Traditionally neo-classical economics has been characterized as a 'marginalist revolution.' And the rational economic man presupposes the diminishing marginal utility of commodities.[63]

Rawls supplements two supporting arguments for the absolute weight of liberty (TJ,p.543). First, even though contracting parties under the veil of ignorance do not know the specific contents of rational plans of life, in order to guarantee full establishment of their plans, they give 'liberty of conscience and freedom of thought' a prior place. Second, regardless of a certain degree of inequality, the significance of self-respect as the main primary social good can be firmly maintained through the equal distribution of fundamental rights and liberties.

The difference principle is the core of Rawls' substantive theory of distributive justice proper, i.e., distribution of social and economic cooperative goods. The general conception of justice is a difference principle of all primary goods, whereas the difference principle in the specific conception is applied as the maximin solution to the remaining social and economic primary goods, except rights, liberties, and self-respect of the first principle. However, there is a division of labor between the principle of fair equality of opportunity and the difference principle for social and economic primary goods. The principle of fair opportunity exercises control over power and opportunities to the official status and benefits attached to the participation of the various socio-political (including educational) institutions. Admittedly, the principle of fair opportunity is that social "positions are to be not only in a formal sense, but that all should have a fair chance to attain them" (TJ,p.73). What this means is that "those with similar abilities and skills should have similar life chances": In other words,

> those who are at the same level of talent and ability, and have the same willingness to use them, should have the same prospects of success regardless of their initial place in the social system, that is, irrespective of the income class into which they are born (TJ,p.73).

But, as Rawls admits, 'perfect equality of opportunity' cannot be practically carried out, at least as long as the institution of the family exists (TJ,pp.301,74). In this regard, he does not pursue the Platonic or the communist abolition of family (TJ,p.511).[64] Rather, he tries to redefine the permissible grounds of social inequalities through the full employment of the difference principle. This means that even though the principle of fair opportunity is theoretically prior to the difference principle, the former practically depends upon the latter.

At this juncture, the difference principle is characterized as a principle of redress to individual differences of natural assets as well as to social and historical influences to individual assets (TJ, 100f). Accordingly, Rawls introduces a concept of individual natural or socially acquired talents and endowments as a 'common,' 'social,' or 'collective asset' (TJ,pp.101,107,179). It is natural that the concept of redress supported by the concept of common asset implies a wide range of egalitarian redistribution of economic goods (income and wealth).

But it is noteworthy that Rawls does not want to sacrifice the efficiency of economic system for an indiscriminate maximization of social minimum of the least advantaged person. In this respect, Rawls indicates 'an appropriate social minimum' (TJ,p.316f). In economic terminology, the appropriate level of social minimum is achieved when a heavy taxational burden for welfare transfers "interferes so much with economic efficiency that the prospects of the least advantaged ... are no longer improved but begin to decline" (TJ,p.286).[65] Rawls at this point reformulates the difference principle into a lexical social welfare function.

The Lexical Difference Principle

In a basic structure with n relevant representatives, first maximize the welfare of the worst-off representative man; second, for equal welfare of the worst-off representative, maximize the second worst-off representative man, and so on until the last case which is, for equal welfare of all the preceding n-1 representatives, maximize the welfare of the best-off representative man (TJ,p.83).

Rawls' lexical difference principle as an overall maximin social welfare function can be regarded as Rawls' answer to the Arrow's Impossibility Theorem. There has been an enormous amount of debate on the viability of Rawls' social welfare function as a solution to the Arrow's Theorem in the domains of theory of justice and social choice.[66] Arrow, as an advocate of utilitarian welfare ethics, himself does not think Rawls' lexical difference principle is a solution. However, Arrow indicates that, in view of formal criteria, contractarian hypothetical thought experiment, or in his own terms, 'extended sympathy' or 'co-ordinal' is illuminating and very likely hopeful.[67]

At any rate, Rawls maintains that his two principles of justice set up "an Archimedean point for assessing the social system" (TJ,p.261). Of course, Rawls admits that "the pace of change and the particular reforms called for at any given time depend upon current conditions." But "the conception of justice, [and] the general form of a just society ... are not similarly dependent" (TJ,p.261).

Now it is time to turn to Rawls' theory of compliance to his two principles of justice. First of all, the aforementioned distinction between strict and partial compliances has to be explained. At the outset of his book, Rawls affirms that "the nature and aims of a perfectly just society is the fundamental part of the theory of justice" (TJ,p.9).[68] This fundamental part is what Rawls calls 'ideal theory,' which presupposes strict compliance: "Everyone is presumed to act justly and to do his part in upholding just institutions" (TJ,p.8). Contrarily, the non-ideal theory deals with partial compliance which "studies the principles that govern how we are to deal with injustice" (TJ,p.8). Partial compliance theory includes such topics as the theory of punishments, civil disobedience, revolution, and questions of compensatory justice. Another assumption attached to the ideal theory is the concept of a well-ordered society: "a society is well-ordered when it is not only designed to advance the good of its members but when it is also effectively regulated by a public conception of justice" (TJ,p.4f). "Thus it is a society in which everyone accepts and knows that others accept the same principles of justice, and the basic social institutions satisfy and are known to satisfy these principles" (TJ,p.453f).

Rawls' strict compliance theory is framed to accord with this idea of society. Thus, in the original position, "[p]rinciples are to be chosen in view of the consequences of everyone's complying with them" or it is "assumed that they will be complied with by everyone" (TJ,pp.132,138). In order to make his contractarian rational ethics complete, Rawls has to show that the original position must be such that the choice made in it by rational men will continue to be rationally acceptable to them when the veil of ignorance is lifted. Rawls' strict compliance theory without the veil has a connection with "the strains of commitment" and "the problem of stability" (TJ,p.183). The strains mean that contracting parties cannot enter into agreements that may have consequences they cannot accept later without the veil. Here Rawls finds his case of rejection of utilitarianism: "A rational person, in framing his plan, would hesitate to give precedence to so stringent a principle" since the utilitarian principle "may authorize the lesser welfare and liberty of some for the sake of a greater happiness of others who may already be more fortunate" (TJ,p.573).

The problem of stability is directly related with FR. We can tentatively admit Rawls' claim that "the rationality of choosing the principles of justice in the original position is not in question" and that "the isolation problem [of PD] is overcome and fair large-scale schemes already exist for producing public goods" (TJ,pp.567,336). However, there are still "two sorts of tendencies leading to instability" (TJ,p.336). The first instability comes from self-interest of FR: "on these occasions [when each person is selfishly tempted to shirk doing his share] any way things proceed much as if free-rider egoism had been acknowledged" (TJ,p.497). The second instability comes from insecure assurance of the other parties to perform their duties: even they are not free-riders, "citizen may be tempted to avoid making a contribution when they believe, or with reason suspect, that others are not making theirs" (TJ,p.336).

In order to solve the problem of stability, Rawls resorts to a combined theory of the moral sentiments and the Platonic congruence between justice and goodness. In section 9 of his book, "Some Remarks about Moral Theory," Rawls calls attention to the fact that his theory of justice is "a theory of the moral sentiments (to recall an eighteenth century title) setting out the principles governing our moral powers, or more specifically, our sense of justice" (TJ,p.51).[69] At the beginning of Part III, "Ends," Rawls points out that "justice and goodness are congruent" and that "the central aim is to prepare the way to settle the questions of stability and congruence" (TJ,p.395). In this regard, many scholars argue that Rawls' congruence project is basically a version of the Platonic congruence theory.[70] In the same way that Gyges' unjust use of the mythical ring, which can make him invisible, challenges Plato, a self-interested rational free-rider challenges Rawls.[71] Eventually, Rawls elaborates the combined theory in section 86, "The Good of the sense of Justice."

Rawls' problem is thus "whether the regulative desire to adopt the standpoint of justice [the sense of justice] belongs to a person's own good when viewed in the light of the thin theory with no restrictions on information" (TJ,p.567). Rawls argues that we cannot share fully in the good to be achieved in a well-ordered society unless we have this sense ourselves. Thus acting from such a sense of justice is something that we directly have a desire to express our nature in doing so, insofar as we think of ourselves as "free and equal moral persons" according to the Kantian interpretation (TJ,p.528). In this regard, Rawls maintains that "justice as fairness appears to be a sufficiently stable conception. The hazards of the generalized prisoner's dilemma [FR] are removed by the match between the right and the good" (TJ,p.577).

Of course, in connection with the Hobbesian problem of coercion, Rawls explicitly acknowledges that "even in a just society it is reasonable to admit certain constraining arrangements to insure compliance, but their main purpose is to underwrite citizen's trust in one another" (TJ,p.577). Accordingly, "these mechanisms will seldom be invoked and will comprise but a minor part of the social scheme" (TJ,p.577). Rawls succinctly summarizes the results derived from his arguments:

> We can say first that, in a well-ordered society, being a good person (and in particular having an effective sense of justice) is indeed a good for that person; and second that this form of society is a good society. The first assertion follows from congruence; the second holds since a well-ordered society has the properties that it is rational to want in a society from the two relevant points of view. Thus a well-ordered society satisfies the principles of justice which are collectively rational from the perspective of the original position; and from the standpoint of the individual, the desire to affirm the public conception of justice as regulative of one's plan of life accords with the principles of rational choice (TJ,p.577).

Rawls finally indicates that "these conclusions support the values of community, and in reaching them my account of justice as fairness is completed" (TJ,p.577).

3. Rawls' Ethics as the Second, Circularity Horn of the Contractarian Dilemma and Critical Comparison with Utilitarian and Libertarian Rationality

As elaborated in our previous discussions, Rawls' rationality *cum* fairness model of the original position under the veil of ignorance is designed to correct the first horn of contractarian ethics, i.e., the moral irrelevancy of Hobbes' rational deduction project. However, Rawls' problem is that his conception of justice as fairness seems so extended that it cannot escape the second horn of the contractarian dilemma, i.e., the circularity of moral assumptions prior to rationality.

It is noteworthy that Rawls is aware of this problem and that he actually tries to avoid the second horn. But, as we will see shortly, Rawls does not sufficiently deal with this problem. In connection with the instrumental concept of rationality, Rawls explicitly acknowledges that "one must try to avoid introducing into it any controversial ethical elements" (TJ,p.14). And in the final section of the book, "Remarks on Justification," Rawls summarizes his position by saying: "I have avoided attributing to the parties any ethical motivation. They decide solely on the basis of what seems best calculated to further their interests so far as they can ascertain them" (TJ,p.584). In this way, "[t]he theory of justice is a part, perhaps the most significant part, of the theory of rational choice" (TJ,p.16).

Rawls' idea in adopting the neutral and instrumental maximizational conception of rationality is that the basic assumption of instrumental rationality and the attendant assumption of mutually disinterested motivation lead to weakness in contractarian premises: "One argues from widely accepted but weak premises to more specific conclusions" (TJ,p.18). Rawls objects against Roderick Firth's sympathetic ideal observer theory and Thomas Nagel's altruistic spectator theory on the ground that these theories[72] presuppose too heavy and strong ethical elements (TJ,pp.184,190). Furthermore, Rawls criticizes W.D. Ross' hardheaded deontological "doctrine of the purely conscientious act" as irrational (TJ,p.477). This doctrine holds that "the highest moral motive is the desire to do what is right and just simply because it is right and just, no other descriptions being appropriate" (TJ,p.477).[73]

However, in order to escape the Hobbesian horn and a strict rational "reductionism which regards ... morality as mere preferences," Rawls has to minimally moralize the original position without resorting to heavy ethical elements as in the cases of Firth, Nagel, and Ross (TJ, p.243).[74] Rawls' rationality *cum* fairness is a result of his endeavor to meet this tricky business. As we have seen, Rawls' original position includes fair initial conditions, i.e., the veil of ignorance and the formal constraints of the concept of right. Thus it produces constraints that are fair and impartial in the sense necessary for the rational contract agreement to constitute a morality:

> [T]he aim is to characterize this situation so that the principles that would be chosen, whatever they turn out to be, are acceptable from a moral point of view. The original position is defined in such a way that it is a status quo in which any agreements reached are fair. It is a state of affairs in which the

parties are equally represented as moral persons and the outcome is not conditioned by arbitrary contingencies or the relative balance of social forces (TJ,p.120).

However, in view of the above passage, the idea of the fair original position is itself a moral notion, so the constraints it generates are morally motivated and themselves embody moral elements. In other words, in confining the rational agreement to a fair initial situation, Rawls cannot derive morality from rationality alone. Instead, Rawls derives morality from "rationality *cum* fairness." Accordingly, Rawls' theory of justice as fairness becomes impaled on the second horn of the contractarian dilemma.[75]

As indicated at the beginning of our discussion, I am not suggesting that Rawls is unaware of this problem. What I am claiming here is that Rawls does not sufficiently treat this problem and consequently that his ethics as the second horn commits a fallacy of circularity in view of the contractarian rational deduction project of morality.

In two places, Rawls acknowledges his problem but he simply disclaims that it is a problem.

[W]hile I have maintained ... that something's being right, or just can be understood as its being in accordance with the relevant principles that would be acknowledged in the original position, and that we can in this way replace the former notions by the latter, these definitions are set up within the theory itself. I do not hold that the conception of the original position is itself with-out moral force, or that the family of concepts it draws upon is ethically neutral. This question I simply leave aside (TJ,p.579).

We can ... define ethical variations of the initial situation by supposing the parties to be influenced by moral considerations. It is a mistake to object that the notion of the original agreement would no longer be ethically neutral. For this notion already includes moral features and must do so, for example, the formal conditions on principles and the veil of ignorance. I have simply divided up the description of the original position so that these elements do not occur in the characterization of the parties, although even here there might be a question as to what counts as a moral element and what does not. There is no need to settle this problem. What is important is that the various features of the original position should be expressed in the simplest and most compelling way (TJ,pp.584-5).

As Rawls admits, if the fairness of the original position is ensured by the formal constraints of the concept of right and the veil of ignorance then the alleged 'conclusive argument' from the maximin strategy must presuppose some of the moral standards which it is intended to justify (TJ, p.153). Recall that the imposition of the veil is derived from the claim that particular facts on individuals' natural endowments and social positions are "arbitrary from a moral point of view" (TJ,p.15). In this case, the preformed constraints are impeccably moral but their acceptance will be rationally optional. Worst of all, if Rawls admits that "We want to define the original position so that we get the desired solution" and specifically that "the original position has been defined so that it is a situation in which the maximin rule applies," Rawls' contractarian argument will be rationally arbitrary (TJ,pp.141,155).

This objection is not that it is inappropriate in general to give a particular characterization (whatever including fairness) of the choice problem. After all, every moral theory employs such a characterization. My objection is limited to the contents of such a characterization (moral circularity of fairness) in view of the contractarian rational deduction project.

The charge of rational optionality and arbitrariness is directly applied to Rawls' claim that his justice as fairness is "the most favored interpretation" of the initial choice situation (TJ,p.121). As Rawls points out, there are many interpretations of the initial situation (TJ,p.121). But "how are we to decide what is the most favored interpretation?" (TJ,p.18). The crucial issue is whether Rawls' justice as fairness is "the unique solution" as he asserts (TJ,p.119).

There are two perspectives on this issue. The first perspective is from within. Even if we accept Rawls' constraints in the original position, it is not clear whether rational men would necessarily choose Rawls' two principles of justice (especially the difference principle) according to the maximin strategy. Here the main debate has taken place between Rawls and Harsanyi. Harsanyi agrees with Rawls that the proper choice model for social justice is the individual choice under uncertainty. However, whereas Rawls uses the maximin criterion, Harsanyi resorts to the equiprobability criterion according to the principle of insufficient reason.[76] Not surprisingly, Harsanyi's approach leads to average utilitarianism since if everybody has equal probability of turning out to hold any position of society, it will be rational for an individual to choose a society which promotes the average utility of society.

Rawls' reasons for rejecting average utilitarianism are that Harsanyi's model lacks the objective ground of equiprobability and that it takes great risks since it does not guarantee the satisfactory social minimum for the least advantaged person (TJ,pp.168f,81). As Rawls indicates, if the parties are viewed as rational individuals who have "no aversion to risk," then the idea of the initial position leads naturally to the average utilitarianism (TJ,p.166). Harsanyi rejoins that "using the maximin principle in the original position is equivalent to assigning unity or near-unity probability to the possibility that one ends up as the worst-off individual in society."[77] And as far as he can see "there cannot be any rational justification whatever for assigning such an extremely high probability to this possibility."[78] Furthermore, he provides several counterexamples to the difference principle. In such examples, the difference principle would require us to give "absolute" priority to the interests of the worst-off individual, "no matter what," even under the most extreme conditions.[79].

The debate over the difference principle and the average utilitarianism is "far from settled" as is the debate about the correct rule for making rational decisions under uncertainty.[80]: "It is hard to think of a more notorious, long-standing, and often outright confused controversy in modern decision theory than the continuing debate on the meaning of 'rationality' in choice under uncertainty."[81] All these considerations suggest that the application of individual rational choice under uncertainty to the social contract or social justice problems is beset with many more difficulties than were heretofore supposed. Thus, in case of the individual choice under uncertainty, the normative outcome depends on apparently arbitrary assumptions about attitudes to risk. I am not suggesting that Rawls himself does not recognize this problem (TJ, pp.447,585). However, Rawls' contracting parties practically have no freedom to choose the principles of rational choice (TJ,p.446). In view of the debate between Rawls and Harsanyi, Rawls' following suggestion is very baffling: "I have suggested that the conception of justice adopted is insensitive with respect to conflicting interpretations of rationality" (TJ,p.447). It is interesting to note that Mueller, Tollison and Willett suggest a reconciliation between Rawls and Harsanyi. Their model is to choose on the basis of "the average degree of risk-averseness among the members of society."[82] However, in this model, the social justice problem is at the disposal of the distribution of attitudes to risk in a certain society.

There is another perspective on the issue of Rawls' claim of "the unique solution." Nozick criticizes Rawls that justice as fairness with the veil of ignorance cannot be accepted by rational individuals. "Why should knowledge of natural endowments be excluded from the original position?" (AST, pp.227f). In brief, Nozick's libertarian project is a defense of the minimal state, which guarantees the entitlement of individual natural property rights. His libertarianism consists of two major parts: a justification of the minimal state and a refutation of any kind of social structure beyond the minimal state, especially an economic redistributive state. The first part is to establish "the original acquisition of holdings" from the Lockean proviso: that "there be 'enough and as good left in common for others' is meant to ensure that the situation of others is not worsened" (AST,p.175).[83] His entitlement theory of distributive justice is primarily that individuals are entitled to the original Lockean acquisition. Secondarily, they are entitled to the voluntary "transfer of holding" (AST,p.151). He terms his entitlement theory of justice a pure procedural "historical principle" whereas he treats Rawlsian theory of (re)distributive justice as an "end-result principle" (AST,pp.153,198). Nozick's motto, "From each as they choose, to each as they are chosen" exemplifies a maximal form of libertarian individual rationality in the procedure of the free market system (AST,p.160).[84]

Nozick's criticism of Rawls is one of the major goals of the second part of his theory; viz., the refutation of theories of distributive justice beyond the minimal state. Nozick identifies his position with "the system of natural liberty" in Rawls' context (AST,p.213). According to Rawls, "the system of natural liberty" asserts that "a basic structure satisfying the principle of efficiency and in which positions are open to those able and willing to strive for them will lead to a just distribution" (TJ,p.66). Here equality is considered as careers open to talents, that is "a formal equality of opportunity" (TJ, p.72). Rawls finds his argument against the system of natural liberty in the following passage: "the most obvious injustice of the system of natural liberty is that it permits distributive shares to be improperly influenced by these factors [natural assets and social contingencies] so arbitrary from a moral point of view" (TJ,p.72).

As we have seen, Rawls draws down the veil of ignorance on these "morally arbitrary" factors.

Nozick points out first that "A procedure that founds principles of distributive justice on what rational persons who know nothing about themselves or their histories would agree to *guarantees that end-state principles of justice will be taken as fundamental*" (AST,pp.198f. emphasis original). And he supposes that if social products fell from heaven like manna, the difference principle chosen under the veil of ignorance might be a suitable rule for their distribution (AST,p.198). But he claims that the difference principle is not the appropriate model for deciding how the individual products made by the known contributions from the known individuals are to be distributed (AST,p.198). How can the contracting parties under the veil in the original position get the right to make this kind of decision? In terms of rationality, Nozick's point is that the maximin strategy reveals "the asymmetry" of rationality only in favor of the least advantaged ones (AST,p.193). Thus the most advantaged persons cannot rationally comply with the difference principle after the veil is lifted.

Nozick maintains that the introduction of the veil is blocking "a person's autonomous choices and actions (and their results)" (AST,p.214). Furthermore, the difference principle requires the most advantaged persons to make sacrifices not only of their freedom but also of their own benefits for the benefits of the least advantaged. Nozick resorts to Rawls' favorite Kantian argument that the difference principle grounded on the concept of collective assets treats persons as mere means (AST,p.228).

However, as Nozick acknowledges, "the entitlement theory's claim that moral entitlements may arise from or be partially based on such facts [of individual natural assets] is what is now at issue" (AST,p.227). Thus he provides his master argument against Rawls' claim that natural assets are morally arbitrary. Nozick interprets Rawls' alleged claim in two ways. The first is "the positive argument": "It might be part of an argument to establish that the distributive effects of natural differences ought to be nullified" (AST,p.216). The second is "the negative argument": "It might be part of an argument to rebut a possible counterargument holding that the distributive effects of natural differences oughtn't to be nullified" (AST,p.216). Against the positive argument, Nozick maintains that any possible premise of the argument is incompatible with Rawls' introduction of the necessity of inequality in distributive shares for productive incentives (AST,p.217). In addition, Nozick indicates that Rawls correctly discards the concept of pure moral desert as unworkable criterion for distributive shares (AST,p.217). According to Rawls, the concept of moral desert is that "justice is happiness according to virtue" (TJ,p.310). Rawls makes it clear that "justice as fairness rejects this conception" (TJ,p.310). In sum, Nozick's kernel point is that Rawls' positive argument is incompatible not only with his introduction of incentives and but also with his rejection of pure moral desert.

Against the negative argument, Nozick asserts that if Rawls rejects any possible premise concerned with the concept of distribution according to natural endowments, Rawls' argument is reduced to an absurdity. "If nothing of moral significance could follow from what was arbitrary, then no particular person's existence could be of moral significance" (AST,p.226). Nozick here presents his famous sarcastic example, i.e., the moral arbitrariness involved in the process of sperm cells' fertilizing egg cells. About this process, he says that "whether or not people's natural assets are arbitrary from a moral point of view, they are entitled to them, and to what flows from them" (AST,p.226).

When we review overall the debate between Rawls and Nozick, it seems impossible to adjudicate it. In view of rationality, Rawls' argument is asymmetric in favor of the least advantaged persons, whereas Nozick's argument is asymmetric in favor of the most advantaged persons. Is there any rational reconciliation between them? And also in view of the introduction of prior moral assumptions, Rawls claims that natural assets are morally arbitrary, whereas Nozick claims that these assets have moral status. Thus it is not surprising to find a charge that both Rawls and Nozick commit a fallacy of begging the question.[85]

It is time to move to Rawls' theory of rational compliance. The charge of moral circularity against Rawls becomes more serious when we carefully scrutinize his theory of rational compliance. As we have discussed, Rawls' strict compliance theory basically deals with the problems of stability, which is aroused by the free rider (FR). Rawls has to show that the sense of justice as "a settled disposition to adopt and to want to act from the moral point of view" accords with the individual's good, possibly even with a free-rider's (TJ. p.491). Rawls basically admits that FR "egoism is logically consistent and in this sense [self-interest maximization] not irrational" (TJ,p.136). However, Rawls' Platonic congruence in a well-ordered society and the Kantian deontological interpretation of human nature as "free and equal moral persons" does not give a sufficient answer to the FR's question, "Why should I be moral?" (TJ,p.528).[86] As Rawls leaves aside the question as to what counts as a moral element and what does not in the original position, he leaves unclear the relationship between "a free and equal rational being" and "a free and equal moral person" in case of the theory of compliance (TJ,pp.252,528).

In the section 86 of *A Theory of Justice*, "The Good of the Sense of Justice" Rawls sets up his aim: "It remains to be shown that this disposition to take up and to be guided by the standpoint of justice accords with the individual's good."; "But congruence is not a fore-gone conclusion even in a well-ordered society. We must verify it" (TJ,p.567). Nevertheless, there are three passages which run against Rawls' avowed aim of the rational deduction project of compliance.[87]

In the first one, Rawls says:

> The main point then is that to justify a conception of justice we do not have to contend that everyone, whatever his capacities and desires, has a sufficient reason (as defined by the thin theory) to preserve his sense of justice. For our good depends upon the sorts of persons we are, the kinds of wants and aspirations we have and are capable of (TJ,p.576).

This passage suggests that compliance derives from a predeter-mined concept of moral person, according to which the contents of desires are fixed. But this is not to say that having such desires is the mark of a rational person or at least a fully rational person with the weak and thin (in the sense of not having substantial moral ideals) instrumental concept of good. It is pertinent here to inves-tigate Rawls' claim that his justice as fairness is a deontological theory (TJ,p.30).[88] In this context, Rawls thinks that "the priority of the right over the good" is a central feature of his theory (TJ,p.32). The reason that Rawls calls his theory of the primary social goods the thin theory of the good can be interpreted in two ways. The first way is to provide a neutral rational foundation for morality which can be compatible with the instrumental concept of rationality, as already defined. The second way is to assert that since the primary social goods do not designate any substantial value, they do not "jeopardize the priority place of the concept of right" (TJ,p.396). However, the second interpretation raises a serious question about the relationship between Rawls' deontology (the priority of the right over the good) and rational compliance theory. Hamlin interprets Rawls' rational approach to mean that "linking rationality and ethics is the use of a particular conception of rationality to derive an ethical position which, once derived, has independent status."[89] However, it seems that the rational deduction project is only applied to the choice in the original position, but not to the posterior compliance. In other words, Hamlin's interpretation is compatible with Rawls' deontology, whereas it is incompatible with Rawls' original avowal of rational compliance theory for the stability of a well-ordered society.

The second passage also has a significant problem.

> Suppose that even in a well-ordered society there are some persons for whom the affirmation of their sense of justice is not a good. Given their aims and wants and the peculiarities of their nature, the thin account of the good does not define reasons sufficient for them to maintain this regulative sentiment. It has been argued that to these persons one cannot truthfully recommend justice as a virtue. And this is surely correct, assuming such a recommendation to imply that rational grounds (identified by the thin theory) counsel this course for them as individuals (TJ,p.575).

In the face of such persons, Rawls' strict compliance theory has to invoke the Hobbesian coercive power, which Rawls had already rejected.

In the third one, Rawls does not properly deal with FR:

> I am not trying to show that in a well-ordered society an egoist would act from a sense of justice, nor even that he would act justly because so acting would best advance his ends. Nor, again, are we to argue that an egoist, finding himself in a just society, would be well advised, given his aims, to transform himself into a just man. Rather, we are concerned with the goodness of the settled desire to take up the standpoint of justice. I assume that the members of a well-ordered society already have this desire. The question is whether this regulative sentiment is consistent with their good (TJ,p.568).

In view of our previous discussion of FR as a serious paradox of rationality, a reliable rational deduction project must provide a sufficient argument against it. However, Rawls' mere assumption of strict compliance practically makes the last question in the passage trivial. Rawls himself admits that "Therefore in this form [of strict compliance] the question is trivial: being the sorts of person they are, the members of a well-ordered society desire ... to act justly and fulfilling this desire is part of their good" (TJ,p.569).

In view of Rawls' double failure in his rational deduction project in the original choice as well as in the compliance theory, I conclude that Rawls' contractarian ethics cannot escape from the second horn of the contractarian dilemma, circularity of moral assumptions prior to rationality. Rawls himself later admits this failure:[90]

> Thus it was an error in *Theory* (and a very misleading one) to describe a theory of justice as part of the theory of rational choice. What I should have said is that the conception of justice as fairness uses an account of rational choice subject to reasonable conditions to characterize the deliberations of parties as representatives of free and equal [moral] persons; and all of this within a political conception of justice, which is, of course, a moral conception. There is no thought of trying to derive the content of justice within a framework that uses an idea of the rational as the sole normative idea. That thought is incompatible with any kind of Kantian [mostly deontological] view.

It is interesting to follow Rawls' recent developments according to his second thoughts on the rational deduction project. I have briefly pursued Rawls' basic ideas in his recent developments in Chapter I and I will not pursue them further.[91]

If we gather together the results of our discussions of Hobbes and Rawls, then the contractarian ethical dilemma is obvious. As a rational foundation for initial agreement and posterior compliance, the contractarian ethics is cornered between the moral irrelevancy of rationality and the circularity of prior moral assumptions. In other words, the contractarian rational deduction project is either irrelevant or circular. In either case, contractarian ethics appears to be doomed to failure. Notwithstanding, as mentioned in Chapter I, this may not be the end of the story. A stimulating attempt to steer between Scylla and Charybdis can be found in David Gauthier's *Morals By Agreement*. Gauthier seems to have a heavy theoretical burden since he has to solve the contractarian dilemma. Furthermore, he has to show that his model of rational choice represents the unique solution to the problems of social justice in face of the indeterminacy between various choice models. Overall, the burden to Gauthier appears as the contractarian trilemma between irrelevancy, circularity, and indeterminacy, as was characterized in Chapter I.

Notes

1 This does not mean that Locke, Rousseau, and Kant have nothing to do with the dilemma, or that they are not important in the history of social contract theory, or that there is no significant difference between them, and between them and Rawls and Hobbes. I will, though briefly, mention their positions in due course. Indeed, there are many other ways to classify contractarianism. Alan Hamlin sets up fourfold distinction, i.e., consensual, compromise or bargaining, global, and local. See his, "Liberty, Contract and the State," in Alan Hamlin and Philip Pettit, eds., *The Good Polity: Normative Analysis of the State* (Oxford: Basil Blackwell, 1989), p.90.

2 Hobbes, *Leviathan*, ed. C.B. Macpherson (Harmondsworth: Penguin Books, 1968). Hereafter abbreviated to LE with numerations of chapter and page. All quotations in the text follow 1651 original edition without any change.

3 For detailed survey of Hobbes' moral and political philosophies, see David Gauthier, *The Logic of Leviathan: The Moral and Political Theory of Thomas Hobbes* (Oxford: Clarendon Press, 1969); Gregory S. Kavka, *Hobbesian Moral and Political Theory* (Princeton: Princeton University Press, 1986); Jean Hampton, *Hobbes and the Social Contract Tradition* (Cambridge: Cambridge University Press, 1986); Daniel M. Farrell, "Taming Leviathan: Reflections on Some Recent Work on Hobbes," *Ethics*, 98 (1988), 793-805.

4 Indeed, I am not unaware that there are other kinds of interpretations. They are divine command theory, a priori formalism, ethics of authorization, emotivism or ethics of passion, even deontological ethics (including rule egoism). I am also not denying that there is textual evidence in the *Leviathan* for these interpretations. In this regard, Hampton says that "These strikingly different interpretations of the book strongly suggest that the ethical position Hobbes is espousing is neither clear nor simple; hence one must move slowly and carefully through the thickets of his text to ensure than one gets Hobbes' view right" (Hampton, p.28). My investigation cannot reach such a level of carefulness. But I try to show how rational choice theoretic interpretation predominates over other interpretations.

5 For a general exposition of Hobbes' philosophical position in connection with contractarian liberalism, see Anthony Arblaster, *The Rise and Decline of Western Liberalism* (Oxford: Basil Blackwell,1984), pp.38-49; pp.132-37.

6 See Aristotle, *The Politics*, trans. T. Sinclair (Harmondsworth: Penguin Books, 1962), bk.I,ii., p.59 (1253a).

7 Hobbes, *De Cive: The English Version: Philosophical Rudiments Concerning Government And Society*, ed. Howard Warrender (Oxford: Clarendon Press, 1983: *De Cive*, 1642: Translation, 1651), p.42.

8 Lukes, *Individualism*, p.80. See n.6 of Chapter II. And also see his "Methodological Individualism Reconsidered," in Alan Ryan, ed., *The Philosophy of Social Explanation* (Oxford: Oxford University Press, 1973), pp.118-29.

9 In his table of sciences, Hobbes explicitly points out that ethics is a science of "Consequences from the *Passions* of Men" (LE,9,p.147). In his English version of *De Cive*, Hobbes classifies "the faculties of Human nature unto four kinds; Bodily strength [sensual movements], Experience [imagination, memory], Reason, Passion." p.41.

10 Hobbes explicitly mentions "a possibility to come out of it [state of nature], consisting partly in the Passions, partly in his Reason" (LE,p.13,188). Hampton divides the passion and rationality accounts of conflict in Hobbes' state of nature and claims that these two accounts are mutually incompatible. See Hampton, pp.58-79.

11 I mentioned Hume already in connection with instrumental rationality. See Chapter II, n.22. For Hume, "Reason is ... the slave of the passions": "'Tis not contrary to reason to prefer the destruction of the whole world to the scratching of my finger." *Treatise*, bk.II, pt.III, sec.iii, p.415, p.416.

12 For a comprehensive discussion of Hobbes' concept of reason in connection with neo-classical economics, see Gauthier, "Thomas Hobbes, Moral Theorist," *The Journal of Philosophy*, 76 (1979), pp.547-559.

13 Myers, *The Soul of Modern Economic Man: Ideas of Self-Interest; Thomas Hobbes to Adam Smith*, pp.28-34. For Hobbes' foundationalism, see Chapter I, n.28. especially Ripstein's and Herzog's works.

14 Here it is problematic that Hobbes should be counted as a natural rights theorist. In view of the fact that, as we will see in the discussion of the second law of nature, it is the transfer of natural right that produces obligation, Hobbes is a natural rights theorist. Yet, as I claimed at the end of previous subsection, Hobbes' concept of natural right has a modern rational foundation, different from medieval natural rights and law theories. Nevertheless, as Macpherson claims, Hobbes' natural right in the above way—the right of every man to everything— is of course unworkable or ineffective. Elsewhere Hobbes himself makes it clear that "But that right of all men to all thing, is in effect no better than if no man had right to any thing" in *Elements of Law Natural and Politic*, Tönnies edition (Cambridge, 1989), I, chap.14, sec.10. quoted in C.B. Macpherson, *Democratic Theory: Essays in Retrieval* (Oxford: Clarendon Press, 1973), Essays xiii, "Natural Rights in Hobbes and Locke," p.226. Hobbes, unlike Locke, was not so attached to the institution of property rights.

15 Arblaster, p.137. See n.5. Andrew Levine, *Liberal Democracy: A Critique of Its Theory* (New York: Columbia University Press, 1981), pp.76,83.

16 In this regard, Hampton relates Hobbes' state of nature to Hume' circumstances of distributive justice. Hampton,p.60. As was pointed out several times, Rawls and Gauthier regard their initial contract situations to be in Hume's circumstances of justice (moderate scarcity of natural resources and subjective disinterestedness toward others).

17 Diffidence is distrust. From diffidence, preemptive anticipatory invasion is required. Perhaps Hobbes' citing glory as the third reason for invasion is just a non-essential addition. In view of this, it is not surprising that Hobbes' thinking incorporated 'feudal' as well as 'bourgeois' elements. Keith Thomas is right to point to Hobbes' stress on honor, glory and reputation as reflecting an aristocratic rather than a bourgeois scale of values; "The Social Origins of Hobbes' Political Thought," in *Hobbes Studies*, ed. K.C. Brown (Oxford: Basil Blackwell, 1965).

18 Hobbes makes a distinction between contract and covenant. Covenant is an individual's part on the mutual contract. According to covenant, an individual performs first and leaves the other to perform his part at some determinate time after and meantime be trusted (LE,14, p.193). However, in the text, I will use the terms of contract and covenant interchangeably.

19 The golden rule is mentioned at Matthew 7:12 and Luke 6:31 in the New Testament. At Luke 6:32, it appears clearly as the rule of love: "And if you love those who love you, what credit is *that* to you? For even sinners love those who love them." In this regard, the golden rule is supposed to replace the strict reciprocal ancient law, "An eye for an eye, and A Tooth for A Tooth" (Matthew 5:38). Furthermore, the unilateral character of the golden rule culminates in the passage that "whoever slaps you on your right cheek, turn him the other also" (Matthew 5:39).

20 Kavka, p.347. See n.3.

21 Rawls, "The Idea of Overlapping Consensus," p.23; Gauthier, MA,p.159; Robert Axelrod, "The Emergence of Cooperation among Egoists," *American Political Science Review*, 75 (1981), pp.306-18. and also his *The Evolution of Cooperation* (New York: Basic Books,1984); Michael Taylor, *The Possibility of Cooperation* (Cambridge: The University Press, 1987), p.135; David Braybrooke, "The Insoluble Problem of the Social Contract," *Dialogue*, 15 (1976),pp.3-37. Rpt. in Campbell and Sowden, p.296. See n.42 of Chapter I.

22 Literature on the PD interpretation of Hobbes' stages is enormous. All books mentioned at n.3 and n.21 treat this interpretation. Rawls and Gauthier do the same (TJ,p.269; MA,p.81).

23 For a comprehensive treatment of coercion, see J.R. Pennock and J.W. Chapman, eds., *Coercion*, Nomos XIV (Chicago: Aldine-Atherton, Inc.,1972) and especially J.W. Sobel, "The Need for Coercion," pp.148-177.

24 See A.K. Sen, "Isolation, Assurance and the Social Rate of Discount," *Quarterly Journal of Economics*, 81 (1967); "Choice, Orderings and Morality," in *Practical Reason*, ed. Stephan Körner (New Haven: Yale University Press, 1974), pp.59f.

25 Ullmann-margalit, p.67. See n.45 of Chapter II. Rawls also points out that "The general belief in the sovereign's efficacy removes the two kinds of instability" (TJ,p.497). The first instability comes from free-rider and the second from insecure assurance of the other parties' performing their duties (TJ,p.336).

26 Gauthier, *The Logic of Leviathan*, pp.79,85.

27 A crucial issue of the rational choice theoretic interpretation of Hobbes' "the original condition of mankind" is whether Hobbes' state of nature can be regarded as hypothetical. As Levine points out, it had been commonplace with the contractarian tradition to confound the historical problem of the origin of the political communities with the normative problem of the foundation of the state (Levine,p.81. See n.15.). Both Hobbes and Locke deal with the objection from history and mention American Indians as historical evidence at their contemporary time (LE,13, p.187); John Locke, *The Second Treatise of Government* in *Two Treatises of Government*, ed. Peter Laslett, rev. ed. (New York: A Mentor Book, 1963), ch.ii. sec.14; ch.viii. sec.105 (hereafter abbreviated as ST with chapter and section numeration). In case of Rousseau, he explicitly notes that his social contract theory is "not taken for historical truths, but only for hypothetical and conditional reasoning": Jean-Jacques Rousseau, *Discourse on the Origin and the Foundations of Inequality Among Men*, in *The First and Second Discourses*, trans. Victor Gourevitch (New York: Harper and Row, 1986), "Exordium," par.6. Returning to Hobbes, it is possible to read his state of nature as an initial hypothetical choice situation: "Howsoever, it may be perceived what manner of life there would be, where there were no common power to feare" (LE,13,p.187).

28 Daniels, "New Preface (1989)," in *Reading Rawls*, p.xvi.

29 In this regard, Gauthier makes a distinction: "In my view, distributive justice contrasts with acquisitive justice; the first constrains modes of cooperation, the second constrains the baseline from which cooperation proceeds." "Bargaining Our Way into Morality: A Do-It-Yourself Primer," *Philosophic Exchange*, 2 (1979), p.26. n.5. However, Rawls subsumes acquisitive justice to distributive justice. As we will see in next section, in the original position under the veil of ignorance, the baseline is assumed to be same for everybody. Rawls' idea is especially clarified in his claim for common assets of individual initial endowments.

30 D.D. Raphael, "Hobbes on Justice," in *Perspectives on Thomas Hobbes*, ed. G.A.J. Rogers and Alan Ryan (Oxford: Clarendon Press, 1988), p.170.

31 Rawls, "The Idea of Overlapping Consensus," p.11.

32 Ibid., pp.2, 23.

33 J.A. Schumpeter, *Capitalism, Socialism and Democracy*, 3rd. ed. (New York: Harper & Row, 1950); Robert A. Dahl, *A Preface to Democratic Theory* (Chicago: University Press of Chicago, 1956). It is noteworthy that Dahl recognizes the problem of his position in his *Dilemma of Pluralist Democracy: Autonomy vs. Control* (New Haven: Yale University Press, 1982) and replies that Rawls' redistribution implies moral tyranny in his other book, *A Preface to Economic Democracy* (Berkeley: University of California Press, 1985), pp.18,138. For a full comparison between Rawls and them, see Macpherson, *Democratic Theory*, pp.77-94.

34 Elizabeth Rapaport, "Classical Liberalism and Rawlsian Revisionism," in *New Essays on Contract Theory*, eds. Kai Nielsen and Roger A. Shiner, *Canadian Journal of Philosophy*, suppl., 3 (1977), p.107.

35 Braithwaite, *Theory of Game as a Tool for the Moral Philosopher*. For a good critical discussion, see Brian Barry, *Theories of Justice* (Berkeley: University of California Press, 1989).

36 Rawls, "Justice as Fairness," p.585. n.11.

37 Dennis C. Mueller, "Public Choice: A Survey," in *The Theory of Public Choice-II*, eds. J.M. Buchanan and R.D. Tollison (Ann Arbor, The University of Michigan Press, 1984), p.50.

38 Rousseau, *Of the Social Contract*, trans. Charles M. Sherover (New York: Harper & Row, 1984), bk.II., ch.6, par.104 (abbreviated as SC with corresponding numeration).

39 See John Plamenatz, "On le forcera d'être libre," in *Hobbes and Rousseau: A Collection of Critical Essays*, eds. M. Cranston and R.S. Peters (New York: Anchor Books, 1972), pp.318-32; Henry David Rempel, "On Forcing People to be Free," *Ethics*, 87 (1976), pp.18-34.

40 Alan H. Goldman, *Moral Knowledge* (London: Routledge, 1988), p.34.

41 Braybrooke, p.293. See n.21 of this chapter.

42 Rawls, "The Idea of Overlapping Consensus," p.2. Psychological egoism is a universal descriptive theory in the sense that all human actions are motivated by self-interest. Generally the concept of power as the general inclination of all mankind ("perpetual and restless desire of power after power"), which we dealt with in the first subsection, is counted for standard textual evidence. However, recently, the issue whether Hobbes actually held that doctrine has been raised according to different textual sources. See, Bernard Gert, "Hobbes and Psychological Egoism," in *Hobbes' Leviathan: Interpretation and Criticism*, ed. Bernard Baumin (Belmont: Wadsworth, 1969), pp.107-26. Rawls also adds a qualification that "Hobbes did not think this form of psychological egoism was true; but he thought it was accurate enough for his purpose [to justify the absolute power in the state of war]." Rawls, "The Idea of ...," p.2.

43 Sobel, p.148. See n.23 of this chapter.

44 Braybrooke, p.279. See n.21.

45 The first and second stages correspond to 'two parts' of Rawls' contractarian ethics (TJ,p.15). Concerning the application, Rawls actually sets up a 'four-stage sequence': first, the stage of the original position; secondly, of a constitutional convention; thirdly, of the legislative; and finally, of the individual judge, administrator, and citizen (TJ,pp.195-201). Compliance theory appears during the first and last stages of this sequence. The distinction between strict and partial compliances is applied here (TJ,p.8). I will elaborate on this distinction in the next subsection. However, I shall not pursue the question of the application except for the initial situation and compliance.

46 Aristotle distinguishes between universal and particular justice. Universal justice is complete virtue related to human actions towards others. Particular justice is classified into distributive and rectificatory justice. Rectificatory justice is again divided into communicative justice for voluntary transactions and retributory justice for punishments. See *Nichomachean Ethics*, trans. David Ross (Oxford: Oxford University Press, 1980), bk.V. 1129a-1131a 10. Rawls points out that Aristotelian universal justice is 'a social ideal' and that his theory of justice concerns distributive justice as a part of the social ideal. Rectificatory or compensatory justice is not considered as primary (TJ,p.8ff).

47 Arblaster, p.335. See n.5. Also see Brian Barry, *The Liberal Theory of Justice* (Oxford: Clarendon Press, 1973), p.32; Robert Paul Wolff, *Understanding Rawls* (Princeton: Princeton University Press, 1977), p.208. Additionally, see Chantal Mouffe, "American Liberalism and Its Critics: Rawls, Taylor, Sandel and Walzer," *Praxis International*, 8 (1988), pp.193-206.

48 The complete enumeration of the 12 conditions of the original position is in TJ,p.146f.

49 See Lester C. Thurow, *The Zero-Sum Society: Distribution and the Possibilities for Economic Change* (New York: Basic Books, 1980); J.K. Galbraith, *The Affluent Society*, 4th. ed. (Boston: Houghton Mifflin, 1984; 1st. 1958). John Gray indicates that the Humean circumstances of justice will surely exclude "some societies and moralities - those of Marxist communism or National Socialism" in *Liberalism* (Minneapolis: University of Minnesota Press, 1986), p.50. As mentioned in Chapter II Section A, neo-classical rationality presupposes the scarcity of natural and social resources and the self-interest motivation. For a helpful comparison between Rawls and neo-classics, see Nicholas Xenos, "Liberalism and the Postulate of Scarcity," *Political Theory*, 15 (1987), pp.225-243.

50 For Kant's distinction between autonomy and heteronomy of the will, see Immanuel Kant, *Groundwork of the Metaphysics of Morals*, trans. H.J. Paton (New York: Harper & Row, 1964), pp.61,88f,108f. And also his *Critique of Practical Reason*, trans. L.W. Beck (Indianapolis, Bobbs-Merrill Educational

Publishing, 1956), pp.117-123. For Rousseau's distinction between individual and general will, see SC,II,3,75f. Even though Rousseau mentions there that "The people is never corrupted, though often deceived," I do not think that the term 'corrupted' completely misleads Rousseau. See Arrow's interpretation of Kant and Rousseau: " ... if the corruptions of the environment were removed." *Social Choice and Individual Values*, p.74.

51 For a general discussion of rational expectation, see Steven M. Sheffrin, *Rational Expectations* (Cambridge: Cambridge University Press, 1983). And also K.J. Arrow and L. Hurwicz, "An Optimality Criterion for Decision-Making under Ignorance," in *Uncertainty and Expectations in Economics*, eds. C.F. Carter and J.L. Ford (Oxford: Oxford University Press, 1972); Sen, "Rationality and Uncertainty." See Chapter II, n.19.

52 See Benedict De Spinoza, *The Ethics*, trans. R.H.M. Elwes (New York: Dover Publications, 1955), p.117: "It is in the nature of reason to perceive things under a certain form of eternity (*sub quâdam aeternitatis specie*)." In view of the fact that the subtitle of Spinoza's Ethics is *Ethica Ordine Geometrico Demonstrata*, Rawls' claim of 'moral geometry' for justice is not merely coincidental (TJ,p.121).

53 For a helpful discussion, see David Keyt, "The Social Contract as an Analytic, Justificatory, and Polemic Device," *Canadian Journal of Philosophy*, 4 (1974),pp.241-252.

54 Czeslaw Porebski indicates that "It is being said for example that the application of formal tools of decision theory in the area of ethical reflection puts demands on our ethical intuitions that can be hardly met." For we are not able to determine the possible rational choice dispute through our intuitions. "The Moral Point of View and the Rational Choice Theory," in *The Task of Contemporary Philosophy*, eds. Werner Leinfeller, Franz M. Wuketis (Vienna: Hölder-Pichler-Tempsky, 1986), p.252. As an example of intuitionist objection, he notes J.D. Sneed, "Political Institutions as Means to Economic Justice: A Critique of Rawls' Contractarianism," *Analyse & Kritik*, 1 (1979), p.132.

55 For a general comment, see William Nelson, "The Very Idea of Pure Procedural Justice," *Ethics*, 90 (1980), pp.502-11. For the issue of proceduralism between Rawls and Nozick, see Scott Gordon, "The New Contractarians," *Journal of Political Economy*, 84(1976), pp.573-90.

56 David Lyons, "Nature and Soundness of the Contract and Coherence Arguments," in *Reading Rawls*, pp.141-167.

57 Daniels, "Introduction," in *Reading Rawls*, p.xix.

58 Luce and Raiffa mention in their *Games and Decisions* the four rational decision criteria (pp.278-86): the maximin criterion, the minimax risk criterion, the pessimism-optimism index criterion of Hurwicz, the criterion based on the principle of insufficient reason (in connection with choice models, which I have already discussed, see Chapter II,n.37). Since the

maximin criterion is to choose an alternative with the best worst state, it represents a very conservative or risk-aversion choice. It has been suggested that the minimax risk criterion is an improvement over the maximin. The minimax risk (loss or regret) is less conservative than the maximin because it seeks to minimize the maximum difference between the best that could happen and what actually happens. Yet the maximin and the minimax criteria are each ultraconservative (or pessimistic) in that, relative to each act, they concentrate upon the state having the worst consequence. Why not look at the best state, or at a weighted combination of the best and worst? This, in essence, is the Hurwicz criterion. Hurwicz criterion is dependent upon the pessimism-optimism index **a** (weighting factor): given $0 \leq a \leq 1$, Hurwicz's **a** ranges from maximin (a=1) to maximax (a=0). Notice that here intermediate utilities have no effect on which act is chosen. Where, then, does **a** come from? or how does one decide what **a** to use? There are many difficult problems for deciding **a** (e.g., is **a** arbitrarily decided by individual attitude? or is there any objective criterion?: see Luce and Raiffa, p.183; Resnik, *Choices*, p.33). The principle of insufficient reason leads to the equiprobability criterion: If there is no sufficient reason to believe objective probability, it is presupposed that each state has the same probability. This is tantamount to the subjective expected utility model of Harsanyi's average utilitarianism which presupposes that if everybody has equal probability of turning out to hold any position of society, it is rational for him or her to choose a society which promotes the average utility of society (see Chapter I. D). Concerning the four criteria, Rawls tries to show that it is rational for contracting parties to choose only his two principles of justice (using the maximin criterion rather than the principle of average utilitarianism according to the equiprobability criterion). Rawls argues against Harsanyi's criterion that there is "no objective grounds in the initial situation for assuming that one has an equal chance of turning out to be anybody" (TJ,p.168). And he adds that average utilitarian choice is "to take great risks" since "the average expectations may be rising although the expectations of the least favored are falling" (TJ,pp.169, 81). Luce and Raiffa illustrate the various decision criteria in the following table (p.285f).

Table 8. The Decision Criteria under Uncertainty
(Ignorance) I

A: acts
S: states

	S1	S2	S3
A1	2	12	3
A2	5	5	-1
A3	0	10	-2

Preferred Choice according to

Maximin criterion	A2
Hurwicz criterion (a=3/4)*	A3
Principles of insufficient reason	A1

* Since the formula is amin+(1-a)max, the a-indices of A3, A1, and A2 are 3/4(-2)+(1/4)10=1, 3/4(-3)+(1/4)12=3/4, and 3/4(-1)+(1/4)5=2/4 respectively. Of the three acts, A3 with the highest a-index utility is preferred (Luce and Raiffa, p.286).

Resnik provides another set of illustration, which includes the minimax regret (*Choices* ,p.38).

Table 9. The Decision Criteria under Uncertainty II

	S1	S2	S3
A1	1	14	13
A2	-1	17	11
A3	0	20	6

The maximin   A1
The minimax regret A2
Hurwicz criterion   A3
   (a=1/2)

Resnik does not include the principle of insufficient reason. However, it is clearly enough that the principle recommends A1.

59 The complete list of the conceptions of justice is in TJ, p.124. In this list, along with his two principles of justice, classical teleological conceptions (total, average utilitarianism, perfectionism), intuitionist conceptions (pluralistic principles with no fixed hierarchy), egoistic conceptions, and the various mixed conceptions are enumerated.

60 See Michael Young, *The Rise of Meritocracy* (London: Thomas and Hudson, 1958). "Distribute to every man his own due" is a basic maxim of meritocracy. What is his own due may be different according to the interpretation of due. Aristotle's concept of distributive justice "in accordance with geometrical proportion" or "according to merit" is generally considered as a typical form of traditional meritocracy. See *Nichomachean Ethics*, Bk.V. 1131a 6-27.

61 Pareto optimality or efficiency is a basic concept of economics, which presupposes unanimous ordinal decision. A social decision is Pareto-optimal if there is no alternative decision which could have made everybody at least as well off and at least one person better off. This is the strong Pareto optimality. The weak Pareto optimality is the condition P (Pareto Principle: If everybody prefers alternatives A to alternative B, then society must have the same preference) which is used in Arrow' social welfare function in Chapter II. For an account of the distinction between weak and strong, see Arrow, "Extended Sympathy and the Possibility of Social Choice," *Philosophia*, 7 (1978), p.228. For a comprehensive treatment, see Sen, *Collective Choice and Social Welfare*, 2.1. The Pareto Criterion. Cf. n.65 of this section.

62 Rawls elaborates the just savings principle in sec.44 "The Problem of Justice between Generations" in TJ. Even though Rawls points out that the difference principle must be consistent with the just savings principle, the consistency is very problematic. As Rawls admits, the difference principle

does not apply to the savings principle. For "there is no way for later generation to improve the situation of the least fortunate first generation" (p.291). Rawls does not set up a thick veil of ignorance between generations since to suppose a general assembly of all actual or possible generations is 'to stretch fantasy too far' (TJ,p.139). Thus contracting parties in the original position become contemporaries of two generations (present time entry). However, in this case, contracting parties, who have the motivation of mutual disinterestedness, find no reason to save resources for the next generation. In order to solve this problem, Rawls changes the status and motivational assumptions of contracting parties. Contracting parties are no longer disinterested individuals. They become 'heads of families' with 'ties of sentiment between successive generations' (TJ,p.128, p.292). Accordingly, in any generation expectations of the least advantaged person are to be maximized "subject to the condition of putting aside the savings that would be acknowledged. Thus the complete statement of the difference principle includes the saving principle as a constraint" (TJ,p.292). But Rawls pays too much (inconsistent motivational assumptions of rationality) for the consistency between the difference principle and the just saving principle. For a helpful discussion, see Arrow, "Rawls's Principle of Just Saving," *Swedish Journal of Economics*, 75 (1973), pp.323-35. Rpt. in *Collected Papers of Kenneth J. Arrow*, Vol.I. *Social Choice and Justice* (Cambridge, Massachusetts: The Belknap Press of Harvard University Press, 1983), pp.133-46.

63   The principle of diminishing marginal utility is that the rate of marginal (i.e., additionally increased) utility of consuming n+1 commodity is decreased when compared to the rate of marginal utility of consuming n commodity. In other words, in general, utility increases at a lower rate as the quantity of commodities increases.   Neo-classical marginalism was first used in value theory as an alternative to the production theory of value of the classics (the value of a certain good as determined by its cost of production).   This production theory of value was developed into the labor theory of value by Ricardo and Marx.   In contrast, neo-classicists thought that it was the marginal utility of a good which would control the price offered by the customers and hence its value. In connection with neo-classical economics, see Bernhard Felderer and Stefan Homburg, *Macroeconomics and New Macroeconomics* (New York: Springer-Verlag, 1987), pp.15-17.   For a full treatment, see Edward Heiman, *History of Economic Doctrine* (London: Oxford University Press, 1945), ch.viii. Neo-classicalism; Joan Robinson, *Economic Philosophy* (Chicago: Aldine Publishing Company, 1962).   In Chapter II, I did not discuss the diminishing marginal utility as an assumption of rational economic man. See C. Dyke, *Philosophy of Economics*, p.51.

64   *The Republic of Plato*, trans. F.M. Conford (London: Oxford University Press,1941).   Bk.IV. "Abolition of Family for the Guardians," 457b-446d. Plato's suggestion of reasons for the abolition (mainly educational) might not be uniquely for the considerations of the principle of fair opportunity.   For the communist conception of the family, see Frederick Engels, *The Origin of Family, Private Property, and the State* (New York: International Publishers Co., 1942; original ed., 1884).

65 Rawls explicitly points out that "it should be noted that the difference principle [as a maximin solution to the problem of social justice] is compatible with the principle of efficiency": "For when the former is fully satisfied, it is indeed impossible to make any one representative man better off without making another worse off, namely the least advantaged representative man whose expectations we are to maximize" (TJ,p.79). However, as the second priority rule shows, the difference principle is prior to the principle of efficiency. The priority of the difference principle ranges over two cases. First, if the basic structure is unjust, Rawls' difference principle will authorize redistributive changes that may lower the expectations of some of those better off. This means that the difference principle requires some changes that are not efficient in the sense of Pareto optimality (TJ,p.79f). Second, Rawls attempts to overcome the indeterminateness of the principle of efficiency by the difference principle (TJ,p.75). The indeterminateness means that there are many configurations which are efficient. For example, the distributions in which one person receives the entire stock of commodities is efficient, since there is no rearrangement that will make some better off and none worse off: "Each efficient arrangement is better than some other arrangements, but none of the efficient arrangements is better than another" (TJ,p.70). Thus "the principle of efficiency cannot serve alone as a conception of justice" (TJ,p.71). Cf. n.61 of this subsection.

66 On the one hand, Rawls' lexical difference principle seems to offend condition D (non-dictatorship) since the preferences of the least advantaged solely represent the preferences of social choice. On the other hand, the preferences of the least advantaged representative person seem to be justified according to the fair and impartial conditions of the original position. See David L. Schaefer, *Justice or Tyranny?* (Port Washington, N.Y.: National University Publications, 1979); Steven Strasnick, "The Problem of Social Choice: Arrow to Rawls," *Philosophy & Public Affairs*, 5 (1975), 241-273.; Peter J. Hammond, "Equity, Arrow's conditions, and Rawls' difference Principle," *Econometrica*, 44 (1976), pp.793-804.; James P. Sterba, "A Rawlsian Solution to Arrow's Paradox," *Pacific Philosophical Quarterly*, 62 (1981), pp.282-92.

67 Arrow, "Current Developments in Social Choice," in *Social Choice and Justice*, p.167. For Arrow's criticisms of Rawls see, his "Some Ordinalist-Utilitarian Notes on Rawls' Theory of Justice," *The Journal of Philosophy*, 70 (1973), pp.245-263.; "Extended Sympathy and the Possibility of Social Choice." See n.87 of Chapter II.

68 I am indebted for the following characteristics of the perfectly just society to W.E. Cooper, "The Perfectly Just Society," *Philosophy and Phenomenological Research*, 38 (1977-78), pp.46f.

69 Major proponents of the theory of the moral sentiments are Hume and Adam Smith. See Hume's *A Treatise of Human Nature* (1739), and *An Enquiry Concerning the Principles of Morals* (1751); Adam Smith's *A Theory of the Moral Sentiments* (1759).

70 *The Republic of Plato*, Bk.IX. "Justice, not Injustice, is profitable:" 588b-592b. Edward F. McClennen, "Justice and the Problem of Stability," *Philosophy & Public Affairs*, 18 (1989), p.8.; Wolff, *Understanding Rawls*, p.176.; Stanley Bates, "The Motivation to Be Just," *Ethics*, 85 (1974-75), p.3.

71 For the myth of the Lydian shepherd Gyges' ring, see *The Republic of Plato*, Bk.II. 359d-360a.

72 Rawls thinks that both theories lead to the classical total utilitarianism. Ideal observer theory says that a social system is right, when an ideally sympathetic observer would approve of it from a general point of view should he or she possess all the relevant of knowledge of the circumstances. In the same vein, if an ideally altruistic and benevolent spectator, who is to split into the many members of society, would acknowledge a certain state, that state is considered as right. See Roderick Firth, "Ethical Absolutism and the Ideal Observer," *Philosophy and Phenomenological Research*, 12 (1952), pp.317-345; Thomas Nagel, *The Possibility of Altruism* (Oxford: The Clarendon Press, 1970).

73 For the notion of the pure conscientious act, see W.D. Ross, *The Right and the Good* (Oxford: the Clarendon Press, 1930), pp.157-60.

74 Lansing Pollock clearly points out that "On the one hand, the conditions must be specific and rigorous enough so that it is clear that rational men would indeed choose Rawls's principles. On the other hand, the conditions must be recognizable as representing the typical circumstances of justice and/or the constraints of having a morality." See his "A Dilemma for Rawls?" *Philosophical Studies*, 22 (1971), p.38.

75 L.W. Sumner, *The Moral Foundation of Rights* (Oxford: The Clarendon Press, 1987), pp.159f; Braybrooke, "Social Contract Theory's Fanciest Flight," p.755; Kraus and Coleman, "Morality and the Theory of Rational Choice," p.747. And also see, Chapter I, n.43, n.47.

76 For the meaning of terminology, see n.58 of this chapter. And also refer to the rational choice model discussed in Chapter II, A.3. Formal Models of Rational Choice Theory.

77 Harsanyi, "Can the Maximin Principle serve as a Basis for Morality?" *The American Political Science Review*, 69 (1975), p.599.

78 Ibid.

79 Ibid., p.597. Harsanyi's counterexamples show that, according to the maximin rule, the following is logically as well as practically possible: in order to increase the minor benefits for the least advantaged persons, it may be necessary for other persons to sacrifice large quantities of benefits. Rawls himself admits:

> I want to conclude this section [26. The Reasoning for the Two Principles] by taking up an objection which is likely to be made against

the difference principle and which leads into an important question. The objection is that since we are to maximize (subject to the usual constraints) the long-term prospects of the least advantaged, it seems that the justice of large increases or decreases in the expectations of the more advantaged may depend upon small changes in the prospects of those worst off. To illustrate: the most extreme disparities in wealth and income are allowed provided that the expectations of the least fortunate are raised in the slight degree. But at the same time similar inequalities favoring the more advantaged are forbidden when those in the worst position lose by the least amount" (TJ,p.157).

Nevertheless, Rawls insists that the above illustrations are just "abstract possibilities" (TJ,p.157).

80   Resnik, *Choices*, p.43.

81   Machina, "Rational Decision Making Versus Rational Decision Modelling," p.163.

82   D.C. Mueller, R.D. Tollison, and T.D. Willett, "The Utilitarian Contract: A Generalization of Rawls' Theory of Justice," *Theory and Decision*, 4 (1974), pp.345-67. For a helpful discussion of their position, see Lessnoff, *Social Contract*, pp.154-57; Dennis C. Mueller, *Public Choice* (Cambridge: Cambridge University Press, 1979), ch.13. Utilitarian Contracts, pp 247-59.

83   Locke, ST,5,27.

84   Milton Friedman formulates another libertarian motto: "The ethical principle that would justify the distribution of income in a free market society is, 'To each according to what he and the instruments he owns produces.'" *Capitalism and Freedom* (Chicago: The University of Chicago Press, 1962), pp.161f.

85   Gauthier claims that "Rawls introduces the conception of moral persons" and that "Nozick introduces natural rights ... as an independent moral element." "Justice as Social Choice," p.267.

86   Kai Nielsen, "Rawls' Defense of Morality, Amoralism and the Problem of Congruence," *The Personalist*, 59 (1978), 93-100. And also see, his "Why Should I Be Moral?" *Methodos*, 15 (1963), pp.275-306; "Is 'Why Should I Be Moral?' an Absurdity?" *Australasian Journal of Philosophy*, 36 (1958), pp.25-32.

87   I am in debt of these passages to K. Nielsen, "Rawls and Classical Amoralism," *Mind*, 86 (1977), pp.19-30.

88   Adopting Frankena's definition, Rawls interprets teleological theory (utilitarianism, perfectionism) that "the good is defined independently from the right, and then the right is defined as that which maximizes the good" (TJ,p.24). In contrast, deontological theory is defined: It "either does not specify the good independently from the right, or does not interpret the right

as maximizing the good" (TJ,p.30). From this general definition, Rawls specifies his position. First, "justice as fairness is a deontological theory in the second way [in the general definition]" (TJ,p.30). Second, he embraces the consequentialism: "It should be noted that deontological theories are defined as non-teleological ones, not as views that characterize the rightness of institutions and acts independently from their consequences" (TJ,p.30). Third, Rawls supposes "with utilitarianism that the good is defined as the satisfaction of rational desire" (TJ,p.30). As we will see shortly, Rawls' deontology reveals a significant problem in relation to the theory of rational choice. For the general definition of deontological and teleological theories, see William K. Frankena, *Ethics* (Englewood Cliffs: Prentice Hall, 1963), pp.14f.

89 Hamlin, *Ethics, Economics and the State*, p.110.

90 Rawls, "Justice as Fairness: Political not Metaphysical," p.237, n.20. For the other portion of this passage, see Chapter I. n.37.

91 For a comprehensive treatment, see ten articles in "Symposium on Rawlsian Theory: Recent Developments," *Ethics*, 99 (1989); Norman Daniels, newly added "Preface" in *Reading Rawls*, pp.xiii-xxvii; William A. Galston, "Moral Personality and Liberal Theory: John Rawls' 'Dewey Lectures,'" *Political theory*, 10 (1982), pp.492-519; Richard Rorty, "The Priority of Democracy to Philosophy," in Merrill D. Peterson and Robert C. Vaughan, eds. *The Virginia Statute for Religious Freedom* (Cambridge: Cambridge University Press, 1988), pp.257-281.

Chapter IV

Gauthier's Neo-Contractarian Ethics

A. Contractarian Moral Agreement As Part of the Theory of Rational Choice

1. The Contractarian Dilemma And Beyond

Gauthier's *Morals By Agreement* uses the advanced game-theoretic technique of rational choice theory in order to establish a contractarian rational deduction project of morality. One commentator depicts Gauthier's triumph as "Social Contract Theory's Fanciest Flight."[1] It is not so difficult to figure out the direction of the flight. Gauthier endeavors to fly over the contractarian nest, which has been contaminated by the contractarian dilemma and trilemma, in order to find a new and viable contractarian habitation. In this chapter, I will describe and assess Gauthier's endeavor. The discussion will be divided into two sections: (a) contractarian moral agreement as part of rational choice theory, (b) bargaining theory of liberal justice and its critical assessment.

Gauthier succinctly summarizes his contractarian ethics according to its following five core ideas.

> We shall ... show how each of our core ideas – the morally free zone afforded by the perfectly competitive market, the principle of minimax relative concession, the disposition to constrained maximization, and the proviso against bettering oneself through worsening others – may be related, directly or indirectly, to Archimedean choice. In embracing these other conceptions central to our theory, the Archimedean point reveals the coherence of morals by agreement (MA,pp.16f: the order of the ideas is adjusted).

None of these five core ideas can be ignored if one is to evaluate Gauthier's major theme of his book, i.e., the contractarian rational deduction project of morality. Thus I will investigate these ideas in the following manner.

The first idea (which will be dealt with in Section A) of the morally free zone is a foil against which it is shown how morality can emerge. The morally free zone is represented by the basic ideal-type assumption of economics: viz., that individual utility maximization leads to the optimal equilibrium in a perfectly competitive market (MA,p.84). If there were such a market harmonized by the Smithian invisible hand, morality would be unnecessary. However, as Gauthier acknowledges, since "the world is not a market, morality is a necessary constraint on the interaction of rational persons. Morality arises from market failure" (MA,p.84). Here Gauthier explicitly admits to holding to a theory of market contractarianism.[2]

The second (the principle of minimax relative concession), third (constrained maximization), and fourth idea (the proviso), which will be treated in Section B, are concerned with the bargaining principle of justice for cooperation, and compliance of contractarian agreement, initial bargaining position respectively. These three ideas are "the argumentative centre of the book" (MA,p.ix). The last core idea, the Archimedean point, represents the widely held idea throughout the history of moral philosophy that it is the essence of morality that "moral principles must be impartially acceptable."[3] Gauthier elaborates his version of the contractarian moral point of view into which the results of rational choice agreement converge and vice versa:

> the moral demand for impartiality can be accommodated within the rational demand for individual utility-maximization by attending to the conditions of agreed interaction among equally rational persons. This completes our theoretical exposition (MA,p.267).

As Gauthier claims, if this reciprocal coherence between morality and rationality can be established, it will be a promising solution to the contractarian dilemma.[4]

Along with his position of market contractarianism, Gauthier explicitly points out that "the ideal actor [of the Archimedean point] is, therefore, not a socialist" (MA, p.261). In this connection, he characterizes various merits of contractarian society of the liberal individual (MA,Ch.XI. The Liberal Individual). In view of the external criticisms of liberalism, especially from the Marxist camp, it is pertinent to evaluate Gauthier's contractarian ethics in the context of the liberal agenda, which will be the major theme of the last subsection of Section B.

The major concern of this section is Gauthier's claim that "A contractarian theory of morals, developed as part of the theory of rational choice, has evident strengths" (MA,p.17). I will delay the discussion of his conception of rationality, and his claims for the appropriate model of rational choice and its resultant relation to the market. My primary concern here, then, is to assess the supposed strengths of the neo-contractarian strategy to escape from the contractarian dilemma in the overall history of social contract theory.

As the *modus operandi* of this study dictates, I have assessed the history of contractarian theory of ethical and political norms and institutions in view of the two radically different and rival versions. "The first conceives the social contract decision to be a complex version of a problem in strategic bargaining, in which concepts such as the status quo, threat advantage and strategy play a key role."[5] This approach was historically developed by Hobbes and recently by James Buchanan.[6] In Buchanan's Hobbesian framework especially in *The Limits of Liberty*, "the agreement on rights of the two parties represents a contractual internalization of an externality relationship that existed in the precontract state of nature."[7] The precontractual position of "anarchistic equilibrium" is arrived at by the attack and defense mechanism of individuals' initial bargaining positions according to the "natural distribution" of initial endowments.[8] Thus he makes an extraordinary suggestion that the status quo must be treated as "legitimate contractually" and that departures from it must be renegotiated, in effect, contractually rather than through normative democratic procedures "that are derived from external ethical criteria."[9]

In the domain of bargaining theory, Nash and Braithwaite have made suggestions about bargaining solutions to the so-called fair division problem, which heavily reflect the status quo point and the threat advantage.[10] I have already indicated why Hobbes and the various Hobbesian frameworks lead to the the first horn of the contractarian dilemma, viz., the moral irrelevancy of rational bargaining.

"The second 'idealizes' the contract decision by conceiving of persons as having to reach a decision from an initial position in which considerations of strategy and relative bargaining power have no place."[11] Its historical roots lie in the writings of Kant and Rousseau but most clearly in the contemporary work of Rawls.[12] Locke's position is also considered as an attempt to moralize Hobbesian state of nature through his famous proviso of property rights, which we have discussed in connection with Nozick.[13] However, Locke's contractarian theory presupposes a pre-existing moral principle (Law of nature): "The State of Nature has a Law of Nature to govern it, which obliges every one." That is, "no one ought to harm another in his Life, Health, Liberty, or Possessions" (ST,2,6). Furthermore, the Lockean proviso on natural rights of property is posited "without the assignation or consent of any body" (ST,5,28).

The non-strategic, non-bargaining approach overall seems to avoid the problems of the Hobbesian contractual version. Nevertheless, as has been made clear, the second version commits itself to the second horn of contractarian dilemma: viz., the circularity of introducing prior moral elements before any rational contractarian agreement is reached.

In view of the above historical significance involved in the contractarian dilemma, it is not an exaggeration to say that the leitmotif and viability of Gauthier's neo-contractarian ethics hinges solely on his strategy for escaping the two devastating horns of this dilemma. After having produced a series of important articles on the relations between rational self-interest and morality, Gauthier presents his final version of contractarian rational deduction project of morality in *Morals By Agreement*. In one of the articles, Gauthier explicitly points out that his future philosophical agenda starts from the following observation: "In the end, rights [of Locke] and rationality [of Hobbes] stand unreconciled, and yet, neither I, nor to my knowledge anyone else, has said anything very convincing about the resolution of *this* conflict."[14]

Gauthier formulates the contractarian dilemma as follows.

Those who claim that moral principles are objects of rational choice in special circumstances fail to establish the rationality of actual compliance with these principles. Those who claim to establish the rationality of such compliance appeal to a strong and controversial conception of reason that seems to incorporate prior moral suppositions (MA,p.17).

According to his version of rational choice theory, Gauthier insists that the premises of the theory must not contain any moral ingredients: "Morality, we shall argue, can be generated as a rational constraint from the non-moral premisses of rational choice" (MA,p.4. cf. pp.6,17). In this respect, Gauthier appears to side with Hobbes and Buchanan against Kant and Rawls. Thus he criticizes Rawls that Rawls' use of veil of ignorance implies "a prior moral conception of the person."[15]

However, Gauthier strongly recognizes that "fair procedures yield an impartial outcome only from an impartial initial position" (MA,p.191). In this regard, he seems to agree with Locke and Rawls against Hobbes and Buchanan. His introduction of the Lockean proviso is promoted in this spirit. Accordingly, he rejects Buchanan's Hobbesian framework of the anarchistic equilibrium, which reflects predatory/defensive interaction in the state of nature (MA,pp.193-99).[16] However, he expresses hesitation here since the pre-contractual introduction of the Lockean proviso seems to commit him to the circularity horn of the contractarian dilemma. Gauthier's strategy is that rational compliance of the contractarian agreement cannot be guaranteed without the fair initial position of the Lockean proviso: "We shall therefore argue that it is both rational and just for each individual to accept a certain constraint on natural interaction" (MA,p.192). As Summer correctly emphasizes, "the rational support which Gauthier claims for the proviso thus promises to steer him safely between the horns of the contractarian's dilemma."[17] Though comparatively long, probably the following passage catches the sense of Gauthier's strategy in the clearest way:[18]

> *Introduction of the Lockean state of nature moralizes the base point for social cooperation. Thus moral factors enter into the derivation of the principles of justice.* But the manner of their entry must be carefully noted. *Only those moral considerations are introduced that are necessary to attain rational compliance with the principles.* In effect, the principles of justice have moral force; they require each person to refrain from seeking his or her greatest expected utility if and insofar as this would conflict with carrying out decisions based on the principles. For this to be rational, a further moral factor must be introduced—the requirement that no one benefit at the expense of others in any interaction taken for granted in determining the base point. But this moral factor is introduced only to ensure the rationality of compliance with the principles of justice. *Thus it, like the principles themselves, are ultimately derived from purely rational considerations. It is not introduced as an inde-*

pendent moral element in the way in which Rawls introduces the conception of
moral persons or in which Nozick introduces natural right (emphases mine).

In view of this quotation, Gauthier offers a demonstration that
rational compliance requires the Lockean constraint in the base
point for agreement. Having made evident what Gauthier's philosophical aim is, the next task is to describe it in enough detail in
order to evaluate it.

2. Morality, Rationality, Preference, and Value.

"What is morality? Moral philosophers have often claimed to
discover the essential characteristics of morality"[19] Indeed, they
have presented us with rival accounts of morality throughout the
history of philosophical ethics and this in turn has been a major
impetus to further reflections on the status of morality. Contractarian ethics, one such account, aims to discover or more accurately
to construct morality as the object of fully voluntary agreement
among rational persons in the hypothetical initial choice situation,
traditionally known as the state of nature (MA,p.9).[20] Admittedly,
an initial theoretical responsibility of contractarian ethics is to
answer the following question. Why should we take any interest in
contractarian hypothetical agreement, moral, rational, or otherwise, if it is not really made? In other words, what is the contractarian rationale for morality?

Gauthier gives his answer to this question:[21]

> The rationale for appealing to a hypothetical contract is to found in the
> supposition that, what ever society actually is, it ought to be only an associa-
> tion for the mutual benefit of its members, so that its practices and institu-
> tions ought to be those which would result from an agreement which each
> would find rational to enter voluntarily.

In view of the implication of this passage, contractarian agreement
is a rational justificatory framework for the normative assessment
of social practices and institutions.

Gauthier's contractarian rationale is founded on "a methodological individualism in our social theory and a moral individualism that demands agreement at the core of our social practices."[22]
How can the double-barreled theory of individualism, in turn, be
supported? Gauthier answers that "only such a society could
command the willing allegiance of every rational individual"

(MA,p.11). This means that no society can pass the test of contractarian rational agreement, which is sustained by "exploitation," "coercive relationships," (MA,pp.11,17), "belief in hell fire," or ideological "false consciousness."[23] However, as will be discussed in Section B, not only Christian fundamentalists, but Marxists and communitarians as well, sharply disagree with Gauthier's contractarian rationale. My primary concern, here, is to relate Gauthier's contractarian rationale to his view on morality. Gauthier embraces Rawls' view of society as "a cooperative venture for mutual advantage" among persons "conceived as not taking an interest in one another's interests" (TJ,pp.4,13; MA,p.10). Like Rawls, Gauthier resorts to the need for cooperation in accord with Hume's characterization of the circumstances of justice (MA,p.112). As pointed out several times, the circumstances have to do with the scarcity of social and natural resources and self-bias.

Accordingly, contractarian morality is supposed to provide a rationale for the transition from "a non-social state of nature" or "pre-moral context" in the circumstances of justice to a mutually advantageous cooperative society (MA,pp.11,9). In order to arrive at this mutual advantage, contractarian morality commands constraints of individual self-interest maximization. If this is the case, morality does not seem to be fully compatible with rationality conceived as individual self-interest maximization, even though morality provides collective mutual advantage. Even though "ex ante" contractarian agreement is rationally made, "ex post" compliance cannot be rationally guaranteed, as exemplified by the Free-rider problem (MA,p.9).

As I mentioned in Chapters I and II, the seminal problem of the relationship between morality and rationality is its apparent conflict between moral constraints and individual self-interest maximization. This apparent incompatibility of morality and rationality issues in "an initial presumption against morality, as a constraint on each person's pursuit of his own interest" (MA,p.8f). The presumption naturally leads to a common belief in the history of ethics: "The belief that duty cannot be reduced to interest, or that morality may require the agent to subordinate all considerations of advantage, is one which has withstood the assaults of contrary-minded philosophers from Plato to the present."[24]

Gauthier thus thinks that "morality ... is traditionally understood to involve an impartial constraint on the pursuit of individual interest" (MA,p.7). He tries to retain the traditional view in a unique manner. "Duty overrides advantages, but the acceptance of duty is truly advantageous" (MA,p.2). As Gauthier admits it, this is a "seeming paradox" since morality as a rational constraint on the maximization of self-interest has "foundation in the interest," viz., in the very concept of rationality as maximization (MA,p.2). Choice is made by rationality as self-interest maximization and also by "a meta-choice, a choice about how to make choices" in view of the very concept of rationality (MA,p.79).

According to Nagel, we can distinguish two kinds of rational moral projects. If the rational project says that the moral is rational, it may be a strong claim that to be immoral is always irrational, or it may be a weaker claim that to be moral is never irrational.[25] Gauthier explicitly points out that "To choose rationally, one must choose morally. This is a strong claim" (MA,p.4).

This claim directly relates to his "pioneering enterprise" that "We shall develop a theory of morals as part of the theory of rational choice" (MA,p.2).[26] Gauthier's rational choice theoretic strategy mainly hinges on his avowed solutions to the "three core problems" — rational cooperation, rational compliance, and rational acceptance of the appropriate initial position (MA,p.v). I will address these problems in detail in the next section. As I discussed it in Chapter II, Gauthier accepts the neo-classical concept of rationality as instrumental self-interest maximization. In his own terms, Gauthier embraces "the *maximizing* conception of rationality" (MA,p.7). The maximizing conception of rationality is a form of "subjective utility-maximization" in the sense that the rational person seeks "the greatest satisfaction of her own interest" (MA,p.7).[27] Gauthier contrasts this conception with "the *universalistic* conception of rationality" where "what makes it rational to satisfy an interest does not depend on whose interest it is" (MA,p.7). The universalistic conception is employed by Kant, Nagel, and Hare (MA,p.6). Both Rawls and Harsanyi also use this conception in their respective formulations of choice under uncertainty. Gauthier agrees with Rawls' charge that "utilitarianism does not take seriously the distinction between persons" (TJ, p.187). Nevertheless, because of the veil of ignorance, he claims that "Rawls [also] violates the integrity of human beings as they are and as they conceive themselves" (MA,p.254). Gauthier, thus, ridicules Rawls' universalistic conception that "each man is every-man — or no-man."[28] In this regard, Gauthier suggests that, even though agreement is hypothetical, "the parties to agreement are real, determinate individuals, distinguished by their capacities, situations, and concerns" (MA,p.9). This suggestion naturally leads to Gauthier's observation that "morality enters in defining it [agreement] for certain strategic environments" (MA,p.21).[29] Gauthier thus maintains that the proper choice model for morality must be "a bargain or agreement among persons who need not be unaware of their identities" (MA,p.5).

In general, Gauthier asserts that his "contractarian theory of morals, developed as part of the theory of rational choice, has evident strengths" (MA,p.17). Basically the strengths are two: "Morality is thus given a sure grounding in a weak and widely accepted conception of practical rationality" (MA,p.17). But, first, one may ask whether Gauthier's appeal to the wide acceptance of the maximizing conception is a convincing argument. The mere appeal to the received opinions in the domains of economic theory, decision and game theory is not a philosophical and logical argument. And also how wide is it? As shown in Chapter II. C.1, sociological and psychological theories strongly reject the maximizing conception. Furthermore, in the domain of rational choice theory per se, the Imperfect and the Extended schools also challenge the conception (see Chapter II. C.2). It is even possible that, against Gauthier's wide acceptance argument, the proponents of the universalistic conception appeal to the time-honored heritage in Western moral philosophy. Ironically, as was mentioned, Gauthier has to invoke the universalistic conception of rationality, probably a mixed conception — a thin veil of ignorance —, in order to guarantee the impartiality of the Archimedean point.[30]

Second, the argument from a weak conception of rationality seems to be more convincing on logical grounds. Gauthier thinks that the weakness in premises is a conceptual virtue (MA, p.8). If morality can be derived from such weak premises as those which rely upon the maximizing conception, then fewer commitments are being made. In order words, the universalistic conception is too strong and demanding in the sense that it requires individuals to erase their integrity as individuals. In any case, the universalistic conception practically brings the same effect of assuming altruistic motivations from the beginning. Gauthier supports this idea with the following argument. "Any consideration affords one a reason for acting on the maximization conception, also affords one such a reason on the universalistic conception. But the converse does not hold" (MA,p.8). Probably this non-converse relation means that moral skeptics like Hobbes' Fool can be convinced of his foolishness by the maximization conception but not by the universalistic conception.

Rawls originally uses this same kind of argument from weakness to support his stance of mutual disinterestedness against the traditional utilitarian assumption of the benevolent and sympathetic ideal observer (cf. Chapter III. B.3). Rawls adds that "one argues from widely accepted but weak premises to more specific conclusions" (TJ,p.18). In turn, Gauthier uses the same weakness-of-premises argument against Rawls' and utilitarian universalistic conceptions of rationality overall. The validity of Gauthier's claim may be clear within an axiomatic deductive system.[31] But I will show in Section B that morality itself changes according to the maximizing conception of rationality.

As an argument for a rational morality, its validity is, needless to say again, directly related to avoiding the second horn of the contractarian dilemma. In order to avoid the problems of circularity or begging the question, which beset the universalistic conception, Gauthier indicates that "our concern, once again, is to do this [rational deduction project] without incorporating into the premises of our argument any of the moral conceptions that emerge in our conclusions" (MA,p.6). "No alternative account generates morals, as a rational constraint on choice and action from a non-moral, or morally neutral, base" (MA, p.17). In this respect, many commentators have pointed out that Gauthier's contractarian deduction project of morality is an example of rational foundationalism.[32] The significance of Gauthier's rational foundationalism, perhaps, cannot be better described than in Hardin's following message.[33]

> The extraordinary value of Gauthier's theory, if it is compelling, is that it potentially resolves *all such problems* [of paradoxes of rationality]. Given

that such problems seemingly abound, we must suppose that Gauthier's theory is wrong, or that people have simply failed to understand their rational self-interest in cooperation. Perhaps even more impressively, we must suppose Gauthier has succeeded in cracking a problem that many of the best social theorists of the past two millennia have recognized as central but have failed to crack. It is an audacious supposition. If it is correct, Gauthier's result is, philosophically, world-historical.

Even though I agree with Gauthier that the maximizing conception of rationality enjoys the status of non-moral premise, it is still problematic whether the concept of self-interest instrumental maximization is purely neutral. Gauthier avows that he does not "defend any particular moral code" in his premises (MA,p.6). In this regard, it is pertinent to investigate the basic concepts of rational choice theory—preference, utility, and maximization. Gauthier's subjective utility maximization concept of rationality appears to be vague if one comes to it without understanding the relationship between those three concepts and his theory of value. In this connection, it is helpful to review various related discussions from Chapter II.

Up to this point, I have introduced Gauthier's theory of rational choice loosely in terms of the satisfaction of advantage or self-interest. Gauthier defines the theory of rational choice as "a precise measure of preference, *utility*, and identifies rationality with the maximization of utility" (MA,p.22). This precise definition is still complicated and demands commentary. First, the theory primarily is concerned with individual preferences between states of affairs conceived as alternative possibilities realizable in action (MA,p.22). Second, utility is defined as a measure of individual preference. If an individual prefers the possible outcomes from the state of alternative A in his action to the outcomes from B, his utility in A is greater than in B. "Utility is thus ascribed to states of affairs considered as objects of preference relations" (MA,p.22). Third, the rational individual maximizes his or her utility in choosing from a finite set of the possible outcomes of his or her action in the states of affairs. Rationality, thus, is defined as the maximization of utility (MA,p.23). In sum, "choice maximizes preference fulfilment given belief" (MA,p.30). In addition, Gauthier embraces the formal conditions of coherent preference, connectedness and transitivity (MA,pp.38-40), which I investigated in Chapter II.[34]

In identifying rationality with the maximization of utility as a measure of preference, Gauthier's theory of rational choice takes an instrumental conception of rationality. His "instrumental conception of rationality is thus linked to the identification of value with utility" (MA,p.26). Consequently, it "disclaims all concern with the ends of action" (MA,p.26). However, Gauthier tries to give a minimum criterion for the contents of rational preferences. Gauthier suggests a theory of considered preference. At this point, Gauthier makes a significant modification of the standard concept of rationality in neo-classical economics. As shown in Chapter II. A.2., like Rawls, Gauthier does not accept the revealed preference theory (MA,p.27).[35] The thrust of the considered preference theory is to posit "an attitudinal dimension expressed in speech" against "a behavioral dimension of preference revealed in choice" (MA,p.27). Overall, "Preferences are considered if and only if there is no conflict between their behavior and attitudinal dimensions and they are stable under experience and reflection" (MA,p.32f).

In view of this, Gauthier clarifies his theory of value. Value is identified with utility as a measure of considered preference, and rational choice involves the overall scheme to maximize value (MA,p.33). More precisely, "Value, then, we take to be a measure of individual preference—subjective because it is a measure of preference and relative because it is a measure of individual preference" (MA,p.59).[36] In his celebrated passage, Gauthier maintains that "Objective value, like phlogiston, is an unnecessary part of our explanatory apparatus, as such is to be shaved from the face of the universe by Ockham's razor" (MA,p.56). Gauthier asserts that his value theory can be free from "ontological and epistemological requirements" —e.g., the Platonic idea of the good and the recollective anamnesis of that idea— which are imposed to the objective value theory (MA,p.57).

In view of the time-honored confrontations between subjectivism and objectivism and between relativism and absolutism in moral philosophy, and the tremendous recent proliferation of literature concerning the debate to all the domains of philosophy[37], a detailed discussion of these confrontations is beyond the scope of

my study. My primary concern is, instead, to evaluate whether
Gauthier's subjective and relative theory of value represents a
neutral foundation for his contractarian ethics. Three issues are
involved here.[38] First, there is the issue of meta-theoretical
predicament of Gauthier's subjectivism. As Piper and Morris
correctly criticize it, Gauthier's rational theoretical emphasis on
the unanimous primacy of mutually unconcerned and self-interested subjective values over altruistic and affectionally related
values invokes theoretical objectivism.[39] Second, there is the relativist predicament issue, which is brought out by Sandel and
Wolfram.[40]   How is it possible to affirm Gauthier's eventual
endorsement of the liberal individualistic way of life without
embracing some vision of the good life, viz., without endorsing
some ends over others? "It would seem we are back to the relativist predicament — to affirm liberal principles without embracing
any particular ends."[41] Third, the second predicament leads to the
general issue of liberal neutrality predicament. Galston complains
that even though liberals mean to provide a neutral foundation for
liberalism, in practice, they covertly employ "a substantial theory of
the good."[42]

All of these three predicaments seem to be confirmed by
Gauthier's introduction of the "four criteria for classifying one way
of life as more advanced than another, as exhibiting a higher stage
of human development," viz., density of population, duration of
life, material well-being, breadth of opportunity (MA,p.288). It is,
however, possible to interpret the four criteria as objective but still
historically relative to "the particular conditions of our own Western society" (MA,p.335; cf. p.289). But Gauthier explicitly indicates that to think of these four criteria as confined only to the
Western society but "neither generally applicable nor ideally
appropriate, is mistaken" (MA,p.335). If this is the case, Wolfram
is right to charge that Gauthier presupposes "objective and absolute" values.[43] These four criteria sound like Rawls' conception of
the primary social goods.

Another related issue concerning neutrality is connected with
the rational economic man, i.e., *homo economicus*, which I
discussed in Chapter II. Gauthier, in this regard, clearly acknowledges that "Morals by agreement capture the understanding of
economic man" (MA,p.345). But Gauthier wants to go one step

further. He is ready to "show that morals by agreement are more than the morals of economic man" (MA,p.329). If I do justice to these two claims together, they probably mean that morality is derived from the rationale of the enlightened economic man in the sense that he or she can admit moral constraints in view of his or her genuine self-interest maximization. However, Gauthier posits exclusively the rationale of *homo economicus* of Western market capitalism in his premises (MA,pp.18f,335). This apparent non-neutral imposition leads to his controversial assertion that the perfectly competitive market is "a morally fee zone, a context within which the constraints of morality would have no place" (MA,p.13).

3. The Perfectly Competitive Market as the Morally Free Zone

I have, until now, investigated Gauthier's basic theoretical starting point of contractarian ethics: the identification of rationality with individual utility-maximization and his characterization of morality as a cooperative constraint on the direct pursuit of individual utility.   In view of this basic relationship between rationality and morality, Gauthier's claim concerning the morally free zone is simple: If there is an ideal place, like a perfectly competitive market, individual rationality is fully employed without any constraint, and there is no need for morality.[44] It is interesting to note here that the essential spirit of Gauthier concerning this claim is the mirror image of the spirit of Rawls' assumption of the perfectly just society, which I have criticized in the previous chapter (B.2). Gauthier's perfectly competitive market (no morality) is a topsy-turvy world of Rawls' perfectly just society (perfect justice).

Traditionally, in economics, individual rationality is fully employed without constraint in the perfectly competitive market where demands and supplies dovetail into an optimal equilibrium. This is the basic assumption of laissez-faire economics, initiated by the famous Smithian conception of the invisible hand. This basic assumption naturally leads to an "abandonment of morals in economics".[45]   In this connection, economics has been mainly regarded as a typical case of value-free social engineering toward material prosperity.[46]

Unlike traditional and contemporary advocates of laissez-faire, Gauthier is not maintaining that the real market is such a morally free zone or that the perfectly competitive market "is realized, or almost realized, or at least could be realized, in most of our economic transactions" (MA,p.93). His claim, however, concerning the perfectly competitive market as the morally free zone is still remarkable. According to Gauthier, the perfectly competitive market is a "foil against which morality appears more clearly" (MA,13). Morality, then, is applicable to the market only in virtue of its imperfection — which is generally known as market failure (MA,p.84).

Needless to say, the normative issues which surround the various economic theories are complex and controversial, and a proper treatment of them requires an enormous amount of ideological discussion.[47] Even though, in Section B, I will take up Marx's and Macpherson's criticisms of primitive capital accumulation and capitalistic exploitation, I am here confining my study only to the viability of Gauthier's arguments for the first core idea, viz., "the morally free zone afforded by the perfectly competitive market" (MA,p.16).

In order to appropriately evaluate Gauthier's first core idea, the following three issues have to be clarified. First, what are the basic assumptions and consequence of the market? Second, what is the exact meaning of the zone? In other words, which aspects of the market are morally free? — conditions? operations? or outcomes? Third, if morality arises from market failure, what counts as the market failure? And how can morality correct the failure? In dealing with these three issues, I will eventually show that Gauthier cannot assert that the perfect market is such a zone, in terms of his own position. Furthermore, I will point out how and why Gauthier changed his position concerning the first core idea in recent articles.

First, what are the basic assumptions and consequence of the perfectly competitive market? Gauthier says that "Individual factor endowments and private goods, free market activity and mutual unconcern, and the absence of externalities — these are the presuppositions of a perfectly competitive market" (MA,p.89). This brief statement needs explanation. The market primarily presupposes private ownership of all products and factors (labor, capital, land) of production. Furthermore, each rational individual is free to use his or her resources as he or she pleases in the process of production, exchange, and consumption. Accordingly, the presupposition of private ownership is divided into two parts: "individual factor endowments, and the free individual market activity" (MA,p.86). The market presupposes a more restrictive form of privacy in the consumption of all products. Each individual exclusively consumes his or her own private goods and excludes other people's consumption of them. In addition, each rational individual is independent of other individuals in the utility of consumption. This presupposition is exemplified by Rawls' aforementioned assumption of mutual disinterestedness. Gauthier embraces it as a requirement of "non-tuism" (MA,p.87). "Private consumption, like private ownership, is thus divided into two parts: private goods, and mutual unconcern" (MA,p.87).

The absence of externalities is a further condition of perfect competitions. An externality arises from the presence of public goods or interdependent utilities. There are two types of externality. The first is a positive externality of non-exclusive public goods, which I have fully discussed with respect to the Free-rider problem (e.g., a lighthouse: a shipowner, who does not pay the cost of construction for the lighthouse, but benefits from the lighthouse). The second is a negative externality of non-exclusive public hazard (e.g., air pollution: air polluting factory owner imposes the cost of air pollution on others. Thus the owner becomes a parasite, who, in obtaining his or her benefit, displaces the cost on to other parties). In sum, "the absence of externalities ensures that no one is affected whether beneficially or harmfully, by any market activity to which she has not chosen to be party" (MA,p.96).

I have, up to now, clarified the basic assumptions of the market. What are, then, the consequences of the market? They are that, under appropriate conditions (those of perfect competition in a free market), if each person acted purely self-interestedly (to maximize his or her own utilities), then the outcome would be Pareto-optimal.[48] This observation of the outcome, which was loosely conjectured by Adam Smith, has received its clearest expression in a theorem of modern neo-classical welfare economics. This is the so-called first, basic, or fundamental theorem of welfare economics.[49] Gauthier is fascinated by the theorem as is clear below (MA,p.89).

The economist now offers his triumphant demonstration that given perfect competition, the market equilibrium must be also optimal—no one could be better off unless someone else were to become worse off.

Now it is time to turn to the second task. How can the optimal equilibrium of the perfectly competitive market be a morally free zone? What aspects of the market are morally free?—conditions, operations, or outcomes? At first glance, Gauthier seems to maintain that all of the three aspects are morally free. But, a careful reading of the text shows that this is not the case. Gauthier explicitly distinguishes the three aspects of the market (MA,p.95). In case of the conditions of the market, Gauthier claims that "neither the operation of the market nor its outcome can show, or can even tend to show, that its initial situation is also either rationally or morally acceptable" (MA,p.94). The initial factor endowment of each person is brought to the market in the operational process of production, exchange, and consumption. Under the fundamental theorem of welfare economics or the invisible hand assumption of laissez-faire, the initial factor allocation is merely given. For Gauthier, if morality is a form of rational constraint, the initial condition of factor endowment is definitely not within the morally free zone. As will be seen in the next section, "each is constrained by the rights of her fellows, as determined by the [Gauthier's version of Lockean] proviso" (MA,p.222). Gauthier still wants to maintain that the proviso is not derived from an independent prior moral element of natural rights. However, in view of his ardent objection to Buchanan's predatory model of natural distribution of initial endowment, the initial condition of the market is not beyond morality. Even though I take seriously Gauthier's endeavor to avoid the circularity horn of the contractarian dilemma, morality —not in the sense of rationally ungrounded morality but in the sense of "rational morality"— is clearly involved in his version of Lockean proviso.[50] At this juncture, if I am right, Gauthier wants to distinguish himself from the advocates of laissez-faire. Of them, Gauthier says that they "failed to appreciate the normative significance of some of the presuppositions of the market" (MA,p.93).

Another crucial issue is the background conditions for the possibility of the emergence of the market. Gauthier definitely indicates that, under the conditions "that force and fraud are absent from interaction, a market emerges" and that "the absence of force and fraud is essential to the workings of the market" (MA,pp.261,85). Gauthier, in this regard, notes that even Adam Smith presupposes a background morality (MA,p.85): "Every man, as long as he does not violate the laws of justice, is left perfectly free to pursue his own interest his own way."[51] If the absence of force and fraud is posited into the definition of the market, Gauthier's claim of the morally free zone is just trivial.[52] Thus it is not strange to find Gauthier's own acknowledgment that "in understanding the perfect market as a morally free zone we shall be led back to its underlying, antecedent morality" (MA,p.85. cf. p.102). Gauthier cannot avoid a charge of "misleading rhetoric."[53] In this respect, I conclude that, as far as the initial conditions and the background morality are concerned, the perfect market does not belong to a morally free zone.

Even if I can interpret the initial conditions and background morality as a "minima moralia", it is still controversial whether the other aspects of the market are beyond any other moral constraints.[54] What about the operation and outcome of the market? According to Gauthier, the relation of operation and outcome to the initial conditions is as follows: "The operation of the market is to convert an initial situation specified in terms of individual factor endowments into a final outcome specified in terms of a distribution of goods or products among the same individuals" (MA,p.94). If there is any justice to Gauthier's claim concerning the zone, it seems to be mainly applicable to the operation (MA,p.95). In view of this, the relation between the three aspects can be more accurately defined. Since "the operation of a market cannot in itself raise any evaluative issues," market outcome is fair if and only if it results from fair initial conditions (MA,p.95). At this point, Gauthier resorts to the familiar conception of pure procedural justice of the market, as seen in the writings of Rawls and Nozick. The basic idea of pure procedural justice is that if there is a correct or fair procedure, the outcome is likewise correct or fair. In plain words, the idea reflects a common sense notion of fair play. However, even if we suppose the initial conditions are fair, in order to agree that the outcome is also fair, the intermediate operational procedure must also be shown to be fair. Here Gauthier carefully approaches this task in view of the contractarian dilemma.

> But we must not simply assume that, because market interaction is rational and morality is not opposed to rationality, the market is therefore morally free. We must argue independently, from our conception of morality as an impartial constraint, if our conclusion is not to beg the question (MA,p.95).

Gauthier's task is to prove that, in the operational interaction of the market, there is no partiality. The best way to decide whether market operation involves partiality is to ask whether any individual could enter "any reasonable complaint or objection against the market outcome" (MA,p.95). The impartiality of the market is supported by Gauthier's version of the so-called "marginal productivity theory of distribution." As Gauthier emphasizes it, "essential to the operation of the perfectly competitive market is the marginal matching of supply and demand" (MA,p.88). The marginal productive theory was initiated by the neo-classical economist as a proper explanation of the optimal equilibrium of the perfectly competitive market.[55] The market leads to an optimal equilibrium at which every factor of production—each lot of labor, of capital, of land, and of enterprise—gets a reward equal to the marginal productivity of its contribution. In plain words, each factor receives an income according to how much it adds to output (indeed, assuming private ownership of the means of production). The theory specifies the Aristotelian time-honored criterion of distributive justice, i.e., "distribute to every man his own."[56] In terms of the theory, his or her own (desert or merit) is determinated by his or her marginal contribution: expressed in the slogan, "to each according to his (marginal) productive contribution."[57] Gauthier, correspondingly, maintains that "the equation of income with marginal contribution ensures just this impartiality" (MA,p.97).

Gauthier supports the impartiality by the presuppositions of the market, viz., the free market activity and the absence of externalities. First, each individual, as a Robinson Crusoe, is free to direct his or her capacities to the services of his or her preferences or incentives (MA,pp.90,97) Second, in the market, there is no beneficial or harmful externalities from free-riders or parasites (MA,P.96). Thus individuals have a right (or possibly a responsibility) to something they have produced themselves, without any reasonable complaint or objection against the market operation and outcome. Overall, Gauthier says "the operation of a market cannot in itself raise any evaluative issues" (MA,p.95).

Even though there are several significant problems concerning free activity and absence of externalities, the more crucial problem concerns the moral status of the marginal productivity theory of distribution.[58] In one sense, the theory is not morally free. Rather it must be considered as a normative argument. The primary reason for this is that the theory generates tremendous constraint against (or a normative claim for ignoring) the other possible impartial criteria of distributive justice. The theory neglects other justice criteria such as need (the marginal product of a disabled or unemployed person, for example, is zero), equality, effort, hazard, etc.[59] Gauthier seems to discuss this neglect without shame or remorse in many places (MA,pp.17,105,225). He says: "Equality is not a fundamental concern in our theory" (MA,p.270). He also says the following.

> The rich man may feast on caviar and champagne, while the poor woman starves at his gate. And she may not even take the crumbs from his table, if that would deprive him of his pleasures in feeding them to his birds (MA,p.218).

At a glance, Gauthier appears to be a libertarian. In this regard, Gauthier understandably criticizes utilitarian welfare economics and Rawls' asset or endowment collectivism, which heavily rely on redistributive programs and disturbs the proper operation of the market—sometimes this disturbance is called government (intervention) failure (MA,pp.110,270)[60]. However, Gauthier, in many ways, departs from Nozickean libertarianism. My argument that the operation of the market is not beyond morality is confirmed by Gauthier's own normative qualifications on the relentless application of the marginal productive theory of distribution.

Gauthier himself seems to acknowledge the practical difficulties of his theory.[61] The more pertinent problems arise from the normative issues. First, Gauthier indicates that the theory must be employed under the condition that each enjoys similar opportunities and receives similar encouragement (MA,p.263). Second, he endorses a conditional license for taxing inheritances: "The right to dispose of one's possessions by gift or bequest is not an integral part of the right to the exclusive use of those possessions that is required for market and cooperative interaction" (MA,p.301). Third, "The market affords each person a return for the factor services she supplies" (MA,p.97). This means that so-called economic factor rent must be totally taxed away. Economic rent is an unearned income, issued from the scarcity of factor endowments, which is a "return over and above the cost of supply" (MA,p.98. cf. pp.272-77).[62] In view of these three qualifications, it is clear that the morally free zone cannot encompass the operation of the market.

Then, is the market outcome beyond morality? Gauthier maintains that "the optimality of the market outcome ensures that any alternative to it that was not worse for everyone would benefit some individuals at the expense of others" (MA,p.97). I have investigated the outcome of, in other words, the consequences of the market in connection with the attraction of Pareto optimality. Gauthier appeals to the mutual advantages or cooperative surplus produced from the Pareto optimal outcome of the market. However, there are many ways of distributing the cooperative surplus and the avowed attraction of Pareto optimality is plagued by its indeterminacy.[63]   Gauthier correctly points out that "affording mutual advantage is a necessary condition for the acceptability of a set of social arrangements as a co-operative venture, not a sufficient condition" (MA,p.11). For Gauthier, as a moral philosopher, the problem of the sufficient condition is the problem of distributive justice, which cannot be beyond morality. Gauthier actually tries to provide the unique sufficient condition with his principle of minimax relative concession, as will be seen in next section.

In sum, I conclude that, in view of Gauthier's own position, neither the condition, operation, nor the outcome of the perfectly competitive market belongs to the morally free zone. This conclusion, derivatively, challenges Gauthier's argument that morality is only a rational remedy for market failure. In connection with the paradoxes of rationality in Chapter II, and the absence of externalities, I have dealt with market failure. In the case of market failure, the supposed coincidence of optimality and equilibrium (Pareto optimality) cannot be held.   Only suboptimal equilibrium has resulted: "Public goods are supplied by the market in manner that is neither efficient nor fair" because of the presence of externalities from the free-rider and parasite (MA,p.270). Thus the exact meaning of Gauthier's claim that morality arises from market failure is as follows:[64]

> Moral constraints arise only in the gap created by conflict between the two rationality properties [optimality and equilibrium], when mutual benefit is not assured by the pursuit of individual gain. We assess outcomes as right or wrong when, but only when, maximizing one's utility given the actions of others would fail to maximize it given the utilities of others (MA,p.93).

I am not arguing against Gauthier's concept of morality as a rational remedy for market failure. Rather I agree with Gauthier that, without proper treatment of market failure, any kind of moral theory, especially the theory of distributive justice, cannot be a viable theory. What I am arguing is that morality is more than the remedy for the market failure as the discussion of the condition, operation, and outcome of the perfectly competitive market has demonstrated. This conclusion is confirmed by Gauthier's recent comment. He suggests "a significant conceptual revision" in his account of morality:[65]

> Rather than treating it as a remedy for market failure, I might rather have introduced it as a condition for market success. Rather than treating, if only implicitly, the coincidence of equilibrium and Pareto-optimum found within the market as the normal form of interaction, so that morality becomes a constraint enabling us to approximate to that form when it is deplorably absent. I might instead have treated the coincidence as an exceptional form made possible only by the prior acceptance of a structure of constraints identifiable with a rational morality.

In view of this revision, Gauthier cannot but admit the criticism that "the market can be regulated by the social contract."[66] However, Gauthier does not think that this revision implies the failure of his contractarian rational deduction project of morality. In this regard, he says: "In effect, morality would then be seen to transcend itself, to find a way of overcoming its directly constraining character, in making possible market interaction, in which each person could straightforwardly seek to maximize his utility."[67] The self-transcendence of morality still remains mysterious to some.[68]

I, rather, interpret the mystery as the paradox of his project, which I mentioned when I gave a general characterization of Gauthier's contractarian rational ethics (A.2). For Gauthier, the revision is merely a transition from a thin form of market contractarianism to a thick form.[69]

It is now time to move to the argumentative center of his market contractarianism (MA,p.ix): viz., the bargaining theory of justice, compliance, and the initial bargaining position. In dealing with these core ideas, I will discuss them against the background of thick market contractarianism. In other words, I will show how the three core ideas fit into his background scheme.

B. The Bargaining Theory of Liberal Justice and Its Critical Assessment

1. The Rational Bargaining Solution to the Principle of Distributive justice: Minimax Relative Concession

In this section, I will explore and assess Gauthier's rational solutions to the three core problems (the initial bargaining position, the bargaining problem, and rational compliance) which frame the argumentative center of his contractarian ethics. The solutions (the Lockean proviso, the minimax relative concession, and constrained maximization) correspond to the afore-discussed triadic structure of Hobbes' and Rawls' contractarian ethics.[70] In view of what was said earlier concerning the failure of Hobbes' and Rawls' ethics (in relation to the triadic structure), it will be appropriate to view Gauthier's contractarian ethics from the same structure. I will follow the order of the topics in accord with Gauthier's presentation.

Gauthier's discussion of the market showed the need for morality as a cooperative rational constraint to overcome the non-cooperative suboptimality of the natural interaction of force and fraud, and of the market failure in the presence of externalities. If morality is a vehicle which takes us from the mutual disadvantages of non-cooperation to the mutual advantages of cooperation, it would seem to appeal to an individual maximizer. In this connection, Gauthier says: "Each can increase his utility by co-operating; hence as a utility-maximizer each must find it rational to co-operate" (MA,p.143). However, as Gauthier makes it clear, mutual advantage is only a necessary condition of cooperative agreement made by individual maximizers since individual maximizers' rational cooperative agreement is mainly dependent upon the mode of distribution of the cooperative surplus. Therefore Gauthier's task is to provide a sufficient condition for the cooperative rational agreement (MA,p.15). This explains why in contractarian ethics the status of the problem of distributive justice is so crucial. As I mentioned in the previous section, Gauthier criticizes Rawls' and Harsanyi's rational choice model (i.e., individual choice under the veil of ignorance or uncertainty) since their model ignores the distinctiveness and integrity of individuals. Thus, for Gauthier, the problem of distributive justice is to provide a sufficient contractarian rational agreement among rational bargainers who need to be aware of their identities.

The problem is addressed in the theory of rational bargaining and is divided into two issues: "The first is the bargaining problem proper, which in its general form is to select a specific outcome, given a range of mutually advantageous possibilities, and an initial bargaining position. The second is then to determine the initial bargaining position" (MA,p.14). In terms of traditional terminology, the first problem is a problem of distributive justice and the second is of acquisitive justice.[71] If we relate the distinction of the two problems to the previous discussion of the market, the optimality of market outcome is determined not only by the operation of the market (productive contribution) but also by the initial market condition (initial individual endowments).

First, Gauthier tackles the bargaining problem proper. "Solving the bargaining problem yields a principle that governs both the process and the content of rational agreement" since "the bargainers are concerned with the distribution of the gains which cooperation may bring them, or with the co-operative *surplus*" (MA,pp.14,130). The simplest process is the two-person bargaining model. Let us assume for the sake of argument that the initial bargaining position of the two can be rationally fixed. And also suppose that cooperation of the two produces a certain amount of surplus. First, each person advances his or her maximal claim for the surplus. In general the maximal claims of the two people are incompatible. Hence, second, each offers a concession by withdrawing some portion of his or her original claim and then proposes an alternative outcome. This process of bargaining continues until a set of mutually compatible claims is reached. In short, the bargaining problem is that "What claims, and what concessions, will rational bargainers make?" (MA,p.133). Gauthier here introduces a measure of relative concession. A bargainer's relative concession is a proportion of his or her absolute concession (maximal claim minus agreed share: $U\#-U$) to his or her complete concession (maximal claim minus initial bargaining holding: $U\#-U^*$). A bargainer's relative concession is thus $[(U\#-U)/(U\#-U^*)]$ (MA,p.136). This relative concession allows comparison of concessions made by different bargainers. The bargainer with a less relative concession must concede. Eventually this process of bargaining leads to the requirement that "the greatest concession, measured as a proportion of the conceder's stake, be as small as possible" (MA,p.14). In other words, Gauthier argues that the agreement point will be selected according to what he calls the principle of minimax relative concession (MRC) (MA,p.137).[72]

The Principle of Minimax Relative Concession

The greatest or *maximum* relative concession ... is as small as possible, or a *minimum*, that is, is no greater than the maximum relative concession required by every other outcome.

Gauthier asserts that "the principle governs both the process and the object of rational choice in bargaining situations" (MA,p.145). If MRC is a principle, which is instructive for the concession procedural aspect of bargaining, the opposite twin, i.e., the principle of maximin relative benefit (MRB) is instructive for the content of bargaining outcome in connection with the cooperative surplus: "the least relative benefit, measured as a proportion of one's stake, be as great as possible" (MA,p.14). The process of bargaining is the same as in MRC. A bargainer's relative benefit is a proportion of his or her expected gain of cooperative surplus (the difference between agreed share - initial bargaining holding) to his or her complete gain of cooperative surplus (maximal claim - initial bargaining holding) (MA,p.155).[73] Gauthier maintains that MRB captures "the ideas of fairness and impartiality in a bargaining situation, and so serves as the basis of justice" (MA,p.14). In sum, "impartiality and rationality coincide in bargaining" (MA,p.155).

As Gauthier acknowledges, the avowed coincidence of rationality and impartiality of MRC/MRB cooperative interaction parallels the rationality and impartiality of market operations (MA,p.118f). This means that Gauthier's alleged claim of fairness and impartiality works only within market contractarianism. MRC/MRB is a mere replica of the marginal productive theory of distribution, which I have explained and criticized in the previous section.[74] In connection with MRC/MRB, Gauthier merely repeats the market rationale for it as follows (MA,p.156).

> ... [O]ur concern is with the choice of a basis for co-operative interaction taking an initial position for granted, and our argument is that in affording equal or equivalent shares of the co-operative surplus to all persons, the principle of minimax relative concession ensures that bargaining impartially relates each person's contribution to co-operative to the benefit he receives from it.

I am not claiming here that MRC/MRB has no meaning in the domain of distributive justice. Perhaps MRC/MRB is necessary and even sufficient for governing the individual incentives for productive activities. However, the full domain of distributive justice is beyond productive activity (cf. the aforementioned other precepts of justice in A.3.) and therefore MRC/MRB is not a sufficient condition for human cooperative society.

Gauthier offers a series of very delicate arguments, which I will not deal with, to support MRC/MRB against the rival solutions to the bargaining problem, especially against the Nash bargaining solution.[75] Furthermore, Gauthier claims that his MRC/MRB is the unique rational solution to the Arrow's Impossibility Theorem (MA,pp.123-25). However, in view of the ongoing controversies in the literature, Gauthier's MRC/MRB appears to be far from the unique solution to the bargaining problem and the Theorem.[76] Even though I will not get involved with the intricate formal axiomatic problems in the domain of social choice or social welfare function theory, I will show what kinds of controversies continue in view of the various criticisms of MRC/MRB.

First, the morality or the fairness and impartiality of MRC/MRB can be questioned because of its limited scope (as we have seen) in connection with the marginal productive theory of distribution. In sum, MRC/MRB probably represents a crucial and necessary but not a sufficient condition for human cooperation.[77]   Second, MRC/MRB as a unique rational solution to the bargaining problem can be questioned.   In this regard, many commentators point out the MRC/MRB lacks the practical rational calculation or application.   Simply put, Gauthier's MRC/MRB can be called "splitting the difference."[78]   The difference is each individual's stake in the bargain, viz., "the difference between the least he might accept in place of no agreement, and the most he might receive in place of being excluded by others from agreement" (MA,p.14). As I explained above, the former is the initial bargaining utility and the latter is the maximal bargaining claim, both of which are necessary for determining the relative concession. Since the initial bargaining position will be treated later, the primary concern here is how to determine the maximal claim.   In view of the above passage on the difference, Gauthier seems to broadly point out that the maximal claim is just below the exclusion point.[79]

Then how can we know and judge where the exclusion point lies not only in one social structure but also in the different social structures?   In this regard, Gauthier says "we should note that the comparison among social structures required to determine potential contribution and maximal social benefit must be restricted to structures that are feasible alternatives" (MA,p.264).   For Gauthier, the operational criterion for MRB/MRC is not an actual contribution but the potential maximal contribution, which an individual would make in the most favorable development of individual capacities and character traits (MA,p.264).   In turn, the feasible alternatives can be selected "given the available technology and the existing conceptual horizon" (MA,p.264).   Finally Gauthier thinks that "these boundaries [of the feasible alternatives] are vague, but they keep the required comparison meaningful" (MA,p.264).

However, many commentators persistently point out the problem of indeterminacy and vagueness of the bargaining shares.   For instance, Barry complains that "how could we establish the maximum amount that any given person could expect to get, if everybody else were maximally cooperative?"[80]   This debate continues between Gauthier and Rawls, even though Gauthier's MRB can be interpreted as a version of Rawls' difference principle, i.e., the proportionate difference principle.[81]   Rawls criticizes Gauthier that "no sense can be made of the notion of that part of an individual's social benefits that exceed what would have been ... [his or her] situation in another society or in a state of nature."[82] Rawls seems to admit that the notion makes sense in the case of associations within society. However, "the parallel calculations when adopting principles for the basic structure have no foundation."[83]

In view of the above criticisms, Gauthier's MRB/MRC appears to be far from the unique fair solution to the problem of distributive justice. Furthermore, whether MRC/MRB is the unique rational solution to the bargaining problem remains open since there are many other delicate axiomatic issues, which vex Gauthier's MRC/MRB.[84]

My final task for the assessment of MRC/MRB is to see how it can be related to Gauthier's overall endeavor to avoid the contractarian dilemma. A common objection to the use of a bargaining model in the domain of justice is that it employs the threat advantage. As I have indicated earlier, Nash's and Braithwaite's bargaining models are victims of the Hobbesian horn, i.e., the moral irrelevancy of rationality.[85] I suggest that Gauthier's idealization of bargaining procedure can be understood as just an attempt to avoid this horn. Gauthier distinguishes his model of ideal bargaining from ordinary bargaining (MA,p.155). In his ideal bargaining, Gauthier presupposes full and undistorted information, no bluff, no threat advantage, equal rationality of bargainers, no difference of bargaining skill and strength (MA,pp.156f). Finally Gauthier assumes that the "bargaining is cost free, in terms of both utility and time" (MA,p.156).

These presuppositions are motivated by his desire to avoid the Hobbesian horn. For Hobbes, the equal rationality of contractors is based upon a roughly equal ability to impose the cost of death.[86] Thus if bargaining is in fact costless in time and utility, it is possible to think that rational bargaining will surely lead to fair outcomes. In other words, in the case of costless bargaining, those who are disadvantaged (in the state of nature and in their maximal bargaining claim) have nothing to lose by refusing to participate in a cooperative venture unless the terms of bargaining are fair. Furthermore, since bargainers are equally rational, they will get fair terms. This assumption of costlessness, which aims at avoiding the Hobbesian horn (at equalizing bargaining power), turns out to have extraordinary normative consequences, which are caught up in the other horn of dilemma, the circularity of prior moral assumptions.[87]

In a sense, the idealization of bargaining procedure is very similar to Rawls' veil of ignorance. The assumption of ideal bargaining, especially of costlessness, makes Gauthier's fair and rational deduction project possible but at the price of over-idealizing the essential character of Hobbesian state of nature.[88] One important thing to be noted is that even the alleged fairness has a limited scope (exclusion of the other precepts of distributive justice, e.g., basic needs) since it is confined to the only fairness in the context of bargaining. Gauthier acknowledges this problem but I do not think he does justice to it (MA,p.156):

> We might suppose that even granting the ideal nature of our bargainers, their circumstances might nevertheless give rise to significant partiality. But problems about circumstances concerns the initial bargaining position, not the process of bargaining.

2. Rational Compliance and the Constrained Maximization

The MRC/MRB defines the content of Gauthier's bargaining theory of justice. As applied to cooperative venture, MRC/MRB constitutes a constraint on the direct pursuit of individual utility. Gauthier has "yet to demonstrate that such action [of constraint] is rational — that each person should rationally comply with the joint strategy to which he has rationally agreed" (MA,p.145). Even though it is supposed that MRC/MRB is a rationally impeccable solution to the bargaining problem, it is not sufficient to show that compliance with MRC/MRB is rationally required. At this moment, Gauthier pays special attention to the compliance problem through distinction between *ex ante* and *ex post* stages of contractarian ethics. As Gauthier admits, "the step from hypothetical agreement *ex ante* on a set of social arrangements to *ex post* adherence may no longer seem straightforward" (MA,p.12). He adds: "We see why one might willingly join the [cooperative] venture, yet not willingly continue with it. Each joins in the hope of benefiting from the adherence of others, but fails to adhere in the hope of benefiting from her own defection" (MA,p.12).

Needless to say again, this *ex post* rational compliance problem derives from the vexing Prisoner's dilemma (PD) and Free-rider Problem (FR), as I have shown in Chapter II and in the discussion of market failure in the previous section. In Chapter III, I investigated Hobbes' and Rawls' failure to solve the rational compliance problem. At this juncture, Gauthier's ambition is to solve the problem with his version of contractarian ethics without resorting to the Hobbesian political coercion or to the Rawlsian deontological supposition of strict compliance. "A Hobbesian sovereign is a replacement for, and not part of a reconstruction of, a moral system."[89] Against Rawls, Gauthier points out that "although he makes some use of rational choice arguments in considering what principles persons in an appropriate initial situation would agree to, he does not show, or attempt to show, the rationality of their compliance with the agreed principles."[90] One of the major aims of this subsection is to evaluate Gauthier's endeavor here with respect to compliance — since his endeavor is significant for his overall scheme, viz., avoiding the contractarian dilemma.

However, Gauthier's endeavor here is not just confined to contractarian tradition. Gauthier also attempts to answer the time-honored question of moral philosophy, i.e., Why should I be moral?[91] This question can be rephrased as: Is it rational for me as a moral skeptic or egoist to be moral? The possible audience of Gauthier's rational solution project with respect to the compliance problem is made up of the various time-honored moral skeptics, viz., the Fool, the sensible knave, and the Lydian shepherd.[92] In this regard, Gauthier's rational solution to the compliance — "motivational reinforcement to the rational requirements of co-operation" (MA,p.351) — is an answer not only to the contractarian failure but also to the traditional question of moral philosophy: viz., "the gap between justification and motivation."[93]

In general, Gauthier aims to generate voluntary, free and rational compliance. Before I enter into his detailed solution, several crucial things have to be made clear in connection with Hobbes and Rawls. First, what is the exact meaning of the "voluntary compliance"? (MA,p.164). Does Gauthier belong to a group of philosophers who "have believed that perfectly good and wise men could do without it [coercion], that perfect men left alone would inhabit utopias"?[94] No, Gauthier does not: "More realistically, we supposed that such enforcement is needed to create and maintain those conditions under which individuals may rationally expect the degree of compliance from their fellows needed to elicit their own voluntary compliance" (MA,pp.164-5). Then, he adds: "Internal, moral constraints operate to ensure compliance under conditions of security established by external, political constraints" (MA,p.165). In this regard, Gauthier's voluntary compliance project has a limited scope.

Second, if Rawls cannot deduce rational compliance from instrumental maximizing conception of rationality, how can Gauthier do this? Rawls gives up the dream of the derivation: "Nor, again, are we to argue that an egoist, finding himself in a just society, would be well advised, given his aims, to transform himself into a just man" (TJ,p.568).[95] Gauthier attempts to realize Rawls' forlorn dream that "the rational economic individual will in fact change his conception of rationality, so that adherence to agreements undertaken to secure mutual benefit will accord with his new standard of rationality."[96] As Gauthier acknowledges, the change or transformation seems to be a paradox: "He [a rational utility-maximizer] makes a choice about how to make further choices; he chooses, on utility-maximizing grounds, not to make further choices on those grounds" (MA,p.158). I think Gauthier's attempt to establish that the instrumental maximization conception of rationality dictates its own constraint is one of the most interesting components of his theory. In other words, Gauthier's attempt is to show moral skeptics and egoists alike that it is rational for them to accept the moral constraints in view of their own commitments.[97]

As we will see shortly, Gauthier's rational compliance project eventually leads to an introduction of the revised conception of rationality. As investigated before in Chapter II and previous section A.2, Gauthier generally accepts the standard neo-classical instrumental self-interest utility maximization concept of rationality, except for the revealed preference theoretical aspect of it. In connection with rational compliance, Gauthier provides a major modification of the standard conception as follows (MA,pp.182-3)[98]:

> The received interpretation ... identifies rationality with utility-maximization at the level of particular choices. A choice is rational if and only if it maximizes the actor's expected utility. We identify rationality with utility-maximization at the level of dispositions to choose. A disposition is rational if and only if an actor holding it can expect his choices to yield no less utility than the choice he would make were he to hold any alternative disposition. We shall

consider whether particular choices are rational if and only if they express a
rational disposition to choose.

In simple terms, "the key" to understanding the above claim is that
rationality is not for particular choices but for a meta-choice having
to do with a disposition (MA,p.183). Gauthier, at this moment,
introduces the distinction between the dispositions of straightforward maximization (SM) and constrained maximization (CM)
(MA,pp.15,167,174). The SM person is disposed to choose
whichever course of action would represent a maximization of his
or her expected utility at the particular time of choice in the interaction with others. The CM person is disposed to choose to
comply with the agreed constraints, at least as long as other are
similarly disposed. Gauthier makes it clear that the CM person is
"conditionally disposed" (MA,p.168). This conditional disposition
of CM reflects the basic idea of Hobbes' conditional compliance
since unilateral compliance is easily exposed to exploitation —
simply according to the "no sucker rule".[99] In sum, "If a CM
believes that the other party will cooperate, the CM will too;
otherwise not."[100]

Of course, first, Gauthier admits that "someone who acts morally
(performs particular morally required actions) need not expect to
do better than if she did not (performed other actions)."[101] In
short, SM is better than CM in the particular case of action in view
of utility-maximization. The reason for this is so clear that if this is
not the case, PD or FR does not happen. Second, he points out
that "constrained maximizers sometimes lose by being disposed to
compliance, for they may act co-operatively in the mistaken expectation of reciprocity from others who instead benefit at their
expense" (MA,p.15). This means that if CM disposition is a conditional compliance, the willing compliance of the CM depends upon
his or her epistemic or probabilistic anticipation of whether the
others are the CMs or SMs. Gauthier originally presumed the
"transparency" of the individual agent's identification as a CM or
SM (person). However, Gauthier was challenged by Parfit's charge
that the transparency assumption is too ideal since it eradicates all
practical possibilities of deception or hypocrisy.[102] Gauthier, now,
presupposes rather "a more realistic *translucency,* supposing that
persons are neither transparent nor opaque, so that their disposi-

tion to co-operate or not may be ascertained by others, not with
certainty, but as more than mere guesswork" (MA,p.174). Thus
Gauthier admits the possible loss of the CM by the exploitations of
the SM as noted above. In respect of those two possible advantages of the SM over the CM, Gauthier's attempt seems to be sterile from the beginning.

Yet, Gauthier is not so easily discouraged. He says: "we shall
show that under plausible conditions, the net advantage that
constrained maximizers reap from co-operation exceeds the
exploitative benefits that others may expect" (MA,p.15). Elsewhere, he says that "My argument turns on the claim that a person
disposed to morality may (under suitable conditions) expect to
have more beneficial opportunities open to her than someone not
so disposed; she gains greater utility, even though she behaves with
constraint given her opportunities, than someone who takes full
advantage of his inferior opportunities."[103]

Given Gauthier's claims, then, my next task is to examine what
the plausible or suitable conditions are and how the CM is better
off than the SM in those conditions. In other words, "Let us
examine the conditions under which the decision to dispose oneself
to constrained maximization is rational for translucent persons, and
ask if these are (or may be) the conditions in which we find
ourselves" (MA,p.174).[104]

Given the presuppositions of conditional compliance and
translucency of agents, it is clear that CMs will seek to exclude
SMs. SMs will also seek out CMs while attempting to conceal their
identities as SMs in the hope of free riding on the CMS. A clever
calculation demonstrates that if there are enough CMs, and their
disposition to cooperate is secure, then it is better to be a CM than
a SM (see n.104). On the one hand, "A [SM], who is disposed to
make maximizing choices, must expect to be excluded from cooperative arrangements which he would find advantageous"
(MA,p.183). On the other hand, "A [CM] may expect to be
included in such arrangements. She benefits from her disposition,
not in the choices she makes, but in her opportunities to choose"
(MA,p.183). From this, Gauthier concludes that "it is rational to
be disposed to [CM] behavior by internalizing moral principles to
govern one's choices" (MA,p.15). In general, a just person is one
who is disposed to comply with the agreed moral principles "in

interacting with those of his fellows whom he believes to be similarly disposed" (MA,p.157).

The first curiosity about Gauthier's position here arises from how Gauthier's dispositional solution is different from the common sense distinctions between immediate/long-term benefits, direct/indirect strategies, or from the dictum, "honesty is the best policy." In this regard, Gauthier makes it clear that [CM] is not [SM] in its most effective disguise" (MA,p.169). Probably long-term or indirect benefits may appeal to moral skeptics. But Gauthier points out that such skeptics exhibit no real constraint (MA,p.170). And also the real answer to skeptics is that of "treating honesty, not as a policy, but a disposition" (MA,p.182). Broadly speaking, Gauthier's dispositional solution modifies the common sense distinctions into the more secure foundation of an internalized disposition. Gauthier often emphasizes that, through internalization of moral principles, rational compliance is genuinely achieved (MA,pp.15,165). Finally, Gauthier says that "Such a [CM] is not able, given her disposition, to take advantage of the 'exceptions'" (MA,p.182).

However, concerning this impossibility of a CM's taking particular exceptional advantages, there arise many complicated questions about the exact meaning or definition of disposition. One the one hand, the impossibility implies that the CM's disposition is a permanent mechanism of certain sort. However, in this case, CM dispositional cooperation cannot be a voluntary, free and rational action. On the other hand, if the CM's disposition is not a permanent mechanism, the other possibility is that it is a preferential choice. However, in this case, the CM's disposition does not make sense since a free and voluntary preferential choice is itself a non-constrained maximizing choice. Gauthier explicitly indicates that moral philosophers "have failed to relate our nature as moral beings to our everyday concern with the fulfilment of our individual preferences. But we have shown how morality issues from that concern" (MA,p.184). In a recent article, Gauthier also points out that "Persons who take an interest in cooperation are, I suggest, likely to prefer to dispose themselves to cooperate with other cooperators."[105] Furthermore, the aforementioned conditional compliance does not permit any room for the mechanistic interpretation. "Thus we have an apparently vicious dilemma: On the mechanism interpretation, Gauthier seems wrong to think of co-operation as voluntary, free, and rational action. On the preference interpretation, he seems wrong to think that it is constrained action."[106]

I do not intend to pursue here all the difficult questions concerning the concept of disposition that arise from the domains of action theory, psychology, and moral philosophy.[107] However, one crucial thing to be noted is that it is not the case that Gauthier alone has to bear the theoretical burden of the rational dispositional solution to the compliance problem. Throughout the history of philosophy moral philosophers have suggested various forms of dispositional solutions. In this connection, witness Aristotle, Hobbes, Dewey, Rawls, MacIntyre, and Williams.[108] If Gauthier supplemented his discussion of rational disposition, while probing the similarity and difference between himself and them, his rational dispositional compliance project would have probably developed into a more comprehensive and perspicuous position.[109]

Returning to rational choice theory, if the rational disposition of CM is the preferential choice, significant questions as to whether Gauthier's rational compliance project can solve PD and FR problems arise. For, as Gauthier worries, "it might seem that a maximizing disposition to choose would express itself in maximizing choices" (MA,p.183). In other words, is the CM disposition utility-maximizing? Does acting from the CM disposition have greater expected utility than acting from the SM, which is extensionally equivalent to acting with the received conception of rationality?[110]

Gauthier claims that "to demonstrate the rationality of suitably constrained maximization we solve a problem of rational choice" (MA,p.170). He means the PD problem here. Gauthier' solution to PD focuses on the so-called one-shot PD game.[111] Gauthier makes it clear that "constrained maximization is not parallel to such strategies as 'tit-for-tat' that have been advocated for so-called iterated [PD]s. Constrained maximizers may co-operate even if neither expects her choice to affect future situations. Thus our treatment of co-operating does not make the appeal to reciprocity" (MA,p.169. n.19).[112]

The following passage is helpful in understanding Gauthier's CM dispositional solution to PD (MA,p.170):

> Suppose ... the familiar [PD] structure; each benefits from mutual co-opera-
> tion in relation to mutual non-co-operation, but each benefits from non-co-
> operation whatever the other does [This is from the dominance argument].
> In such a situation, a [SM] chooses not to co-operate. A [CM] chooses to co-
> operate if, given her estimate of whether or not her partner will choose to co-
> operate, her own expected utility is greater than the utility she would expect
> from the non-co-operative outcome. [CM]s can thus obtain co-operative
> benefits that are unavailable to [SM]s, however far-sighted the latter may be.

Gauthier's general strategy is to appeal to the collective optimiza-
tion against individual maximization. "Moral theory is essentially
the theory of optimizing constraints on utility-maximization"
(MA,p.78). As we have seen in Chapter II, both prisoners know
that collective optimizing is better than individual maximization.
However, according to the dominance argument, both end up
confessing. Gauthier's strategy is, then, to show that, under the
suitable conditions, the dominant argument does not work. In
other words, "this [dominant] argument would be valid only if the
probability of others acting co-operatively were, as the argument
assumes, independent of one's own dispositions" (MA,p.172).
Contrarily, Gauthier's dispositional solution relies on the
"probabilistic dependence" thesis.[113] In a one-shot PD game, the
probabilistic dependence thesis works in the present because individual decisions in one-shot games cannot affect future situations.
But Gauthier's dispositional solution needs to take into account
the effects on the future situations since his solution depends on
the exclusion of SM disposed persons from the benefits of the
future opportunities, which only CM disposed persons obtain.
Therefore, to suppose that a CM disposition is rational is question-
begging in the present context of a one-shot PD game.

Gauthier is exposed to an unavoidable inconsistency, as is clear
in the two following passages:

> Constrained maximizers may co-operate even if neither expects her choice to
> affect future situations (MA,p.170. n.19).

> The essential point in our argument is that one's disposition to choose affects
> the situations in which one may expect to find oneself (MA,p.183).

Especially, in view of the latter, Goldman's interpretation shows
just this inconsistency: "For either tit-for-tat or Hobbes's strategy
(co-operate only when others are co-operating) to be rational, we

must expect present interactions to influence opportunities for later ones. This requirement is dropped in the new variation [of Gauthier's]."[114]. In view of this inconsistency, Gauthier's dispositional solution—"it is not the choice itself, but the maximizing character of the disposition in virtue of which it is choiceworthy, that is the key to our argument" (MA,p.183)— just provokes many difficult questions concerning levels of rational decision making.[115]

What is to be said of the FR problem as it relates to Gauthier's dispositional solution?   Gauthier's solution to it is structurally similar to PD. Gauthier's exclusion thesis of the SM free-riders from cooperative society by the CMs relies on the epistemic presupposition of sufficient translucency of other minds (MA,p.177). This exclusion thesis on the foundation of sufficient translucency puts an additional burden on the CMs: the cultivation of their ability to read other minds (MA,p.181). If the CMs fail to develop this ability, they cannot benefit from their CM disposition. "And it can then appear that constraint is irrational. But what is actually irrational is the failure to cultivate or exercise the ability to detect other's sincerity or insincerity" (MA,p.181).   Gauthier's argument here seems to make sense in view of conditional compliance and of the no sucker rule. Nevertheless, sufficient translucency is practically indistinguishable from transparency in view of the strong requirement to cultivate the ability. In other words, Gauthier's distinction between transparency and translucency is blurred. "If [CM] defeats [SM] only if all persons are transparent, then we shall have failed to show that under actual, or realistically possible, conditions, moral constraints are rational" (MA,p.174).

Probably, cultivating the ability to read other people's minds, and the condition of the sufficient translucency are perfectly possible in the small and stable isolated society. Indeed, Gauthier may be still suffering from Rousseau's nostalgic yearning for the small Greek polis (SC,III,15,291). However, the contemporary world of mass society leads to a stubborn mistrust of innocent strangers or to the totalitarian punitive world of scarlet letter S (to be worn by the SMs).[116] Gauthier's liberal individuals do not want to be members of this kind of society.

The question-begging character of Gauthier's dispositional solution on the ground of the probabilistic dependence thesis becomes more serious when we consider the conditional compliance of the

CM disposed persons. In many places, Gauthier emphasizes that: "to avoid being exploited, a [CM] behaves as a [SM], acting on the individual strategy that maximizes her utility given the strategies she a [CM] expects the others to employ" (MA,p.169). He adds: "A [CM] makes reasonably certain that she is among like-disposed persons before she actually constrains her direct pursuit of maximum utility" (MA,p.169; cf. pp.155,160,167). In sum, if a CM believes that the other party will cooperate, the CM will too; otherwise not. I am disposed to comply if you will. You are disposed to comply if I will. But that does not settle what each of us will do. First, a CM must take into account the probability of CMs in a given population, but this probability cannot be determined in advance because of interdependent conditional compliance. Furthermore, even this probability calculation is meaningless in the sense that a CM must expect the actual compliance of other CMs before he or she develops a readiness to cooperate, as emphasized above. From these considerations, I can infer that Gauthier's rational compliance project is circular.[117] Gauthier's own textual evidence shows this well. Listen to his qualifications here: "taking other's dispositions as fixed"; "given sufficient security"; "if followed by all"; "enough are like minded"; "if we find ourselves in the company of reasonably just persons, then we too have reason to dispose ourselves to justice" (MA,pp.171,162,167, 177,182).

Overall, then, what should be said of Gauthier's rational dispositional compliance project in view of his avowed endeavor to avoid the Hobbesian and Rawlsian contractarian dilemma? On the one hand, if it is the case that Gauthier's dispositional solution heavily relies on the exclusion of SMs from cooperative arrangements, how much is his solution different from Hobbesian sovereign's coercive punishment of SMs? As Gauthier acknowledges, "Hobbes's argument that those not so disposed may not rationally be received into society, is the foundation on which we shall build" (MA,p.165). Perhaps Gauthier's exclusion thesis might be a version of liberal (not Hobbesian political absolutistic) communitarian excommunication. Nonetheless, as Hume charges, a social contract presupposes the moral community or custom of promise keeping.[118] In Heideggerian terminology, Gauthier's CMs are "Being-already-in-the-[moral]-world" or "Being-already-alongside[-with-CMs].[119]

Thus Gauthier is forced to move to the other horn. On the other hand, if it is the case that the CM's disposition mainly hinges on a preestabilished society of similarly disposed people, how much is Gauthier's solution different from Rawls' presupposition of strict compliance? As Gauthier acknowledges, "A community in which most individuals are disposed to comply with fair and optimal agreements and practices, and so to base their actions on joint cooperative strategies, will be self-sustaining" (MA,p.182).

In conclusion, Gauthier's solution is torn between the rational but non-moral non-voluntary Hobbesian political compliance and the circular moral presupposition of strict compliance in Rawlsian perfectly just society.

3. The Lockean Proviso as the Initial Bargaining Position and Its Critical Comparison with Marxism.

In this second section, I have, until now, explained and assessed Gauthier's MRC/MRB principle, and CM dispositional compliance against the general background of individual maximizing rationality. As I emphasized on occasions, MRC/MRB and CM compliance along with the Lockean proviso, to which I now turn, comprise the argumentative center for Gauthier's contractarian rational solutions to the three core problems: bargaining problem, rational compliance, and initial bargaining position. Gauthier's rational project presented so far is incomplete because the initial bargaining position has yet not been defined. Before I discuss this position in detail, it is pertinent to indicate the range of this incompleteness.

In the last subsection of Section A, I have shown why Gauthier has to change his position from thin market contractarianism to thick market contractarianism. Gauthier's thick market contractarianism means that his contractarian ethics is not only designed to be a rational and impartial remedy for market failure, but also designed to represent the rational and impartial initial conditions which are needed for market success.[120] As we have seen, the conditions of market success presuppose private ownership and free use of individual factor endowments and products. Unlike laissez-faire welfare economists who take initial factor endowments as given, Gauthier raises a serious question about them: "Each product and each factor of production is owned by some individual who may use it as she pleases as far as production, exchange, and consumption are concerned, but why should individuals exercise this control?" (MA,p.94). As discussed in Chapter III, the rejection of market presuppositions concerning individual endowments is a crucial part of Rawls' theory of justice and the issue has been a focal point of much dispute between Rawls and Nozick. One of the major aims of Gauthier's appeal to a modified Lockean proviso is to settle the dispute between Rawls and Nozick: by taking "a position between the simple individualism of Robert Nozick and the implicit collectivism of John Rawls" (MA,p.268).[121]

Even though Gauthier generally adopts Nozick's use of the proviso, he thinks that Nozick's theory of natural property rights presupposes an independent moral element.[122] When Gauthier acknowledges that "Indeed, one may reject the very idea of an endowment [as arbitrary]," he is probably thinking of Rawls (MA,p.99). As we will see shortly, Gauthier replies to Rawls that Rawls' morality licenses free riders (MA,p.220). At this juncture, Gauthier's aim is to show that free use of individual factor endowments and its resultant property rights are not "arbitrary, but rather fully justified by the (yet to be shown) rationality and impartiality of the proviso" (MA,p.210).

In the first subsection of this section, I have shown that, according to Gauthier's alleged claim, MRC/MRB is a rational and impartial bargaining theory of justice, which is applied to the distribution of the cooperative surplus. As specified there, the bargaining problem is divided into two sub-problems. The first is the bargaining problem proper, the second the initial bargaining position problem. In the traditional terminology, the first is the distributive justice problem, the second the acquisitive justice problem. According to Gauthier's rational choice theoretic terms, the first is the internal rationality of co-operation, the second, the external rationality of co-operation problem (MA,p.118). In the former, co-operation is taken for granted, whereas, in the latter, Gauthier calls "co-operation into question and demand[s] its rationale as a mode of interaction" (MA,p.118). In analyzing the internal structure of MRC/MRB, I have indicated that the thrust of MRC/MRB is "splitting the difference." The difference is between the maximal claims and the initial bargaining claims of bargainers. For the application or calculation of the MRC/MRB, the initial bargaining claims of bargainers have to be determined in advance. Gauthier clearly points out that "the application of [MRC/MRB], or more generally, the emergence of either co-operative or market interaction, demands an initial definition of the actors in terms of their factor endowments" (MA,p.222). The initial bargaining endowments "provide, the starting point for, and not the outcome of, agreement. They are what each person brings to the bargaining table, not what she takes from it" (MA,p.222).

At the second subsection, I have discussed the CM dispositional solution to the rational compliance problem. However, my criticism concerning the unique rationality of complying with MRC/MRB is still incomplete since the problem whether the initial bargaining shares of MRC/MRB are fair or impartial is to yet be solved. Even though we suppose that MRC/MRB is fair, the fairness of the initial position is still at stake. Gauthier himself makes this point clear. He says: "compliance is rationally grounded only within the framework of a fully co-operative venture, in which each participant willingly interacts with her fellows. And this leads us back to the second issue addressed in bargaining theory—the initial bargaining position" (MA,p.15).

If we relate this issue to the background of the thick market contractarianism, it is that "[m]arket outcomes are fair if, but, of course only if, they result from fair initial conditions" (MA,p.95). Accordingly, the rational compliance problem is to be rigorously specified. At this juncture, Gauthier introduces the distinction between a "narrowly compliant" and "broadly compliant" disposition (MA,p.178). A bargainer is broadly compliant if he or she is disposed to comply with any outcome of a bargain that gives him or her more benefit than the non-cooperative outcome. Contrarily, a narrowly compliant bargainer is disposed to comply with the outcome of fair bargaining (in the sense that it satisfies MRC/MRB *cum* the proviso). In order to show the rational ground of compliance, which is also morally admissible, Gauthier has to prove that that narrow compliance for fair cooperation is uniquely more rational than broad compliance for unfair cooperation.[123]

The proviso, to emphasize it once more, is Gauthier's pivotal strategy for overcoming the contractarian dilemma and trilemma, which I have featured in Section A. Since I have shown how the proviso is deeply correlated with the whole configuration of Gauthier's contractarian ethics, I will be able to properly assess the viability of Gauthier's rational deduction project in the subsequent critical discussion of the proviso. Making such a claim is not an exaggeration since the most crucial problem of contractarianism is how to construct the initial hypothetical situation, viz., the state of nature.

Throughout the history of social contract theory up to the contemporary times, there have been numerous characterizations of the state of nature. Why does Gauthier resort to the Lockean proviso? As we have seen in Chapter III, Nozick's adoption of the proviso is mainly to establish the legitimate initial acquisition of property rights. Gauthier's thrust for the adoption of the proviso is caught up in his endeavor to escape from the Hobbesian horn of contractarian dilemma, viz., the moral irrelevancy of rationality. Thus it is understandable why Gauthier rejects both Buchanan's natural interaction of coercive initial position and Nash's bargaining model of threat advantage, which I have treated in Section A.1. and Section B.1. respectively. In short, Gauthier thinks that Locke's theory of acquisition or property moralizes the Hobbesian state of nature which he calls "that condition of unlimited predation" (MA,p.201).[124] However, Gauthier criticizes both Locke and Nozick for bringing a prior moral element of natural rights into the contract. In other words, they are victims of the second horn of the contractarian dilemma.[125]

Gauthier's strategy is: (1) to show how the proviso is used to constrain natural interactions in the non-coercive and non-threat initial situation and consequently how it can be a proper initial bargaining position for market and social cooperation; (2) to show how the proviso guarantees the establishment of property rights, and furthermore the fairness and impartiality of them; and (3) to show how it is rational for individual utility-maximizers to accept and comply with the proviso. I shall follow Gauthier's strategy in these three tasks, and then I shall assess whether his strategy succeeds in avoiding the contractarian dilemma.

(1) Gauthier takes up the basic idea of the Lockean proviso as a general constraint of natural interactions in the state of nature. This means that, for Gauthier, interpreting the proviso as the

establishment of people's exclusive property rights from the beginning is begging the question (even though he will eventually move in that direction). As we have seen, the proviso is a specific theory of property rights, viz., the acquisition or appropriation of external objects. Locke starts from one of the early versions of the labour theory of value or property, or *homo faber* (transformation of nature through one's labor) and moves to the exclusive property rights under a specific condition of abundance[126]: "For this *Labour* being the unquestionable Property of the Labourer, no man but he can have a right to what is once joyned to, at least where there is enough, and as good left in common for others" (ST,5,27). Gauthier claims that a suitable reading of the proviso is to think of it as a constraint of "natural interactions in order to make society possible" (MA,p.202).

In this regard, Gauthier evaluates Nozick's interpretation of the proviso, and then modifies it to suit his own purpose. As pointed out in Chapter III, Nozick says: "Locke's proviso that there be 'enough and as good left in common for others' ... is meant to ensure that the situation of others is not worsened" (AST,p.175).[127] According to Gauthier, Nozick's interpretation means that natural interaction must exclude activities that worsen the situations of any person, whether by predation or parasitization. However, Gauthier claims that Nozick's interpretation is too strong for rational utility-maximizers since there are some situations in which they could satisfy the Nozickean proviso only by worsening their own position. Thus Gauthier modifies Nozick's interpretation of the proviso that "it prohibits worsening the situations of others except this is necessary to avoid worsening one's own position" (MA,p.203).

In this context, Gauthier also criticizes Rawls that his original position controlled by the maximin strategy is too strong for rational utility-maximizers. Since Rawls' original position enjoins bettering one's own situation only by bettering that of others (especially that of the least advantaged persons), it permits free rides (MA,p.206). Gauthier's argument until now is that in the natural interactions both free-ridership and parasitism must be excluded. In other words, "a stronger constraint on natural interaction than the proviso would license free-ridership, a weaker constraint would license parasitism" (MA,p.206). Gauthier's interpretation of the proviso is to provide a minimal condition for the possibility of social cooperation or market competition by excluding the external influences upon free use of individual endowments.[128]

Before we move to Gauthier's second task, viz., to show how the proviso actually determines initial factor endowments and how it eventually establishes fair and impartial property rights, there still remains one delicate problem. That is, "How are we to understand worsening — and, conversely bettering — someone's situation, where that someone may be oneself or another?" (MA,p.203). At this point, Gauthier makes a crucial distinction between worsening someone's situation and failing to better it and asserts that the proviso excludes only the former, not the latter (MA,p.204). An example is here of a man drowning in the river. If I push him into the river and leave him to drown, under these conditions, I definitely violate the proviso. If I had not pushed him or if I had not been there, he would have been better off. But if he falls into the river and I just do nothing about it, under these conditions, he would not have been worse off in spite of my presence. Hence I have not worsened him. However, if I had saved him, his position would have been bettered. Hence I have failed to better his situation.[129] But, for Gauthier, this does not mean that I violate the proviso.

In view of this example, Gauthier says that "the base point for determining how I affect you, in terms of bettering or worsening your situation, is determined by the outcome that you would expect in my absence" (MA,p.204). There seem to be several significant logical problems concerning the counterfactual test of absence.[130] However, my major concern is not with logical problems but with the relationship of this absence test to individual basic endowments. At this point, Gauthier uses Robinson Crusoe for his purposes once again.[131] "Even though Robinson Crusoe is in fact solitary, we may define her *basic endowment* as what she can make use of, and what no one else could make use of in her absence" (MA,p.100). In view of this, Gauthier proposes his final interpretation of the proviso (MA,p.205):

> We interpret the Lockean proviso so that it prohibits worsening the situation of another person, except to avoid worsening one's own through interaction

with that person. Or, we may conveniently say, the proviso prohibits bettering one's situation through interaction that worsens the situation of another.
This, we claim, expresses the underlying idea of not taking advantage.

(2) In order to establish property rights, Gauthier constructs a
comprehensive four-step procedure. Through this procedure, he
endeavors to show that the establishment of property rights is fair
and impartial. The first step is to establish exclusive personal rights
to each person's basic endowment of physical and mental capacities. Gauthier claims that these personal rights are naturally
derived from the first task of the absence test. "Thus the proviso,
in prohibiting each from bettering his situation by worsening that
of others, but otherwise leaving each free to do as he pleases, not
only confirms each in the use of his own powers, but in denying to
others the use of those powers, affords to each the exclusive use of
his own" (MA,p.209).

The second step is to extend these exclusive personal rights to
use rights. Suppose that in the state of nature, I cultivate a plot of
land, intending to consume its produce. In view of the costs and
expectation of cultivation (viz., my own labor and my intended use
of those goods), if some other person seizes the produce of the
cultivated land, he violates the proviso. In order to use my products, he or she has to provide full compensation for my cost.
Gauthier thus asserts that "the proviso affords a right *in* the fruits
of one's labour and so to full compensation" (MA,p.211).
According to Gauthier, the first and second steps complete the
conversion of the pure state of nature. The remaining two steps
concern "the transition from natural interaction to market and cooperative interaction" (MA,p.211).

The third step is to demonstrate that "in both market and cooperative interaction, all of the costs of one person's activities that
fall on others within the sphere of interaction are displaced costs,
requiring compensation if proviso is not to be violated"
(MA,p.213). A simple example is helpful in understanding this
step. In polluting the river in order to sell the products from one's
factory, one must compensate the costs to the fisherfolk alongside
the river. In the first two steps, one's disposal of his or her wastes
and its consequential killing of the fish in the river do not violates
the proviso (MA, p.211).[132] However, in this third step, polluting

the river violates the proviso since the cost of the pollution is displaced to the fisherfolk.[133] Thus Gauthier maintains that "the internalization of costs necessary to the emergence of the market" is required (MA,p.211).

The final and fourth step is crucial for Gauthier. It "defines the full endowment of each individual, [and] introduces exclusive rights to land and other goods" (MA, p.214). In this step, the use rights in the first three steps are transformed into so-called possessive or private property rights.[134] What is the essential difference of this step from the first three steps? Gauthier answers that the first three steps are for "the creation of a framework of common use among interacting persons" but not for "exclusive rights of posses- sion to external objects" (MA,p.214). Gauthier provides us, once again, with a simple example. One person or family takes a "sufficiently small" portion of land and makes the land "more productive" through intensive cultivation rather than common use (MA,pp.216, 215). The person or family seeks an exclusive right to the portion of the land. How can Gauthier vindicate the proposed right? First, we must ask "whether someone, in seeking exclusive use of the land or other goods, violates the proviso, bettering her situation through worsening that of others" (MA,p.215). Because the taking is only of a sufficiently small portion, he or her does not violate the proviso. Second, "If not, then we must ask whether some other person, in interfering with a claim to exclusive use, violates the proviso" (MA,p.215). The answer is yes because he or she does not provide compensation. In this case, Gauthier means market compensation. "If so, then the proposed right is estab- lished" (MA,p.215). At this last step, the right-holder has a private right in the full sense: "A right *to* land or goods is a right not only to the fruits of use, but also to the fruits of exchange" (MA,p.215). Gauthier finally resorts to Pareto-optimality (appropriation may enable everyone to improve his or her own situation through the new opportunities for trade or exchange of the products) and the mutual benefits of the division of labor in the emerging market (MA,pp.216f).

An important remaining task for Gauthier is to show that the established exclusive property right is fair and impartial. Gauthier's claim for the supposed fairness and impartiality is that the proviso prohibits taking advantages of others, viz., no free rider and no parasite. However, as Gauthier admits, "advantage is thus not taken, but equality is not assured" (MA,p.217). It is plain that the cumulative result of the exclusive property right might be extreme inequality. In view of this, Gauthier' task is more specified: "We must show, then, that the inequality allowed by the proviso is no indication of partiality" (MA,p.217).

This task is nothing new since what are "justifiable inequalities" is the catch phrase of the free market capitalistic property system (cf. MA,pp.270f). Once more, Gauthier resorts to Robinson Crusoe's free entitled use of his endowments (only this time he postulates sixteen Robinson Crusoes, each living on a different island; MA, pp.218f). This example is just a replica of the supposed impartiality of the free market, which I investigated in Section A.3.: viz., "any principle other than the one allowing each Crusoe to benefit himself would be unfair and partial, in requiring some to give free rides to others, or to be hosts for their parasitism" (MA,p.219). From this example, Gauthier thinks that he can safely derive the following conclusion: "The proviso, in determining the rights persons have on the basis of what they do, and in treating what persons do from the standpoint of the individual actor, ensures the impartiality of interaction" (MA,p.221). Against the broad background of the market contractarianism, this claim turns out as follows (MA,p.270):

> Pure market societies are frequently criticized for the inequalities that allegedly they promote. But where market inequality is a legitimate basis for criticism, it is the failure of the market occasioned by the presence of externalities, giving rise to free-ridership or to parasitism, that is the true source of fault.

(3) Through his first and second tasks, Gauthier has tried to show that "fair procedures yield an impartial outcome only from an impartial initial position" (MA,p.191). But he still has to show that the impartial initial position must be a rationally acceptable initial position. More exactly he has to show that "it is rational for utility-maximizers to accept the proviso as constraining their natural interaction and their individual endowments, in so far as they anticipate beneficial social interaction with their fellows" (MA,p.193). Gauthier's strategy here is to appeal to the rational compliance of the proviso. The distinction between a broadly and

narrowly compliant disposition, which was mentioned at the beginning of this subsection, plays a significant role. Gauthier wants to prove why the narrow compliant disposition is uniquely rational through the expectation of cooperation and the equal rationality of contractors. First, if all persons were broadly compliant (i.e., refusing to act voluntarily on the proviso), then cooperative mutual advantage would be impossible (MA,p.226). This means in Hobbesian terms that the Fool's broadly compliant behavior leads back to the state of war, which is inimical to all the contractors.[135] Second, if some persons are less compliant, then cooperation is possible only if others are more compliant. But Gauthier maintains that this violates equal rationality since non unilateral but conditional compliance is a form of rational compliance (MA,pp.226f).[136] Furthermore, Gauthier argues that "If you will [broadly] comply for any benefit whatsoever, then in interacting with you I should dispose myself to comply with a joint strategy only if it offers me, not a fair share, but the lion's share of the cooperative surplus" (MA,p.226). This means that the narrowly compliant could always expect to do better, and hence it is rational to be narrowly compliant. Therefore Gauthier concludes (MA,p.227):

> The proviso, forbidding the taking of advantage, represents the weakest constraint rationally acceptable to persons who avoid costly interaction with others, and the strongest constraint rationally acceptable to persons who would be free to benefit themselves. Thus the proviso reflects the equal rationality of persons who must constrain their natural interaction in order to enter into mutually beneficial social relationships.

Gauthier's alleged impartial and rational proviso seems to be very impressive since the long-standing controversies concerning the relationship between morality and rationality (e.g., the contractarian dilemma) might find their solution here. However, as Gauthier later admits, "in appealing to a revised form of the Lockean proviso ... I have, at least in my own view, ventured on a far more precarious construction than in developing minimax relative concession or in arguing for constrained maximization."[137] Where does the precariousness come from? I will show its location in terms of Gauthier's three tasks concerning the proviso.

The first task is to introduce the modified proviso as a fair constraint to the natural interactions in the noncooperative state of nature. The crucial issue here is how Gauthier can match the seemingly abundant state of nature with the scarcity situation of the bargaining. As I mentioned in the previous chapters, contractarianism and rational choice theory presuppose the scarcity of external goods and social resources. Gauthier explicitly embraces the presupposition of scarcity, viz., the Humean circumstances of justice as a general background of his bargaining theory (MA,pp.113f).[138] If Gauthier still holds that "one must leave enough and as good for others" (MA,p.203), how can the proviso suitable for this abundant situation of the state of nature apply to the scarce social situation of bargaining?[139] Perhaps the afore-mentioned sixteen Robinson Crusoes in the sixteen islands may welcome the proviso. Nonetheless, I am not arguing here that Gauthier totally ignores the scarcity problem. Because of this problem, I believe, he modifies Nozick's interpretation of the proviso into that "it prohibits worsening the situation of others except where this is necessary to avoid worsening one's own position" (MA,p.203).

Gauthier's modified proviso, however, has its own problem too. Since the modified proviso "allows us to worsen the position of others to an arbitrarily large degree to avoid worsening our own slightly,"[140] it seems to be too weak (even though it is right that Gauthier considers the Nozickean proviso as too strong). I have alluded to the drowning man case for the proper understanding of the modified proviso. Gauthier has another more interesting example of two castaways, Joanna and Jonathan (MA,p.206). Gauthier is quite right that it is irrational for Joanna to run any risk whatsoever to save Jonathan from the sharks in the lagoon. Nonetheless, in their relation, Gauthier admits, "an understanding to co-operate may place each of them under a rational and moral obligation to endeavor to save the other even at real risk to oneself" (MA,p.207). "Each insures himself or herself against being left to whatever perils there may be by agreeing to seek to rescue the other" (MA,pp.207f). When we compare ignoring the drowning man (proviso not violated) with these castaways (possible risk taking), the application of the modified proviso seems too different. In order to make these two cases consistent, Gauthier needs a proportionality test of risk.[141]

When we recall that the debate between Rawls and Harsanyi concerning the proper model of individual choice under uncertainty hinges on risk aversion or taking, it might not be just coincidence that Gauthier's rational contractors (without the veil of ignorance) have to meet the same problem. This reveals just how much Gauthier's modified proviso is precarious as a general constraint on the natural interactions in the state of nature or in the contractarian hypothetical initial position.

Gauthier's second task is his state-of-the-art presentation of his theory of transformation from the state of nature to the cooperative society or market. The four-step justification of impartial exclusive property right is perhaps the most sophisticated version of property right theories in recent times.[142] Gauthier seems to show how well the standard argument for the justification of liberal market capitalism works, that is, how well capitalism can drive "human beings in more efficient and productive ways" (MA,p.216). Furthermore he also seems to show how perfectly the supposed impartiality of property rights dovetails with the traditional natural rights theory (even though he does not merely presuppose natural rights from the beginning).

Nonetheless, there are many problems with Gauthier's position here as he moves from stage to stage. I will have time to deal with only one of them: viz., the impartiality or fairness of the exclusive property right — which pivots on Gauthier's more important claim that "the inequality allowed by the proviso is no indication of partiality" (MA,p.217). At this juncture, it is pertinent to see what kinds of objections Marx and Marxists can make against Gauthier.

Before turning to Marxists, however, it is necessary to raise the following preliminary question. How does Gauthier's justification of property rights differ from the other traditional justifications of the capitalistic property rights? He appeals to many arguments: the Pareto efficiency or optimality, mutual advantage, productivity, and free and fair uncoerced use of individual endowment (no free rider and no parasite). In view of mutual advantage, I think, he can also embrace the "trickle-down theory" (i.e., the theory that claims that benefits to the rich will eventually reach the poor and in that way prosper the whole society).[143] However, Gauthier does not employ the assumptions of "the history of economic original sin" or the Weberian "Protestant ethics" of frugality or abstinence of capitalists.[144] And also he does not directly appeal to social Darwinism of the survival of the fittest.[145]

Marx's criticism of capitalism has been well known through his views on exploitation, alienation, labor theory of value, and the theory of surplus-value.[146] But he still has to explain how capital came into existence in the first place. His theory of surplus-value is still incomplete since surplus-value cannot proliferate without capital to start with. In the famous chapter on "primitive accumulation" in *Capital*, Marx seems to acknowledge that the original primitive accumulation of capital is not a "result of the capitalistic mode of production but its starting point"[147] In this regard, Marx and Gauthier do not differ. Furthermore, Marx's criticism on "the history of economic original sin" has nothing to do with Gauthier since Gauthier does not embrace this concept into his rational reconstruction of property rights. Against this idyllic vision of history, Marx observes that "[i]n actual history it is notorious that conquest, enslavement, robbery, murder — briefly, force — play the great part."[148]

Admittedly, the economic structure of capitalism had grown out of the economic structure of feudalism. The dissolution of the latter set free the elements of the former, and so free laborers emerged. Marx, however, observed that "[f]ree labourers, in the double sense that neither they themselves form part and parcel of the means of production, as in the case of slaves, bondsmen, &c., nor do the means of production belong to them, as in the case of peasant-proprietors; they are, therefore, free from, unencumbered by, any means of production of their own."[149] In short, freedom has the double sense: emancipation and expropriation. It is in this double sense of freedom where the secret of primitive accumulation lies:[150]

> The so-called primitive accumulation, therefore, is nothing else than the historical process of divorcing the producer from the means of production. It appears as primitive, because it forms the prehistoric stage of capital and of the mode of production corresponding with it.

With respect to this passage, it is not surprising for Marx that "[t]he whole movement [of the historical process] ... seems to turn in a vicious circle."[151]

In spite of Marx's double meaning of freedom, Gauthier seems to confine his discussion only to the first. He points to the liberation effect or "equalizing force" of the market compared to the feudal caste society (MA,p.270).[152] But he does not seriously take into account the pejorative sense of freedom, having to do with the separation of the producers from the means of production. This seems to drive him to make a series of hard-headed proposals in favor of free market capitalism. He says, for example, "[e]quality is not a fundamental concern in our theory" (MA,p.270); "we should not be surprised that the natural inequalities that would be manifested by different Robinson Crusoes reappear as market inequalities" (MA,p.270); "the proviso says nothing about equalizing," or "meeting needs" (MA,p.218). He adds: "we think of rich and poor within a social context, and we think that his wealth and her poverty are in some way related. If so, then in examining how the situation came about, we may well find a violation, if not of the proviso, then the principle of minimax relative concession" (MA,p.218).[153]

It is hard to believe that Gauthier does not know about Marx's charge concerning Rousseau's contract theory as an adventure story of Robinson Crusoe.[154] Unfortunately we have seen how deeply Gauthier's justification for the emergence and impartiality of exclusive property rights relies on the small and great adventure stories of Robinson Crusoe (the stories of single Crusoe, of two castaways, and of sixteen Crusoes, etc.). Here, I am not maintaining that Marx is right in his negative or positive visions of capitalism, socialism, and communism. Indeed, I agree with Gauthier that Marx has his own problems.[155] Perhaps the most serious one is that his communist economic arrangement is irrational (rationality in the sense of efficiency).[156] If it is possible to assess Marx according to the contractarian rational deduction project, Marx would be a victim of the second horn of circularity (in the sense that his vision of equality as a prior moral ideal is rationally optional).[157] It is worthwhile to note that, within the Marxist camp, so-called market socialism has emerged to meet the rationality problem. But this kind of socialism is still a myth to those in the capitalistic liberal camp.[158]

Returning to Gauthier's proviso, there is another serious problem (besides the limited scope of the proviso —callous neglect of basic needs and equality). What exactly his proviso means is not clear. Is it the case that property rights have been actually established according to the proviso? If not, Gauthier has to develop a compensation project for the discrepancy between descriptive and normative emergence of property rights. As Marx does, Gauthier observes real history as follows: "Blood and the Sword have been the bonds of human society throughout, and before, recorded history."[159] If this is the case, Gauthier's idyllic fantasia of natural inequalities of Robinson Crusoe has nothing to do with correcting the historical injustice. Although Gauthier does not adopt Hobbesian predation and threat advantage exemplified by Buchanan and Nash, this concession is not an effective reply to Marx. He lacks even Nozickean explicit consideration for past injustice (let alone Rawlsian consideration): "The existence of past injustice (previous violations of the first two principles of justice in holdings) raises the third major topic under justice in holdings: the rectification of injustice in holdings" (AST,p.152. cf. p.231).[160]

In this connection, Macpherson has made a formidable challenge to the contractarian liberalism from the Marxist point of view. His comparison between Hobbes and Locke restates the contractarian dilemma. He says: "The natural rights doctrines which we have examined *are* inconsistent with them [social contract theorists], because of their postulate of possessive individualism, which makes men's rights either ineffective (Hobbes) or grossly unequal (Locke)."[161] Since we examined Hobbes already, our primary concern at this point is Macpherson's criticism of the Lockean proviso. About this he says: "[Locke] justifies, as natural, as a class differential in rights and in rationality, and by doing so provides a positive moral basis for capitalist society."[162]

Consonant with Marx, Macpherson relates this point with respect to capital accumulation. He does not seriously object to personal rights of free labor and use of individual endowments and property rights to external goods guaranteed by the Lockean proviso. For him, these kinds of personal and property rights are limited by their derivation, since "there are still enough, and as good left; and more than the yet unprovided could use" (ST,5,33). Additional limitation is that, for any individual, "it [is] a foolish thing, as well as dishonest, to hoard up more than he could make use of" (ST,5,46). In sum, there are three limitations to rights here: the labour, sufficiency, and spoilage.[163]

However, Macpherson claims that expansion from those initial rights to the exclusive unlimited property rights of external goods leads to extreme inequality, and that these expanded kinds of rights are not natural. For Locke, the exclusive unlimited right to external goods is guaranteed "without the assignation or consent of any body" (ST,5,28). As a faithful follower of Locke, Gauthier also asserts that "[r]ights provide the starting point for, not the outcome of, agreement" (MA,p.222). But, Macpherson accurately points out, Locke requires one kind of consent, i.e., tacit consent to the use and invention of money (ST,5,36;5,45). Because of money, the original limitation that one must possess external goods as long as one can use them has no meaning. For money can be accumulated without decaying or spoiling. Finally, Locke transcends the three limitations set up by his initial justification from the proviso (ST,5,50):

> Life of Man in proportion to Food, Rayment, and Carriage, has its *value* only from the consent of Men, whereof Labour yet makes, in great part, *the measure*, it is plain, that Men have agreed to disproportionate and unequal Possession of the Earth, they having by a tacit and voluntary consent found out a way, how a man may fairly possess more land than he himself can use the product of, by receiving in exchange for the overplus, Gold and Silver, which may be hoarded up without injury to any one, these metalls not spoileing or decaying in the hands of the possessor.

In view of this, Macpherson flatly asserts that "Locke's natural man is bourgeois man: his rational man is man with a propensity to capital accumulation. He is even an infinite appropriator."[164] Locke was not a mere exponent of the traditional law of nature: "he has put into it quite a new content, the right to unlimited accumulation"[165]

Generally speaking, Macpherson's charge that contractarianism is a historically and ideologically conditioned product of a certain aspect of modern society (viz., its possessive liberal capitalism) is well taken. However, whether his positive suggestion, which lies "within sight of a society of abundance," is right or not is quite different matter.[166]

Indeed, Gauthier might have been influenced by Macpherson since Gauthier composes the contractarian dilemma in terms of Hobbes and Locke and, furthermore he once thought of contractarianism as an ideology.[167] However, in *Morals By Agreement*, he no longer considers contractarian ethics as just an ideology. Rather, as we have seen, he tries to prove that his fifth core idea, the Archimedean neutral point, is congruent with the individual rational bargaining choice and that the resultant liberal individuals are ideologically free. In short, he claims that the contractarian rational test is the real test of neutrality, fairness, and impartiality. In order to see whether this is the case, we have to move to Gauthier's third task, i.e., rational compliance to the proviso.

The two crucial supporting arguments for rational compliance, more exactly the narrowly compliant disposition, are expectation of cooperative mutual benefit and equal rationality. Rationality issues can be divided into two. The first is whether the proviso is rational, but partial and unfair. The second is whether the proviso is perhaps impartial and fair, but irrational. The first issue is, in other words, whether the proviso is too weak. This is directly related to Marx's and Marxists' criticisms of the proviso. Analytic Marxist John Roemer argues that unless you start with a certain amount of wealth in the capitalistic society, you are only "free to lose."[168] I do not need to retell Gauthier's position on this matter. Recently, in replying to various criticisms that the proviso is too weak, Gauthier claims that "I do not think that any attempt to strengthen the proviso is likely to succeed. The real question is whether it is not already too strong."[169] Gauthier's point is that since coercion and threat advantage are prohibited by the proviso, those who are least favored in personal endowments and property assets cannot rationally complain.

For Gauthier, the more serious problem is "Why should an individual seeking to maximize his utility not take advantage of his fellows?" (MA,p.223). Gauthier's strategy is to justify choosing rational compliance, more exactly the narrowly compliant disposition, by the expectation of mutual advantage from cooperative and market society and by equal rationality. First, the expectation argument is generally dependent upon the expected-utility theory of rational choice.   Nonetheless, if this argument is used for complying with the proviso, it seems to lead to the second horn of the contractarian dilemma, viz., circularity.   In other words, if, as Gauthier clearly admits, complying with the proviso is conditional — complying when enough others are complying as well — (MA,p.193), the appeal to the mutual benefit derived from complying with the proviso seems to beg the question.[170]   Needless to say, the case of the narrowly compliant disposition is more difficult.   In case of the CM dispositional solution to the MRC, there might exist a moral community already.   But, in the proviso case, the issue is whether entering into a moral or whatever cooperative community is rational or not.   From this point of view, Gauthier's following argument is suspicious.   It states that "it is rational for utility-maximizers to accept the proviso as constraining their natural interaction and their individual endowments, in so far as they anticipate beneficial social interaction with their fellows" (MA,p.193).   In connection with the unique rationality of the narrowly compliant disposition, the following criticism by Kraus and Coleman of the circularity horn is devastating:[171]

> [I]n the absence of a preexisting large population of narrow compliers, it is not and will never be rational for anyone to become a narrow complier. ... But if this is so, then there will never be any population of narrow compliers, for it will never be rational for any individual to become narrowly compliant in the first place!

Second, the equal rationality argument is also very problematic. As Gauthier himself explicitly acknowledges, the avowed link between rationality and morals is loosened by the following three factors: ideological, historical, and technical (MA,pp.231-2). Gauthier discusses the first two (ideological beliefs and historical institutional practices) by giving feminist examples. His first example deals with ideological unfair beliefs which affect the terms of cooperation.   Many people believe that a woman's place is in the home. Given these beliefs, a woman who does not find her place or role at home satisfying will find it impossible to claim her fair shares by interacting with others.   His second example deals with those historical practices which pertain to a wage system unfavorable to women.   Under these practices, no individual woman can rationally expect to claim equal pay for equal work.   In general, then, it is rational for an individual person to increase his or her preference-utility within status quo conditions (e.g., of male dominance). In other words, it is not rational to change the contents of his or her preference in face of social pressure, let alone to change the historically unfair social practices.

Male dominant social practices happen regardless of "whether these [practices] satisfy the proviso or not" (MA,p.231). When we recall Gauthier's concept of instrumental rationality ("which disclaim all concerns with the ends [or contents] of action"; MA,p.26), Gauthier's contractarian rationalism seems to be challenged by feminism. However, Gauthier does not mean by the above examples that contractarianism is against the feminist position or that contractarianism is a victim of ideological false consciousness.[172] Gauthier points out that the first two factors "may, ultimately depend on irrational beliefs" (MA,p.231). Gauthier's excuse to the feminist is that, "[t]he identification of value with the measure of preference, and the rationality of preference-based choice, are not affected by these failings of beliefs" (MA,p.30; cf. our previous discussion of the identification in A.2. of this chapter). Nevertheless, for ardent feminists' thought, the irrational beliefs cannot be corrected or erased by contractarian rational ethics.[173]

Third, technological factors posit a very vexing problem to equal rationality and the link between rationality and impartiality. "Without their guns, a small number of Spaniards would never have been able to overcome the Indian civilization of the Americas" (MA,p.231). But, Gauthier supposes that "the unequal rationality brought about by technological differences between societies is accidental" (MA,p.231). I do not think Gauthier's supposition is convincing. Over and above international or intersocietal relations, many claim that the imperialism of technocrats in the contemporary society is ubiquitous.[174] For technological inferiors, acquiescence to the superiors represents more a rational response than seeking for an agreement which is impartially or narrowly compliant (cf. MA,p.230)—even though I do not believe in the possibility of "happy slaves" in contemporary times.[175]

In sum, concerning the three factors, I can infer that the two crucial supporting arguments (expectation of cooperative mutual benefit and equal rationality) for rational compliance of the

Lockean proviso fail. Now I want to assess Gauthier's use of the Lockean proviso in a broad perspective. In this connection, consider the following passage (MA,p.232):

> In reconciling reason and morals, we do not claim that it is never rational for one person to take advantage of another, never rational to ignore the proviso, never rational to comply with unfair practices. *Such a claim would be false.* We do claim that justice, the disposition not to take advantage of one's fellows, is the virtue appropriate to co-operation, voluntarily accepted by equally rational persons. Morals arise in and from the rational agreement of *equals* (emphases mine).

In so far as such a claim cannot be made by Gauthier, his contractarian rational deduction project has no hope. Even its supposed equality is ephemeral. Quite apart from Marx's so-called laws of motion in capitalism,[176] the monopolistic trends in the free market screen out inferiors among even equal starters and finally, without proper control, only one superior will prevail. Gauthier could very well reply, "[b]ut why is this morally objectionable?"[177]

What, then, does he finally say about unequals? "Among unequals, one party may benefit most by coercing the other, and our theory would have no reason to refrain" (MA,p.17). "Animals, the unborn, the congenitally handicapped and defective, fall beyond the pale of morality tied to mutuality" (MA,p.268). It is proper to note here that Rawls also acknowledges that the scope of contractarian morality is limited.[178] I do not expect that contractarian ethics has to provide solutions for the problems of all the domains of morality, including animal rights, respect for nature, supererogatory acts, etc. As Gauthier insists, contractarianism is not for conventional morality: "We shall find no simple fit, or lack of fit, between our theory and the supposedly 'plain duties' of conventional morality" (MA,p.269).[179] Perhaps its essentials belong to a certain specific kind of human relationship. For Althusser, for example, contractarianism is an ideology, which "represents the imaginary relationship of individuals to their real conditions of existence."[180] Worse than that, the imaginary relationship is very dim. Sumner's comment here is that: "the greater the natural advantage of one agent over another the weaker the constraint which it will be necessary for the former to accept in dealing with the latter and, conversely, the stronger the constraint which it will be necessary for the latter to accept in dealing with the former."[181]

However, if this is so, there is no unique rational solution to the Lockean proviso in the sense that there are now many provisos. This means that Gauthier cannot solve the indeterminacy between Rawls, Nozick, and Harsanyi within the framework of liberal rationality, let alone the tension between liberalism and socialism. One might suppose that Gauthier would try to resolve this indeterminacy through bargaining. But this is not an option he has since the Lockean proviso is not an object of bargaining.[182]

Therefore "the state of nature will yield not convergence on a common proviso but observance of different provisos in interaction between equals and unequals."[183] This means that the Lockean proviso cannot escape from the contractarian dilemma and trilemma. As Gauthier develops it, perhaps he has "constructed, not a theory linking morality to rational choice, but a portrayal of moral constraints and maximizing choice in an ephemeral market society" (MA,p.354).[184] If this is the case, the Lockean proviso has no justificatory power. It merely indicates where the status quo point lies. According to Hobbes, "the Entire Right" or "the First Possession" is determined by "Lot" (LE,15,213).[185] All of these considerations make it sterile to inquire further whether there is a grand coherence between the individual rational bargaining choice and the Archimedean choice, which I discussed in the first section. Thus Gauthier's market liberal individuals are not a result of the rational choice, or Archimedean choice, or whatever, but just of presupposition.[186]

His overall aim, then, to achieve a world-historical project of rational foundationalism is well off its mark. Perhaps the best that can be said for it is that although it fails, it fails heroically.[187]

Notes

1 David Braybrooke, "Social Contract Theory's Fanciest Flight," *Ethics*, 97 (1987), pp.750-64.

2 Jules L. Coleman, "Market Contractarianism and the Unanimity Rule," in Ellen Frankel Paul et al. eds., *Ethics and Economics* (Oxford: Basil Blackwell, 1985), pp.69f. Sometimes, a broader term, "Market Liberalism" is used. See Samuel Brittan, *A Restatement of Economic Liberalism* (Atlantic Highlands, NJ: Humanities Press International, 1988), pp.211f. I adumbrated the term in connection with the discussion of the relation between the various types of market failure and the need of contractarian morality in Chapter II. B.2.

3 T.M. Scanlon, "Contractarianism and Utilitarianism," in Amartya Sen and Bernard Williams, eds., *Utilitarianism and Beyond* (Cambridge: Cambridge University Press, 1982), p.121. Also see Jean Hampton, "Can We Agree on Morals?" in Symposium on David Gauthier's *Morals by Agreement, Canadian Journal of Philosophy*, 18 (1988), p.344; Stephen L. Darwall, *Impartial Reason* (Ithaca: Cornell University Press, 1983).

4 This reciprocal coherence sounds like his version of Rawlsian congruence project between justice and goodness (TJ, p.395), which we discussed in the previous chapter B.3. As Alan Nelson correctly indicates, if impartiality is "our pretheoretical conception of *morality*", Gauthier has to, but does not, discuss whether the Archimedean point is circular in appealing to moral sense of 'impartial' and 'fair' prior to the rational bargaining solution. See his "Economic Rationality and Morality," in *Philosophy and Public Affairs*, 17 (1988), p.154. n.7.

5 C.A. Hooker et al. eds., *Foundations And Applications of Decision Theory*, vol.II. *Epistemic And Social Applications* (Dordrecht: D. Reidel Publishing Co., 1978), "Preface," p.xii.

6 Buchanan is one of the leading figures in the domain of the public choice school and political economy. Starting from *The Calculus of Consent: Logical Foundations of Constitutional Democracy* (Ann Arbor: The University of Michigan Press, 1962), which he co-authored with Gordon Tullock, he has attempted to construct his "constitutional contractarianism" with the help of the theory of rational choice. Since then, he has developed it further in his books: *The Limits of Liberty: Between Anarchy and Leviathan* (Chicago: The University of Chicago Press, 1975); *Freedom in Constitutional Contract: Perspectives of a Political Economist* (Austin: Texas A & M University Press, 1977); *What Should Economists Do?* (Indianapolis: Liberty Press, 1979) – especially pt.iii. Economics as Moral Philosophy – ; and six more books published recently.

7   Buchanan, *The Limits of Liberty*, p.25.

8   Ibid., pp.67, 23f.

9   Ibid., pp.85, 86. In this regard, Buchanan works within the Schumpeter-Dahl model of liberal democracy, which was discussed in Chapter III. A.3.

10 For Braithwaite's suggestion, which I dealt with in connection with Rawls' criticism of its Hobbesian vein (TJ,p.134f. n.9), see Chapter II. A.3. Nash's solution will be elaborated in the next section. Here it is noteworthy that Sen reproaches them in *Collective Choice and Social Welfare*, p.123:

> [T]he solutions put forward by Nash, Braithwaite ... might be relevant for predicting certain outcomes of bargains and negotiations, but they seem to be very unattractive solutions in terms of widely held value judgments about principles of collective choice. The special importance attached to the status quo point and to threat advantages ... seem to rule out a whole class of ethical judgments that are relevant to collective choice.

11 Hooker et al., "Preface," p.xii.

12 Rousseau's position is tricky.   Even though I have not investigated Rousseau's criticisms of Hobbes and Locke in *Of the Social Contract* and *Discourse on the Origin and the Foundations of Inequality Among Men*, I have followed Rawls' interpretation of Rousseau in placing him in the anti-Hobbesian or the Kantian line (TJ, p.264) in Ch.II. B.1. It is commonplace that Rousseau's consent theory is interpreted as non-instrumental as Joseph Raz does: "The other approach, deriving from Rousseau, regards consent non-instrumentally.   The consent is a constitutive element both of the condition of the person who gives it and of the society resulting from it, which is good in itself." See his *The Morality of Freedom* (Oxford: The Clarendon Press, 1986), p.80. In this respect, it is not eccentric to view Rousseau in terms of a communitarian or Marxist line.   However Rousseau himself seemed to acknowledge the basic theme of contractarian rational morality: "In this investigation I shall always strive to ally what right permits with what interest prescribes, so that justice and utility may not be divided" (SC,I,Prefatory Note,2). Furthermore, he said that "This passage from the state of nature to the civil state produces in man a very remarkable change, by substituting in his conduct justice for instinct, and by giving his actions the morality that they previously lacked" (SC,I,8,55). In this regard, it is perfectly possible to reformulate Rousseau in the context of the theory of rational choice. See W.G. Runciman and A.K. Sen's article, "Games, Justice and the General Will," *Mind*, 79 (1965), pp.554-62.

13 See Chapter III. B.3.

14 Gauthier, "Economic Rationality And Moral Constraints," in Peter A. French et al. eds., *Midwest Studies in Philosophy*, vol.III. *Studies in Ethical Theory* (Morris: The University of Minnesota, 1978), p.95.

15 Gauthier, "Justice as Social Choice," p.256.

16 Buchanan develops a comprehensive rejoinder to Gauthier. I cannot follow all the details here. However, one thing relevant to the contractarian dilemma must be mentioned. Notably, Buchanan acknowledges that

> my own construction is conceptually *explanatory* in a sense that Gauthier may not intend for his justificatory alternative. For his purposes, the independent existence of the individual provides the normative benchmark from which cooperative gains are counted. In my enterprise, by contrast, parties to potential contract commence from some status quo definition of initial positions because, quite simply, there is no other place from which to start. This existential acceptance of the status quo, of that which is, has no explicit normative content and implies neither approbation nor condemnation by any criterion of distributive justice.

"The Gauthier Enterprise," in Ellen Frankel Paul et al. eds., *The New Social Contract: Essays on Gauthier* (Oxford: Basil Blackwell, 1988), p.85. Thus Buchanan submits that "the contractarian exercise does not require rectification of prior injustices before application to relevant forward-looking questions" (Ibid., p.87). But I agree with Gauthier that "What is the status of prior injustices in Buchanan's theory?" and "Is it, then, unjust to remedy injustice?" in his "Morality, Rational Choice, and Semantic Representation: A Reply to My Critics," in the same book, p.201. Probably, Buchanan wants to describe or explain contractual constitutionalism as a decision procedure which provides the framework for settling conflicts among competing interests groups for distributable goods. Quite apart from the accuracy of his explanation or description, Buchanan's contractual constitutionalism is clearly not suitable for a normative contractarian ethics.

17 L.W. Sumner, *The Moral Foundation of Rights* (Oxford: Clarendon Press, 1987), p.161.

18 Gauthier, "Justice as Social Choice," pp.266f.

19 Neil Cooper, *The Diversity of Moral Thinking* (Oxford: Clarendon Press, 1981), "Introduction," p.1. Also see William K. Frankena, "The Concept of Morality," *The Journal of Philosophy*, 63 (1966), p.688.

20 The reason "construct" is more accurate than "discover" is that Gauthier thinks that "morality is to be understood as conventional, not natural [in the sense of ontological objects to recollect, intuit, or perceive]". Gauthier, "The Social Contract: Individual Decision or Collective Bargain?" in *Foundations and Applications of Decision Theory*, vol.II, p.66. Gauthier also makes it clear that, among the four species of contractarian theory (original, explicit, tacit, and hypothetical), hypothetical contractarianism is proper for ethical and political philosophy. See his "David Hume, Contractarian," *The Philosophical Review*, 88 (1979), pp.11-3.

21 Gauthier, "The Social Contract," p.47.

22 Gauthier, "Morality, Rational Choice, and Semantic Representation," p.221.

23 Ibid., p.182. Concerning false consciousness, see "The Social Contract as Ideology," p.132; "Moral Artifice: A Reply," *Canadian Journal of Philosophy*, 18 (1988), pp.387-9.

24 Gauthier, "Morality and Advantage," *The Philosophical Review*, 78 (1967), pp.460-75. Rpt. in his ed., *Morality and Rational Self-Interest* (Englewood Cliffs: Prentice-Hall, 1970), pp.166-180; pp.166-7.

25 Thomas Nagel, *The View From Nowhere* (Oxford: Oxford University Press, 1986), p.200.

26 In view of Rawls' recent disclaimer concerning this enterprise, Gauthier is proud that he is undertaking a pioneering enterprise. See "Morality, Rational Choice, and Semantic Representation," p.173. Also see MA, p.5.

27 For the term, "subjective utility-maximization" see Lars Bergström, "Some Remarks Concerning Rationality in Science," in Risto Hilpinen, ed., *Rationality in Science: Studies in the Foundations of Science and Ethics* (Dordrecht: D. Reidel Publishing Co., 1980), p.4.

28 Gauthier, "Justice and Natural Endowment," p.9.

29 Cf. Gauthier's distinction between parametric and strategic choices (MA,p.21). With parametric choice, the rational agent takes his or her environment as fixed, and is solely concerned with his or her utility-maximization. With strategic choice, the agent recognizes that the outcome of choice depends in part on the choices of other rational agents.

30 In contrast to Rawls' thick veil of ignorance (see Chapter III. B.1), the thin veil of ignorance means that individuals know the concrete situations of their society and their specific individual endowments distribution (a, b, ... n) but they do not know which individual endowments they will have. Cf. R.M. Hare, "Rawls' Theory of Justice," in *Reading Rawls*, p.90; "Justice and Equality," *Dialectics and Humanism*, 6 (1979), p.25. For Hare's use of the thin veil and a general critical discussion of his recent position, see Douglas Seanor and Nicholas Fotion, eds., *Hare and Critics* (Oxford: Clarendon Press, 1988). Even though Sumner correctly indicates that "the two simple conceptions which Gauthier outlines clearly leave room for a mixed account" he does not realize that Gauthier actually employs the mixed conception later. See Sumner, "Justice Contracted," p.527. As a textual evidence, I can point out the following passage. In connection with his fifth core idea, the Archimedean point, Gauthier asks:

> How may we represent choice from the Archimedean point so that each person, aware of his capacities and preferences, is able to identity with it as the choice he would have made lacking this awareness? (MA,p.245).

31 Christopher W. Morris, "The Relation between Self-Interest and Justice in Contractarian Ethics," in *The New Social Contract*, vii. "SI as a 'Weak' Assumption," p.133. The paradigm for the weakness argument is proof in axiomatic disciplines. If a theorem can be derived from weak axioms, then that is a rationale for assuming the weak rather than the stronger. However, it is notable that this argument can work only for proofs of the same theorem. Gauthier himself acknowledges that "we must not suppose that the moral principle we generate will be identical with those that would be derived on the universalistic conception" (MA,p.8).

32 There are many versions of foundationalism. In case of epistemological and ontological foundationalisms (the given: sense-data theory; reductive analysis: logical atomism; certainty; innate ideas, etc.), see Jonathan Dancy, *Introduction to Contemporary Epistemology* (Oxford: Basil Blackwell, 1985), Ch.V. "Foundationalism." In case of ethical foundationalism, Morris' distinction between "reductive foundationalism" and "simple moral foundationalism" is helpful. Simple moral foundationalism rests on a set of basic or self-evident moral facts or judgments and that moral theory can be founded on the set. Traditional foundationalism includes natural law and natural rights theories as well as intuitionist theories and moral will, conscience, virtue theories. If Rawls' and Nozick's theories are foundational, they are foundational in this sense (fairness and natural rights respectively). Reductive moral foundationalism argues that moral theory can be founded on non-moral facts and judgments (various forms of ethical naturalism and teleology: utilitarianism-pleasure; eudaimonism-happiness; rational self-interest, etc.). If Hobbes' radical contractarianism and Gauthier's strong deductive project are foundational, they are foundational in the reductive sense. See Christopher W. Morris, "Foundationalism in Ethics," *Ethics: Foundations, Problems, and Applications*, E. Morscher and R. Stranzinger, eds. (Vienna: Hölder-Pichler-Tempsky, 1981), pp.134-36. Also see, S. G. Clarke and E. Simpson, eds., *Anti-Theory in Ethics and Moral Conservatism* (Albany: State University of New York Press, 1989), "Introduction," p.4; Carol C. Gould, *Rethinking Democracy* (Cambridge: Cambridge University Press, 1988), Chap.III. "Social Ontology and the Question of Foundationalism in Ethics," pp.114-32. Cf. Chapter I. n.28.

33 Russell Hardin, "Bargaining for Justice," in *The New Social Contract*, p.66.

34 In place of the term, "connectedness," Gauthier uses the term, "completeness." In addition to the two formal requirements for ordinal preference, Gauthier imposes a cardinal interval measure: monotonicity and continuity (MA,p.44). These two additional formal requirements are too technical to be easily explained. However, I will show why they are needed in connection with the minimax relative concession. The basic idea is that in order to calculate the relative concession, two interval scales of utility difference or subtraction must be made (maximal bargaining claim utility minus settled bargaining point utility, and maximal bargaining claim utility minus initial bargaining position utility) (MA,p.136). For a helpful inquiry for measuring utility in general, see Hans Van Den Doel, *Democracy and*

Welfare Economics, pp.23-25; Sen, *Collective Choice and Social Welfare*, Chap.viii. "Cardinality with or without Comparability."

35 When I dealt with the theory, I did not mention its philosophical inception. Interestingly enough, Arblaster notes that Mill's famous passage is the initial formulation of the theory: "the sole evidence it is possible to produce that anything is desirable, is that people do actually desire it." in *Utilitarianism*, Ch.IV. par.3., p.438.   See Arblaster, *The Rise & Decline of Western Liberalism*, p.351.

36 Since the terms are far from being clear, they need to be clarified. First, "to conceive of value as dependent on [preference] affective relationship is to conceive of value as *subjective* (MA,p.47). In contrast, "to conceive of value as objective is to conceive of it as existing independently of the affections of sentient beings, and as providing a norm or standard to govern their affections" (MA,p.47). Second, "to conceive of value as dependent on each individual's own affective relationship is to conceive of value as *relative* (MA,p.50). In contrast, "an absolute [or universal] conception holds that values are the same for all persons, or for all sentient beings" (MA,p.50). Gauthier's position is of a linkage between subjectivism and relativism: "the view that value is dependent on appetite or preference with the view that value is relative to each individual" (MA,p.51). Comparisons with other positions are conducive to proper understanding.   Utilitarianism is a subjective and absolute value theory (MA,p.52). Perfectionism of a specific natural kind — perfectionism or excellence of human race — is an objective and relative value theory (MA,p.51).

37 See, Shia Moser, *Absolutism and Relativism in Ethics* (Thomas Springfield, Ill: Thomas, 1968); Michael Krausz and Jack W. Meiland, eds., *Relativism: Cognitive and Moral* (Notre Dame: University of Notre Dame Press, 1982); M. Krausz, ed., *Relativism: Interpretation and Confrontation* (Notre Dame: University of Notre Dame Press, 1989); Geoffrey Sayre-McCord, ed., *Essays on Moral Realism* (Ithaca: Cornell University Press, 1988);   Nicholas Rescher, *Moral Absolutes: An Essay on the Nature and Rationale of Morality* (New York: Peter Lang, 1989).

38 Two standard arguments have been advanced against moral relativism: First, "it permits the justification of any action as moral and thus allows for no moral discrimination or criticism whatever; for discussion across or between alternative (relativistic) moral frameworks has no rational basis for criticism or persuasion, since these frameworks are taken to be conceptually and practically incommensurable by the relativist." Second, "it may be argued that moral relativism is self-refuting since it itself makes a universal and nonrelative value claim about the relativity of values." Gould, *Rethinking Democracy*, p.118. The first argument is not relevant to Gauthier's individual value relativism. Even though contractarian ethics starts from the non-moral individual relativism, contractarianism as an ethical theory of justice eventually produces a moral distinction: "Morals by agreement offers a contractarian rationale for distinguishing what one may and may not do" even though an individual "initially draws no distinction between what he may and

may not do" (MA,p.9). The three issues discussed in my text are an enlargement of the second argument. For the second argument in detail, see Jack W. Meiland, "Is Protagorean Relativism Self-Refuting?" *Grazer Philosophische Studien*, 9 (1979), pp.51-68.

39 Adrian M. S. Piper, "Instrumentalism, Ojectivity, and Moral Justification," *American Philosophical Qurarterly*, 23 (1986), pp.373-81; Morris, pp.119,148f. See n.31 of this chapter. Cf. MA,p.51f.

40 Michael Sandel, ed., *Liberalism and Its Critics* (New York: New York University Press, 1984), "Introduction."; Sybil Wolfram, "Review of Gauthier's *Morals by Agreement*," *Philosophical Books*, 28 (1987),pp.130,133f. Cf. Gauthier, "Reply to Wolfram," p.133.

41 Sandel, p.3.

42 William Galston, "Defending Liberalism," *The American Political Science Review*, 76 (1982), p.625.

43 Wolfram, p.130.

44 The basic idea of the morally free zone was conceived by Gauthier's early article, "No Need for Morality: The Case of the Competitive Market," *Philosophic Exchange*, 3 (1982), pp.41-54.

45 Walter A. Weisskopf, "The Moral Predicament of the Market Economy," Gerald Dworkin, et al., eds., *Markets And Morals* (Washington: Hemisphere Publishing Corporation, 1977), p.36.

46 Sen, *On Ethics and Economics*, pp.4f. The methodology of so-called 'positive economics' represents the idea of social engineering in economics. Cf. Chapter II. n.71. For a comprehensive criticism of the value-free social engineering, see Norma Haan, et al., eds., *Social Science as Moral Inquiry* (New York: Columbia University Press, 1983). Another relevant book is John Lewis, *Max Weber & Value-Free Sociology: A Marxist Critique* (London: Lawrence And Wishart, 1975).

47 When we confine the normative issues to the free market, we can find the following important literature. Allen Buchanan, *Ethics, Efficiency, and the Market* (Totowa, New Jersey: Rowman & Allanheld, 1985); Richard B. McKenzie, *The Fairness of Markets: A Search for Justice in a Free Society* (Lexington, Massachusetts: Lexington Books, 1987); John W. Chapman and J. Roland Pennock, eds., *Markets And Justice, Nomos* 31 (New York: The University Press, 1989).

48 I have discussed the Pareto optimality in connection with Rawls' position. See Chapter III. n.61. 65.

49 Sen, "The Moral Standing of the Market," in *Ethics And Economics*, p.9. Also See, Coleman, "Market Contractarianism And the Unanimity Rule," in the same book, p.70. See n.2. In Coleman's article, the comprehensive

presuppositions of the market (including the other presuppositions not discussed in this sub-section) are listed: A sufficient number of buyers and sellers, etc. For a full discussion, see Joseph E. Stiglitz and G. Frank Mathewson, eds., *New Developments in the Analysis of Market Structure* (Cambridge: The MIT Press, 1986).

50 In view of Gauthier's' criticism of Buchanan, it is interesting to note that Buchanan himself makes this observation in "The Gauthier Enterprise," p.89. See n.16.

51 Smith, *The Wealth of Nations*, vol.II. bk.iv. ch.ix, p.208.

52 Daniel M. Hausman, "Are Markets Morally Free Zones?" *Philosophy and Public Affairs*, 18 (1989), p.319.

53 Peter Danielson, "The Visible Hand of Morality," *Canadian Journal of Philosophy*, 18 (1988), p.367.

54 I borrow the term from Theodor Adorno, *Minima Moralia* (London: New Left Books, 1974).

55 Traditionally neo-classical economics has been characterized as a "marginalist revolution." Neo-classic marginalism was first used in value theory as an alternative to the production theory of value in the classical theory (the value of a certain good as determined by its cost of production). This production theory of value was developed into the labor theory of value by Ricardo and Marx. In contrast, neo-classicists thought that it was the marginal utility of a good which would control the price offered by the customers and hence its value. For a detailed inquiry, see Richard D. Wolff and Stephen A. Resnick, *Economics: Marxian Versus Neoclassical* (Baltimore: The Johns Hopkins University Press, 1987).

56 For the Aristotelian concept of distributive justice, see Ch.III. n.46. Rawls criticizes the theory as a principle of distributive justice (TJ,p.308). For a comprehensive discussion (including historical one) of the theory as a principle of distributive justice, see Stephen T. Worland, "Economics and Justice," in Ronald L. Cohen, ed., *Justice: Views from the Social Sciences* (New York: Plenum Press, 1986), pp.47-84.

57 Karol Edward Soltan, *The Causal Theory of Justice* (Berkeley: University of California Press, 1987), p.148.

58 In short, the issues of moral freedom and pecuniary externalities are involved. See Hausman, pp.322,329. See n.52.

59 Scott Gordon, *Welfare, Justice, and Freedom* (New York: The Columbia University Press, 1980), p.97. Rawls also shows how the precept of contribution runs cross of the other precepts, ability, need, effort, training, experience, etc. in sec.47. "The precepts of Justice" in TJ.

60 For a helpful discussion of the failure in the political area, see Vincent Ostrom, "Why Governments Fail: An Inquiry into the Use of Instruments of Evil to Do Good," in James Buchanan and Robert Tollison, eds., *The Theory of Public Choice II* (Ann Arbor: The University of Michigan Press, 1984), pp.422-35. For the economic area, in connection with the market failure, see Tyler Cowen, *The Theory of Market Failure: A Critical Examination* (Fairfax, Va.: George Mason University Press, 1988).

61 Gauthier mentions (in MA. p.98. n.11) Gordon's book, *Welfare, Justice, and Freedom* (See n.58. in the text). In the book (pp.97-9), Gordon lists the five problems of the theory: (1) undetermined marginal productivity in case of a dynamic economy (introduction of a new technology and its resultant changes in demands and supplies) (2) interdependent production and the impossibility of calculating the exact marginal productivity (3) the unjustifiable prior assumption of initial factor endowment as given (4) the normative issue involved in the transition from non-personal resources (capital, land, facilities) to personal incomes (problems of private ownership) (5) economic rent from the scarcity of productive factor as a fortunate possessor of monopoly. Gauthier deals with problems (2), (3), (4), (5) in terms of the minimax relative concession, Lockean proviso, inheritance taxation, economic rent control respectively. However, Gauthier is not correct to think that problem (1) is a unique one for utilitarian welfare economics, but not for his theory. Cf. MA. pp.107-9. Problems (4), (5) will be discussed later in this subsection.

62 The basic conception of economic rent is easily understood according to the law of supply and demand explained in any elementary economic text book. Full explanation is as follows: "The recipient of rent benefits from the scarcity of the factors she controls — a scarcity which is of course entirely accidental from her standpoint, since it depends, not on the intrinsic nature of the factors, but on the relation between them and the factors controlled by others. She receives more than is needed to induce her to bring her factors to the market; rent is by definition a return over and above the cost of supply" (MA,p.98). In this regard, Gauthier criticizes Nozick's famous example, Wilt Chamberlain's entitlement to his total income $250,000 (AST,p.161). Gauthier claims that if his cost of supply (in economics this is defined as his opportunity cost, i.e., as the income he could have earned in the best alternative employment) is $100,000, his economic factor rent (total income - opportunity cost: $250,000 - $100,000) $150,000 must be taxed away (MA,p.275). Even though there are several technical problems concerning the determination of the opportunity cost, Gauthier's idea is clear. In this respect, he is on the side of Rawls (MA,p.277). For the technical problems and the possible disturbance of the market price system, see John C. Harsanyi, "Review of Gauthier's *Morals by Agreement*," *Economics and Philosophy*, 3 (1987), "5. The Market Economy and the Problem of Factor Rents," pp.345-8.

63 I have sufficiently investigated indeterminacy in my discussion of Rawls (Ch.III. n.65). Gauthier also emphasizes that "this [Pareto optimality] rule

assigns equal social welfare to all those outcomes among which any serious question of selection arises. ... Slavery is just in any society in which the slave owners could not be fully compensated for its abolition. It seems evident that the Pareto-extension rule is inadequate." See his "Justice as Social Choice," p.254.

64 The conceptions of optimality and equilibrium were made clear in the discussion of the paradoxes of rationality in Chapter II. The optimal equilibrium of the perfectly competitive market is the very antithesis of the PD (suboptimal equilibrium—since there is a chance that both prisoners can be better off). Gauthier makes exact definition of the two conceptions in MA,pp.65,76.

65 Gauthier,"Morality, Rational Choice, and Semantic Representation," p.203.

66 Gauthier, "Moral Artifice," p.413. The criticism is from Danielson's "The Visible Hand of Morality," p.372.

67 Gauthier, "Morality, Rational Choice, and Semantic Representation," pp.203f.

68 Hausman, "Are Markets Morally Free Zones," p.320.

69 Coleman distinguishes market contractarianism into the two. Thin market contractarianism grounds the rationality of political or moral association in the failure of perfect market competition. Thick market contractarianism sees the need for political or moral association in realizing the conditions of market success as well as in remedying market failure. See "Market Contractarianism and the Unanimity Rule," pp.69f. Also See n.2 of this chapter.

70 These are the state of nature/the laws of nature/the sovereign power for compliance; the original position/the two principles of justice/the congruence project between justice and goodness for the strict compliance respectively.

71 Gauthier, "Bargaining Our Way into Morality: A Do-It-Yourself Primer," p.26. n.5. The problem of acquisitive justice is to determine the baseline from which bargaining proceeds. Cf. Chapter III. n.29.

72 Gauthier explicitly points out that MRC is held "among several persons" (MA,p.137). This means that his bargaining model is an n-person bargain. In this regard, Gauthier makes the distinction between two-person and n-person models (MA,p.140). It is helpful to state the principle as an axiom and to give an example at this point. First, MRC is formalized in "the principle of minimum equal relative concession" in case of two-person model (MA,p.140). The principle requires the smallest equal concessions, measured relatively, from the bargainers' point of view (MA,p.140). This is the so-called Kalai-Smorodinsky solution (solution G) (MA,p.130,n.14.; cf. p.136). The formula (relative concession) in the text is directly related to the solution G. It can be restated as follows.

Table 10. Minimax Relative Concession as the Solution G

iniU: initial bargaining position utility
maxU: maximal claim utility
resU: resultant bargain point utility

- -

the absolute magnitude of expected concession: maxU-resU
the absolute magnitude of complete concession: maxU-iniU
the relative magnitude of concession: maxU-resU / maxU-iniU

- -

Solution G: for all i,j, equal relative concessions

$$[(maxUi-resUi)/(maxUi-iniUi)] = [(maxUj-resUj)/(maxUj-iniUj)]$$

Table 11. Monetary Illustration of the Solution G

Mable: investment fund $600
single non-cooperative expected gain $180

Abel: investment fund $400
single non-cooperative expected gain $80
cooperative fund $1000   cooperative surplus $500

Mable: iniU: base-point return $180
maxU: $420 ($500-$80: cooperative surplus
- Abel's iniU $80)

Abel: iniU: base-point return $80
maxU: $320 ($500-$180: cooperative surplus
- Mable's iniU)

If Mable gets $x, then Abel gets $500-$x. Their maximum concession is minimized when their two concession are equal.

$$\frac{\$420 - \$x}{\$420 - \$180} = \frac{\$320 - \$(500-x)}{\$320 - \$80}$$

Solving for x, we find that $x = $300; Mable receives a gain of $300 and Abel $200. This example comes from Gauthier's "Justice as Social Choice," p.261. However, as Gauthier admits, Roth demonstrates that MRC is not always the case with solution G in a n-person model (MA,p.140). Thus Gauthier finally formulates MRC as a modified Solution G (Solution G') as stated above. In other words, MRC as Solution G' is that the minimax relative concession made at the bargaining outcome must be less than the minimax relative concession made by any alternative outcomes in the bargaining region. I will not follow the complicated axiomatic formulation of solution G'.   See

Gauthier's "Bargaining and Justice," in Ellen Frankel Paul et al. eds., *Ethics and Economics* (Oxford:Basil Blackwell,1985), pp.36-7.

73   MRB is max{(resU-iniU)/(maxU-iniU)}. In this way, Gauthier's MRB is a bargaining version of Rawls' difference principle, which is derived from the maximin rule. Gauthier originally suggested MRB as "the proportionate difference principle" in "Justice and Natural Endowment," p.20. Cf. "Bargaining and Justice," p.40.

74   I do not mean that MRC/MRB is the unique representation of the marginal productive theory. In this connection, see the debate between Gauthier's MRC/MRB versus Hampton's "the principle of proportionality of contribution" which considers only the original proportional contribution, but does not consider the maxU of MRC. Gauthier points out that "we [Gauthier and Hampton] can agree that distribution will be based on marginal product where this [MRC] is defined. But then we disagree." See Gauthier, "Moral Artifice," p.398.; Jean Hampton, "Can We Agree on Morals?," p.335.

75   The Nash solution is more exactly the Zeuthen-Nash-Harsanyi solution (MA,p.147). The solution is formally expressed as max {(resUi - iniUi) x (resUj - iniUj)}. This means that the solution is to maximize the products of each bargainer's expected excess utility over the initial bargaining position. Gauthier criticizes the solution not only from rationality but also from fairness. The argument from fairness is that the solution cannot avoid the threat advantages from those who have a better initial bargaining position (MA,pp.199f). I have already showed what kind of problem the Nash solution has in connection with the contractarian dilemma. See previous section n.10. Another good observation is from Jon Elster, *The Cement of Society: A Study of Social Order* (Cambridge: Cambridge University Press, 1989), Chap.II. Bargaining, p.57.

> From a normative point of view, this solution [Nash Solution] has no special appeal. ... Indeed, it might appear positively unattractive, because of the following property. If we assume that a poor man and a rich man are bargaining over the way to divide some amount of money large enough to be very important to the poor man, the Nash solution will assign most of it to the rich man, because he can more credibly make a proposal favorable to himself and say, 'Take it or leave it'.

76   For Harsanyi's rejoinder to Gauthier, see his "Review of Gauthier's *Morals by Agreement*," p.344 (see n.62 of the text). Harsanyi still thinks that "Nash's model has much better properties from a game-theoretic point of view." For an advanced treatment of the bargaining problem debate, see William Thomson and Terje Lensberg, *Axiomatic Theory of Bargaining With a Variable Number of Agents* (Cambridge: Cambridge University Press, 1989); Alvin E. Roth, ed., *Game-Theoretic Models of Bargaining* (Cambridge: Cambridge University Press, 1985). In connection with Arrow's Impossibility Theorem, see Arrow's, Gauthier's and others' articles in the symposium on "Equality and Justice in a Democratic Society," *Philosophia*, 7 (1978).

Especially see Gauthier, "Social Choice and Distributive Justice," pp.239-53; Arrow, "Extended Sympathy and the Possibility of Social Choice," pp.223-238.

77   Cf. John Roemer, "The Mismarriage of Bargaining Theory and Distributive Justice," *Ethics*, 97 (1986), p.90.

78   Brian Barry, *Theories of Justice* (Berkeley: University of California Press, 1989), p.388.

79   Gauthier says that "if someone were to press a claim to what would be brought about by the co-operative interaction of others, then those others would prefer to exclude him from agreement" (MA,p.134).

80   Barry, *Theories of Justice*, p.252. Also see, David Braybrooke, "The Maximum Claims of Gauthier's Bargainers: Are the Fixed Social Inequalities Acceptable?" *Dialogue*, 21 (1982), pp.411-429; cf. Gauthier, "Justified Inequality?" *Dialogue*, 21 (1982), pp.431-43; Braybrooke, "Inequalities Not Conceded Yet: A Rejoinder to Gauthier's Reply," pp.445-48.

81   See n.73.

82   Rawls, "The Basic Structure as Subject," in A. I. Goldman and Jaekwon Kim, eds., *Values and Morals* (Dordrecht: D. Reidel Publishing co., 1978), p.62.

83   Ibid.

84   In view of Gauthier's mention of the exclusion point in bargaining (n.79), MRC/MRB seems to imply a bargaining coalition. In case of the n-person model, if we admit exclusion and coalition, MRC/MRB is inapplicable. Gauthier admits that "MRC needs refinement." Because of the possibilities of coalition "the application of MRC to multi-person interactions ... raises a problem of determining the appropriate cooperative infrastructure" ("Moral Artifice," pp.339,397). Another crucial issue concerns immorality of sub-group trust or coalition. According to MRC, those acts are perfectly rational. However, in view of the whole community including consumers group, those acts are rational but immoral. Cf. Larry May, *The Morality of Groups: Collective Responsibility, Group-Based Harm, and Corporate Rights* (Notre Dame: The University of Notre Dame Press, 1987). Gauthier admits that "I do not attempt to deal with the relation between macrolevel fulfillment of MRC and microlevel principles for interaction." "Moral Artifice," p.390. Gauthier tries to meet the problem in "Morality, Rational Choice, and Semantic Representation." However, I do not think his argument is convincing since if he introduces the constraint (disutility) from the anti-trust law to bargaining, this means that the introduction puts the collective or community utility before individual utilities of individual bargainers (the sole foundation of his bargaining model).

> Bargaining ... gives rise to co-operative interaction but is itself non-co-operative. This distinction is *of great importance* ... for ... in co-operating persons must at times constrain their utility-maximization

behavior, but in bargaining itself persons accept no such constraint (MA,p.129. Emphasis mine).

85 See n.10, n.75.

86 Hobbes says that "The Nature hath made men so equall, in the faculties of body, and mind. ... For as to the strength of body, the weakest has strength enough to kill the strongest, either by secret machination, or by confederacy with others, that are in the same danger with himselfe" (LE,13,p.183). Cf. Chapter III. A.2.

87 Kraus and Coleman, "Morality and the Theory of Rational Choice," pp.747-8. Cf. Jan Narveson, "Review of Gauthier's *Morals By Agreement,*" *Canadian Philosophical Review,* 7 (1987), pp.271-2.

88 Elster classifies the cost of bargaining as the inefficiency of bargaining into the following categories: The cost of bargaining failures, the cost of preparing for bargaining, the cost of conducting bargaining, the cost of decentralized bargaining. See his *The Cement of Society,* pp.94-6.

89 Gauthier, "Morality, Rational Choice, and Semantic Representation," p.177.

90 Ibid., p.179.

91 For a comprehensive treatment of the question, see Kai Nielsen, *Why Be Moral?* (Buffalo, NY: Prometheus Books, 1989).

92 Gauthier, "Three against Justice: The Foole, the Sensible Knave, and the Lydian Shepherd," in Peter A. French, Theodore E. Uehling, JR., and Howard K. Wettstein, eds., *Social and Political Theory,* vol. vii. *Midwest Studies in Philosophy* (Minneapolis: University of Minnesota Press, 1982), pp.11-29. I treated the Foole from *Leviathan* and the Shepherd from *Republic* in Chapter III. Section A and B. The Sensible Knave is from Hume's *An Enquiry concerning the Principles of Morals* in Selby-Bigge ed., *Enquiries concerning Human Understanding and concerning the Principles of Morals* (Oxford: Clarendon Press, 3rd ed. 1975), pp.282-3. Hume says about the Knave: "That *honesty is the best policy,* may be a good general rule, but is liable to many exceptions; and he, it may perhaps be thought, conducts himself with most wisdom, who observes the general rule, and takes advantages of all the exceptions." Gauthier's main idea in "Three against Justice" is repeated in MA,pp.163, 182, and especially in Ch.X. "The Ring of Gyges."

93 David Copp, "Introduction," in *Morality, Reason and Truth,* p.14. For the observation that the possible audience for the rational compliance project is moral skeptics, see Gregory S. Kavka, "The Reconciliation Project," in the same book, p.297. And also see Sumner, "Justice Contracted," p.523. For a general treatment of moral skepticism, see Renford Bambrough, *Moral Scepticism and Moral Knowledge* (London: Routledge & Kegan Paul, 1979); Panayot Butchvarov, *Skepticism in Ethics* (Bloomington: Indiana University Press, 1989).

94 Sobel, "The Need for Coercion," p.148. See Chapter III. n.23,43. For another helpful general discussion, see Alan Wertheimer, *Coercion* (Princeton: Princeton University Press, 1988).

95 See Chapter III. B.3. Rawls might have to try the transformation project since "egoism is logically consistent and in this sense not irrational" (TJ,p.136).

96 Gauthier, "Economic Rationality and Moral Constraints," in Peter A. French, Theodore E. Uehling, Jr., and Howard K. Wettstein, eds., *Studies in Ethical Theory*, vol.iii. *Midwest Studies in Philosophy* (Minneapolis: University of Minnesota, 1980), p.91. The thrust of rational compliance was initiated from his "Reason and Maximization," *Canadian Journal of Philosophy*, 4 (1975), p.430, as follows:

> Hence a rational person who begins by adopting the policy of individual utility-maximization, in accordance with the condition of straightforward maximization, will, following that policy, choose a different conception of rationality, and will prefer a policy which requires agreed optimization whenever possible, to his original policy, and possibly to any alternative policy."

97 Even though I pointed out that instrumental self-interest maximization conception of rationality is not the unique rationality of egoist, it is thinkable that the conception may appeal to egoistic rationality. Cf. Chapter II. A.2. and n.95 above. Also cf. Gauthier, "The Impossibility of Rational Egoism," *The Journal of Philosophy*, 71 (1974), pp.439-56; The Irrationality of Choosing Egoism," *Canadian Journal of Philosophy*, 10 (1980), pp.179-87.

98 For an instructive discussion of Gauthier's modifications of the standard conception of rationality, see Joseph Mendola, "Gauthier's *Morals by Agreement* and Two Kinds of Rationality," *Ethics*, 97 (1987), pp.766-7.

99 Richmond Campbell, "Critical Study: Gauthier's Theory of Morals by Agreement," *The Philosophical Quarterly*, 38 (1989), p.349. In connection with Hobbes, see Chapter III. n.21.

100 Ibid., p.350.

101 Gauthier, "Reply to Wolfram," p.135.

102 Derek Parfit, *Reasons and Persons*, pp.18-19. Here, Parfit criticizes Gauthier's transparency assumption employed in "Reason and Maximization." See n.96.

103 Gauthier, "Reply to Wolfram," pp.135-6.

104 At this juncture, Gauthier employs a most complicated calculation of expected utility maximization. I interpret its gist as follows (MA,pp.175-7).

Table 12. The Probabilistic Calculation of the expected utility of Rational Compliance

---

probability

    p: the probability of CMs' mutual recognition and cooperation

    q: the probability of CMs' failure of recognition of SMs and its resultant exploitation of CMs by SMs.

    r: the probability of randomly chosen member as a CM

expected utility

    defection: 1   cooperation: 2/3
    non-cooperation: 1/3   being exploited: 0

            expected utility of rational compliance

$$p/q > (r+1)/r$$

According to Gauthier's long chain of calculation, the expected utility of being a CM is higher than the expected utility of being a SM just in the above case. Relying on this calculation, Gauthier concludes (MA,p.177):

> Suppose a population evenly divided between [CMs] and [SMs]. If the [CMs] are able to cooperate successfully in two-thirds of their encounters, and to avoid being exploited by [SMs] by in four-fifths of their encounters, then [CMs] may expect to do better than their fellows. ... [I]t will be rational for the [SMs] to change their disposition. These persons are sufficiently translucent for them to find morality rational.

If I put what Gauthier says into the above formula, since p is 2/3 (CMs' cooperation), r is 1/2 (evenly divided population), q is 1/5 (avoid being exploited by 4/5 of SMs), 2/3 / 1/5 > (1/2 + 1) / 1/2. Thus 10/3 > 6/2. However, Gauthier's demonstration depends on the arbitrary presuppositions of p/q and r. First, if CMs are conditionally disposed, the mere determination or givenness of r does not make sense. As Nelson correctly points out, "Why is the case that when some agent decides whether to be a CM or a SM he can take a value of r as given?" See Nelson, "Economic Rationality and Morality," p.158. n.11. I will employ this idea to show a circularity of Gauthier's rational compliance in the text shortly. Second, how are the values of p and q determined? In order to demonstrate that the expected utility of CMs is higher than that of SMs, Gauthier must show that it is the case that p increases and q decreases. Gauthier himself acknowledges this problem (MA,pp.180-1). At this point, Gauthier has to resort to the "sufficient translucency," a condition which puts a heavy epistemic burden on CMs. He adds: "what is actually irrational is the failure to cultivate or exercise the ability to detect other's sincerity or insincerity" (MA,p.181). Nelson again envisages that Gauthier's world of CMs is that of Nathaniel Hawthorne's *The Scarlet Letter*, in which a scarlet A is worn (in case of Gauthier, it is thinly veiled—not transparent but sufficiently translucent) as a punitive mark of adultery. See Nelson, pp.155, 159.

105   Gauthier, "Moral Artifice," p.402.

106   Duncan MacIntosh, "Two Gauthiers?" *Dialogue*, 28 (1989), p.48.

107   They are: occurrent versus dispositional actions; current-time-slice actions and dispositional actions in continuous time; disposition formation procedures of internalization and socialization; disposition and moral freedom, education, and inculcation; psychological control over dispositions, etc. As far as I know, the most comprehensive treatment is Ramio Tuomela, ed., *Dispositions* (Dordrecht: D. Reidel Publishing Company, 1978). When we confine the various issues to Gauthier's case, the following articles are helpful. Paul Weirich, "Hierarchical Maximization of Two Kinds of Expected Utility," *Philosophy of Science*, 55 (1985),pp.562-82; Duncan MacIntosh, "Libertarian Agency and Rational Morality: Action-Theoretic Objections to Gauthier's Dispositional Solution of the Compliance Problem," *The Southern Journal of Philosophy*, 26 (1988),pp.499-525; Jordan Howard Sobel, "Maximizing, Optimizing, and Prospering," *Dialogue*, 27 (1988),pp.233-62; Richmond Campbell, "Moral Justification and Freedom," *The Journal of Philosophy*, 85 (1988),pp.192-213; Laurence Thomas, "Ethical Egoism and psychological Dispositions," *American Philosophical Quarterly*, 17 (1980),pp.73-78.

108   Aristotle, *The Nicomachean Ethics*,1106a5-7: "but in respect of the virtues and the vices we are said not to be moved but to be disposed in a particular way."; Hobbes (LE,28,p.353): "Punishment is ... to the end that the will of men may thereby the better be disposed to obedience."; Dewey, *Theory of the Moral Life* (New Delhi: Wiley Eastern Private Limited, 1967; original ed., 1932),p.8: "the first business of moral theory is to obtain in outline an idea of the factors which constitute personal disposition. ... The formula was well stated by Aristotle."; Rawls, TJ,p.567: "It remains to be shown that this disposition to take up and to be guided by the standpoint of justice accords with the individual's good." Contemporary neo-Aristotelian communitarians, like MacIntyre and Williams, strongly resort to the dispositional solution. MacIntyre, *After Virtue*, p.244: "For since a virtue is now generally understood as a disposition or sentiment which will produce in us obedience to certain rules, agreement on what the relevant rules are to be is always a prerequisite for agreement upon the nature and content of a particular virtue. But this prior agreement in rules is ... something which our individualistic culture is unable to secure."; Bernard Williams, *Ethics and the Limits of Philosophy* (Cambridge: Harvard University Press,1985), pp.51,53: "we may ask the question 'what has to exist in the world for that ethical point of view to exist?' The answer can only be, 'people's dispositions.' There is a sense in which they are the ultimate supports of ethical value. ... The preservation of ethical value lies in the reproduction of ethical dispositions."

In p.53, "No one has yet found a good way of doing without those [Aristotelian] assumptions."

109 Another related issue is the distinction between levels of choices, viz., particular action versus disposition, which bears a close parallel to an issue much discussed in recent years by moral theorists, viz., the issue of act versus rule utilitarianism. For a brief explanation of the parallel, see McClennen, "Rational Choice and Public Policy," p.369; Goldman, *Moral Knowledge*, p.46. For a general introduction to the utilitarian debate, see Michael D. Bayles, ed., *Contemporary Utilitarianism* (New York: Anchor Books, 1968). Gauthier and Harsanyi have something to do with this debate. See, Gauthier, "Rule-Utilitarianism and Randomization," *Analysis*, 25 (1964-5),pp.68-9; Harsanyi, "Rule Utilitarianism and Decision Theory," in Hans W. Gottinger and Werner Leinfellner, eds., *Decision Theory and Social Ethics* (Dordrecht: D. Reidel Publishing Co., 1978), pp.3-31.

110 Campbell, "Critical Study: Gauthier's Theory of Morals by Agreement," p.349.

111 Campbell and Sowden, *Paradoxes of Rationality and Cooperation*, p.40.

112 Tit for tat strategy is to repeat the other partner's previous move. In this sense, tit for tat is more cautious and less cooperative than Gauthier's conditional compliance. This strategy comes from Axelrod, see Chapter III. n.21. Also see, Peter Danielson, "The Moral and Ethical Significance of Tit for Tat," *Dialogue*, 15 (1986),pp.449-470. Gauthier himself presents a comparative discussion. See his "Moral Artifice," pp.399-402.

113 Richmond and Sowden, p.18. See Table 12.

114 Goldman, *Moral Knowledge*, p.46

115 In order to assess whether Gauthier's solution to PD is a real solution, a series of highly technical discussions is needed. See Campbell and Sowden, pp.1-41. Also see, Martin Shubik, "Game Theory, Behavior, and the Paradoxes of the Prisoner's Dilemma: Three Solutions," *The Journal of Conflict Resolution*, 14 (1970), pp.181-93; David M. Kreps et al., "Rational Cooperation in the Finitely Repeated Prisoners' Dilemma," *Journal of Economic Theory*, 17 (1982), pp.245-52.

116 Cf. n.104. For FR problem in the mass society, see Anthony de Jasay, *Social Contract, Free Ride: A Study of the Public Goods Problem* (Oxford: Clarendon Press, 1989), p.64.

117 Cf. Campbell, "Moral Justification and Freedom," p.178; "Critical Study: Gauthier's Theory of Morals by Agreement," pp.350-1. In the latter, he suggests a way out. But I do not think his suggestion (something like "red nose" property of CM) is convincing. Cf. also Nelson's charge of circularity (n.104).

118 Hume, *A Treatise of Human Nature*, bk.III, pt.ii, sec.7, p.542.

119   Martin Heidegger, *Being and Time*, trans. John Macquarrie and Edward
       Robinson (New York: Haper & Row, 1962), p.237. To probe whether the
       original terms of Heidegger's imply ethical meaning is interesting, but this is
       not my concern.   For Heidegger's view on ethics, see his "Letters on
       Humanism," in *Martin Heidegger: Basic Writings*, ed. David Farrell Krell
       (New York: Haper & Row, 1977).

120   The thin market contractarianism aims to be only a remedy for market
       failure. I have adopted the distinction from Coleman. See n.69 of the
       previous section.

121   Besides the proviso, Gauthier's argument for the distribution of economic
       factor rent (see n.62) is midway between Rawls (asset collectivism) and
       Nozick (libertarian asset individualism).

122   Gauthier, "Justice as Social Choice," p.267. I cannot deal with the many
       intricate issues of the doctrine of natural rights in detail. See Rex Martin and
       James W. Nickel, "Recent Work on the Concept of Rights," in K.G. Lucey &
       Tibor R. Machan, eds., *Recent Work in Philosophy* (Totowa: Rowman and
       Allanheld, 1983), pp.205-225; Tibor Machan, "Some Recent Work in
       Human Rights Theory," *American Philosophical Quarterly*, 17 (1980),
       pp.103-115.   In connection with the natural law theory (especially the so-
       called Grisez-Finnis revolution), see Russell Hittinger, *A Critique of the New
       Natural Law Theory* (Notre Dame: University of Notre Dame Press, 1987).

123   For a helpful comment on this point, see Alan Nelson, "Economic Rationality
       and Morality," pp.162f.

124   Cf. Richard J. Arneson, "Locke versus Hobbes in Gauthier's Ethics," *Inquiry*,
       30 (1987), pp.295-316.

125   In case of Nozick, see n.122. Against Locke, Gauthier explicitly points out
       that "How is Locke able to show that I have a right to my body and its
       powers, except by presupposing it and so begging the question of establishing
       a rational and impartial bargaining position?" (MA,p.202). Against natural
       rights theory, Gauthier also clearly indicates that his theory of property right
       is "not inherent in human nature" and that it does not "afford each individual
       an inherent moral status in relation to her fellows" (MA,p.222). With the
       help of Macpherson's comment, I have investigated Hobbes and Locke in
       connection with natural rights theory.   See Chapter III, n.14.   For a
       comprehensive discussion on the related issues, see Ellen Frankel Paul, "Of
       the Social Contract within the Natural Rights Traditions," *The Personalist*, 59
       (1978), pp.9-21; Ian Shapiro, *The Evolution of Rights in Liberal Theory*
       (Cambridge: Cambridge University Press, 1986).

126   Cf. n.55. for the labor theory of value. For a helpful discussion of Locke's
       state of nature concerning the property rights, see A. John Simmons,
       "Locke's State of Nature," *Political Theory*," 17 (1989), pp.449-70.

127   Nozick uses the proviso for justifying "the original acquisition of holding".
       See Chapter III. B. 3. Husain Sarkar criticizes Nozick that the proviso does

not dovetail with his theory of entitlement, but this is not my concern here. See "The Lockean Proviso," *Canadian Journal of Philosophy*, 12 (1982), pp.47-59.

128 "Each person's endowment includes whatever he acquires without worsening the situation of his fellows" (MA,p.203). When we relate Gauthier's proviso with his market contractarianism, he just excludes the market failure situation (presence of externalities: free-riders and parasites). "The absence of externalities" is among the presuppositions of the perfectly competitive market. See Section A.3. However, he is still in the thin level since, in order to arrive at the thick level, he should have to establish the principle of property rights.

129 Additional distinctions can be made here. Gauthier says that "Were I, for whatever reason, completely incapable of doing anything to help you, then I should not have bettered your situation, but I should not have failed to better it" (MA,p.204).

130 Baier raises a question whether eating one's own children violates the proviso. In my absence, they would not have been born. Thus eating one's own children (their non-existence) does not worsen their situation in my absence (their non-existence). If we consider the accompanying pains of the children and biological affective bond, Baier's objection might lose its point. However, Gauthier's individual maximizers do not have affective or (total) utilitarian considerations in their minds. See Annette C. Baier, "Pilgrim's Progress," *Canadian Journal of Philosophy*, 18 (1988), pp.318-322. Gauthier seems to admit Baier's objection from the logical point of view, but he answers her that "it [the proviso] constrains interaction only with a view to cooperation, and Baier's cannibals have no reason to envisage cooperation." in "Moral Artifice," p.404. Donald C. Hubin and Mark B. Lambeth raise a similar objection (parents' sexual abuse of their own children) along with the distinction between absolute non-existence and momentary absence. See their "Providing for Rights," *Dialogue*, 27 (1988), p.492.

131 See Section A.3. in connection with the free market activity.

132 Gauthier's claim is that although the polluting person worsens fisherfolk in view of the absence test (what fisherfolk can expect in the absence of the person), he does not better his own situation through interaction with the fisherfolk. In other words, he is no better off than he would be were no one to live downstream from him.

133 The natural human being in the first two steps emerges as "potential partners in social relationship" in this step (MA,p.214).

134 Since Macpherson's *The Political Theory of Possessive Individualism*, social contract theory has been branded with the label "possessive individualism" (cf. Chapter I, n.60). Marx himself used the term "private property" in the passage that "*communism* is the positive expression of the abolition of private property." *The Economic and Philosophical Manuscripts* in *Early Writings*, p.152. In *The Communist Manifesto*, he also declared that "the theory of the

communists may be summed up in the single sentence: Abolition of private property." *Marx and Engels: Basic Writings on Politics & Philosophy*, Lewis S. Feuer, ed. (New York: Anchor Books, 1959), p.21. However, it is noteworthy that Marx did not want to abolish "personal property" that resulted from one's labor. See *Manifesto*, p.22: "personal property is not thereby transformed into social property." By private property, Marx meant bourgeois capital as the means of production. Thus perhaps Marx's possible objection to Gauthier is confined to the partial bourgeois aspect of this last step.

135 Cf. Chapter III. A.2. As Jan Narveson indicates, Gauthier attempts to "resuscitate Lockean natural rights on an essentially Hobbesian basis." "McDonald and McDougal, Pride and Gain, and Justice," *Dialogue*, 27 (1988), p.504. For a very helpful comment on the related issue, see A. Zaitchik, "Hobbes's Reply to the Fool," *Political Theory*, 10 (1982), pp.245-66; Gregory Kavka, "Hobbes's War of All against All," *Ethics*, 93 (1983), pp.291-310.

136 I have discussed the conditional compliance in the previous subsection.

137 Gauthier, "Morality, Rational choice, and Semantic Representation," p.200.

138 Cf. Chapter I. n.2; II. n.9; III. n.49.

139 In this regard, J.H. Bogart asserts that "we have no reason to prefer ideas tied to abundance of resources to ideas tied to scarcity of resources" in "Lockean Provisos and State of Nature Theories," *Ethics*, 95 (1985), p.836. For a comprehensive treatment on this issue, see Guido Calabresi and Philip Bobbitt, *Tragic Choices: The Conflicts Society Confronts in the Allocation of Tragically Scarce Resources* (New York: W.W. Norton & Company: 1978); Gus Tyler, *Scarcity* (New York: Quadrangle/The New York Times Book Co., 1976). I am not overlooking the fact that Gauthier himself worries about this problem: "There cannot be enough of what is scarce, so that if one takes sufficient for himself, what is left for others is not as good. This literalistic reading of Locke's proviso would simply fail to define persons for the purposes of bargaining—or market" (MA,p.202f). However, I still do not know what the non-literalistic reading is. Perhaps, it means the following (MA,p.217):

> We may assume that Eve, who first takes land for her exclusive use, will take the best portion; no other person is then able to make an equally advantageous appropriation. Eve does not leave her fellow 'as good' to appropriate, although in taking for herself she leaves them as well off, and indeed better off, than before. The proviso ensures that at every stage in interaction, each person is left as much as she could expect from the previous stage.

This non-literalistic reading of the proviso seems to resort to the actual utility maximization of those who did not appropriate before and after Eve's appropriation. In other words, the proviso eventually appeals to the welfare of the disadvantaged non-appropriator. If this is the case, I do not see any difference between Gauthier and Rawls. But, as we have seen, Gauthier criticizes Rawls that his proviso licenses free riding of the least advantaged persons. Then the difference is only that Rawls introduces the proviso of the difference principle from the beginning, whereas Gauthier still sticks to the fading invisible hand to "promote an end which was no part of her intention" (MA,p.217).

140 Hubin and Lambeth, "Providing for Rights," p.491.

141 Ibid., p.493.

142 Cf. n.122, n.125. Also cf. Andrew Reeve, *Property* (Atlantic Highlands: Humanities Press International, 1986). Henry Veatch, *Human Rights: Fact or Fancy?* (Baton Rouge: Louisiana, 1985). For a commentary on the latter, see Fred D. Miller Jr. and Patrick Steinbauer, "A New Defense of Natural Rights," *Humane Studies Review*, 4 (1987), pp.3-6.

143 For a good comment, see Lloyd A. Fallers, *Inequality: Social Stratification Reconsidered* (Chicago: University of Chicago Press, 1973); ch.3. "A Note on the 'Trickle Effect'." Also see, Henry Shue, "The Current Fashions: Trickle-Downs by Arrow and Close-Knits by Rawls," *The Journal of Philosophy*," 71 (1974), pp.319-27.

144 Marx mentions the history in *Capital*, vol.I. (New York: International Publishers, 1967; 1987 printing. Original ed., 1867), p.667. The theological concept of original sin tells us how Adam came to be condemned to work for his bread by the sweat of his brow. History takes this idea as economic discrimination. The diligent and frugal man prospers whereas the lazy and prodigal one falls into poverty. Max Weber fully embraced the concept in *The Protestant Ethics and the Spirit of Capitalism*, trans. Talcott Parsons (London: Unwin Paperbacks, 1985; original ed., 1904-5). Also see J.M. Keynes, *The Economic Consequences of the Peace* (London: Macmillan, 1919).

145 R. Hofstadter, *Social Darwinism in American Thought* (Boston: Beacon Press, 1955). I have mentioned Gauthier's conception of rationality in relation to evolutionary sociobiology in Chapter II. C.2.

146 Detailed discussion of all of them is beyond the scope of this study. In recent times, a vast literature deals with Marx's theory of justice. For a helpful guide, Norman Geras, "The Controversy about Marx and Justice," *New Left Review*," pp.46-85; N. Scott Arnold, "Recent Work on Marx," *American Philosophical Quarterly*, 24 (1987), pp.277-293.

147 Marx, *Capital*, vol.I, p.667.

148 Ibid., p.668.

149 Ibid. This double sense relates to Marx's distinction between political and human emancipation in *On the Jewish Question*, p.8. Cf. n.59 of Chapter I.

150   *Capital*, vol.I, p.668.

151   Ibid, p.667.

152   Unfortunately even this is not all true since Marx as well as Weber point out the following in *Capital*, vol.I., p.711. and in *General Economic History* (New Brunswick: Transaction Books, 1981), p.82. respectively.

> Whilst the cotton industry introduced child-slavery in England, it gave in the United States a stimulus to the transformation of the earlier, more or less patriarchal slavery, into a system of commercial exploitation. In fact, the veiled slavery of the wage-workers in Europe needed, for its pedestal, slavery pure and simple in the new world.

> The mechanical utilization of the product led to entirely opposite effects in Europe and America. In the former, cotton gave the impulse to the organization of a free labour force, the first factories developing in Lancashire in English, while in America the result was slavery.

> I am here indebted to Robert Miles, *Capitalism And Unfree Labour: Anomaly or Necessity?* (London: Tavistock Publications, 1987), "Introduction."

153   Cf. A.3. in context of marginal productive theory.

154   See Chapter I. n.59.

155   I think Gauthier's following criticism can be addressed to Marx himself. He says: "The effect of subordinating the market to some form of political control is typically to reintroduce violations of the proviso and to run roughshod over fairness in the terms of co-operation, as the so-called socialist societies of the Eastern bloc bear eloquent witness" (MA,p.270). Nonetheless, Gauthier mentions that "the appearance of market exploitation may be brought about ... by non-market features of society ... such as the initial distribution of factors, taken as given in market interaction. And this may help to explain why the Marxist argument has convinced so many people, even though it is in fact incoherent and misdirected" (MA,p.112). In view of this, his criticism of Marx's vision as utopia is not so helpful (MA,p.334). Rather Gauthier must provide a better argument against Marx's secret of primitive accumulation. For Gauthier's other criticisms of Marx, see MA, pp.89,110,260,334. and also "The Social Contract as Ideology," pp.161-2.

156   In the Austrian economic tradition (Böhm-Bawerk, Mises, Hayek are classified into this tradition), the Marxist project of suppressing market institutions is condemned as leading to calculational chaos and to a system in which capital and labor alike are subject to political exploitation. See John Gray, *Liberalisms: Essays in Political Philosophy* (London: Routledge, 1989), p.161. For a helpful discussion, see Israel M. Kirzner, "Some Ethical Implications for Capitalism of the Socialist Calculation Debate," Ellen Frankel Paul et al, eds., *Capitalism* (Oxford: Basil Blackwell, 1989), pp.165-

182; David Gordon, *Critics of Marxism* (New Brunswick: Transaction Books, 1986).

157 Cf. James P. Sterba, "A Marxist Dilemma for Social Contract Theory," *American Philosophical Quarterly*, 19 (1982), pp.51-59; Cf. Chapter II, n.97, and n.166 of this chapter.

158 For market socialism, see Oskar Lange and Fred M. Taylor, ed. with an Introduction by Benjamin E. Lippincott, *On the Economic Theory of Socialism* (New york: McGraw-Hill Book Co., 1964). And for the critical debate, see Ernest Mandel, "The Myth of Market Socialism," *New Left Review*, 169 (1988), pp.108-120; David Miller, "Marx, Communism, and Markets," *Political Theory*, 15 (1987), pp.182-204. Cf. TJ,p.273.

159 Gauthier, "Social Choice and Distributive Justice," p.239.

160 For the two principles, see Chapter III. B.3.

161 Macpherson, *Democratic Theory*, p.235. I have already mentioned this point in Chapter III, n.14.

162 Macpherson, *The Political Theory of Possessive Individualism*, p.221.

163 Ibid., pp.203-223.

164 Macpherson, *Democratic Theory*, p.232.

165 Ibid.

166 Ibid., p.237. For a good critical discussion, see William Leiss, *C.B. Macpherson: Dilemmas of Liberalism and Socialism* (New York: St. Martins' Press, 1988).

167 Gauthier, "The Social Contract as Ideology," also "Justice and Natural Endowment: Toward a Critique of Rawls' Ideological Framework."

168 John E. Roemer, *Free to Lose: An Introduction to Marxist Economic Philosophy* (Cambridge: Harvard University Press, 1988).

169 Gauthier, "Morality, Rational Choice, And Semantic Representation," p.202.

170 Concerning the dispute on compensation for natural interactional costs, "[a]ppeal to the proviso would beg the question, since we are seeking its rationale" (MA,p.224).

171 Kraus and Coleman, "Morality and Rational Choice," p.745.

172 Gauthier explicitly mentions that "[a]cceptance by workers and women of the contractarian view of human beings would lead to their refusal to remain excluded from truly human, appropriative activity." in "The Social Contract as Ideology," p.163. Gauthier's position is tricky. Even though he believes that contractarianism as ideology is descriptively plausible, he tries to "undermine its normative plausibility as ideologically effective." Ibid., p.130. The latter means that he aims at a normative transformation of the

Hobbesian radical contractarianism and standard maximizing conception of rationality into the Lockean proviso and constrained maximization.

173   Virginia Held, "Non-Contractual Society," in *Science, Morality, and Feminist Theory*, Marsh Hanen and Kai Nielsen, eds., *Canadian Journal of Philosophy*, 13, suppl. (1987), pp.111-38; Annette Baier, "Trust and Antitrust," *Ethics*, 96 (1986), pp.231-260. Especially see a section, "The Male Fixation on Contract."

174   It is interesting to note that Canadian scholars—McLuhan, Grant— mainly make this point. Especially see George Grant, *Technology and Empire* (Toronto: Anansi, 1969); *Technology & Justice* (Notre Dame: University of Notre Dame Press, 1986). Cf. Gauthier's review of the latter, "George Grant's Justice," *Dialogue*, 27 (1988), pp.121-134. For a general introduction to technology, see Ian G. Barbour, *Technology, Environment, and Human Values* (New York: Praeger, 1980). Especially see Ch.III. Technology as Liberator, as Threat, and as Instrument of Power.

175   Don Herzog, *Happy Slaves*: *A Critique of Consent Theory* (Chicago: The University of Chicago Press, 1989). Cf. Louis Dumont, *Homo Hierarchicus*: *The Caste System and Its Implications*, trans. Mark Sainsbury (London: Weidenfeld and Nicolson, 1970).

176   American Marxist Joseph Gillman proposes a complex of the four laws of motion of capitalism—increasing concentration and centralization of capital, increasing severity of economic cyclical crises, increasing misery of the working class, and a falling rate of profit in his *The Falling Rate of Profit: Marx's Law and Its Significance to Twentieth Century Capitalism* (New York: Cameron Associates, 1985). Marx himself did not propose exactly these four laws. In *Economic and Philosophical Manuscripts* (in *Early Writings*, pp.123-4), he mentions six "laws of political economy" for tendencies of the alienation of the worker. He also mentions the four general laws of capital accumulation, including the famous "Industrial Reserved Army," in ch.25 of *Capital*, vol.I. In vol.III, pt.iii, he proposes "the Law of the Tendency of the Rate of Profit to Fall." I am not claiming here that these laws of motion of capitalism are all correct. See George Catephores, *An Introduction to Marxist Economics* (New York: New York University Press, 1989).

177   Gauthier, "Morality, Rational Choice, and Semantic Representation," p.201.

178   Elsewhere, Gauthier takes this issue very seriously. See "The Social Contract," where "the scope of contract" is discussed. (pp.61-63). Rawls indicates that *A Theory of Justice* "would not cover ... our relations to other living things and to the natural order itself." "The Domain of the Political and Overlapping Consensus," *The New York University Law Review*, 64 (1989), p.248.

179   However, Gauthier elsewhere expects the fit: "many of our actual moral principles and practices are in effect applications of the requirements of [MRC] to particular contexts"—"promise-keeping, truth-telling, fair dealing" (MA,p.156).

180 Louis Althusser, "Ideology and Ideological State Apparatuses," trans. Ben Brewster in *Lenin and Philosophy and Other Essays* (London: Monthly Review Press, 1971), p.162. For an instructive comment, see Quentin Skinner, ed., *The Return of Grand Theory in the Human Sciences* (Cambridge: Cambridge University Press, 1985), "8. Louis Althusser" by Susan James.

181 Sumner, "Justice Contracted," p.538.

182 "[T]he idea of morals by agreement may mislead, if it is supposed that rights must be the product or outcome of agreement. Were we to adopt this account, we should suppose that rights were determined by the principle of [MRC]. ... They are what each person brings to the bargaining table, not what she takes from it" (MA,p.222). However, in a recent article, Gauthier changed his mind. He says: "Danielson is right to insist that 'the market can be regulated by the social contract'." in "Moral Artifice," p.413. This means that not only operations of but also presuppositions (including initial individual endowments and rights) of market can be regulated. I have already commented on this possibility in the context of why Gauthier has to move from thin market contractarianism to thick one. For this and Danielson, see A.3. n.66.

183 Sumner, p.538.

184 As far as I know, the most comprehensive treatment of this issue is *Markets and Justice*, especially pt.I. Contractarianism and Capitalism (see A.3. n.47). Cf. Arthur DiQuattro, "The Market and Liberal Values," *Political Theory*, 8 (1980), pp.183-202.

185 In this connection, the problem of luck must be reconsidered. See Richard A. Epstein, "Luck," in Ellen Paul et al. eds., *Capitalism* (Oxford: Basil Blackwell,1989), pp.17-38; Peter Breiner, "Democratic Autonomy, Political Ethics, and Moral Luck," *Political Theory*, 17 (1989), pp.530-74. At the American Philosophical Association annual meeting (Eastern Division: Atlanta, 1989), Nicholas Rescher delivered his presidential address, "Luck." See *Proceedings and Addresses of the American Philosophical Association*, 64, #3 (1990), pp.5-19. For a general approach to ethics, see Thomas Nagel, "Moral Luck," in *Mortal Questions* (New York: Cambridge University Press, 1979); Bernard Williams, "Moral Luck," in *Moral Luck: Philosophical Papers 1973-1980* (New York: Cambridge University Press, 1981).

186 Cf. Arthur Ripstein, "Gauthier's Liberal Individual," *Dialogue*, 28 (1989), pp.63-76. Also cf. Fred M. Frohock, *Rational Association* (Syracuse: Syracuse University Press, 1987), ch.5. "Liberal Models in Collective Choice."

187 See n.33 of this chapter and n.49 of Chapter I.

Chapter V

Conclusion: The Lessons of Contractarian Liberal Ethics and the Agenda for the Future of Ethics

A. The Contractarian Dilemma and Trilemma: To be Solved or Deepened?

It is often said that moral and political philosophies are now in vogue or have a privileged status. When compared with three or four decades ago (when existentialism on the Continent, and emotivism in the English-speaking countries were dominant[1]), they are surely in vogue. They receive much attention not only from the domain of philosophy, but also from the social sciences.

Considerable vogue or privilege notwithstanding, contemporary moral and political philosophies are endlessly varied. Although this study has assessed some of the more important of those philosophies and their debates, many others have not been mentioned, much less discussed or assessed. I have not even mentioned the following (let alone various forms of applied ethics — medical ethics, military ethics, and so on): Habermas' and Apel's *diskursethik* of the ideal communicative community, Hans-Georg Gadamer's hermeneutical ethics, Michel Foucault's genealogical ethics or ethics of the care of the self, Jean-François Lyotard's postmodern ethics of just gaming, Richard Rorty's postmodernist bourgeois liberalism, Derrida's an ethic of discussion, Levinas' concept of ethics as first philosophy, and Miller and de Man's ethics of reading, etc. In the liberal camp, I have not referred to Ronald Dworkin, Bruce Ackerman, and others. In the communitarian camp, I have also not discussed Michael Walzer, Charles Taylor and others.

This endless proliferation of contemporary moral and political philosophies is quite a vertiginous garden in which "one hundred flowers bloom", or a land of one thousand dances of different paradigms, or a tower of Babel.[2] As Kai Nielsen points out, "[t]he differences in conception are such that it may well be the case that no comparisons can be usefully made, not to mention the scouting out of anything like a unified project."[3]

However, is it not the case that this study of contractarian liberal ethics and its critiques presupposes a common language (or measure of what is at issue and of what gives different answers to the almost same question, i.e., the question of practical rationality)? I do not know whether both methodological and substantial assumptions of this study can expand to cover the above mentioned varieties. Throughout this study, I have made my discussion of contractarian ethics and its critiques consistent only in view of the question of rationality. Perhaps the expansion is partially possible since the varieties, I think, have something to say about contractarianism, foundationalism, and liberalism. In dealing with the relationship between contractarian ethics and the theory of rational choice, I have covered the two important aspects of contractarian ethics (i.e., the methodological aspect of foundationalism and the substantial aspect of liberalism). These two aspects correspond to the internal problems and external criticisms of contractarian liberal ethics.

This concluding chapter is not the place for a long retelling of what I have done. Rather it is a place for commenting in passing on what I have not done. Further, since what I have done is mainly a negative enterprise (showing the impasse of contractarian rational and foundational deduction project of morality, and the non-neutral liberal presupposition of contractarian ethics), it is pressing for me to suggest a sympathetic way out. If not a sympathetic way, it is at least useful for me to explore the viability of non-contractarian liberal ethics or of non-liberal communitarian and Marxist ethics as alternatives to contractarian liberal ethics.

In Chapter I, as a background scheme, I identified the four grand methodological foundations of contractarian ethics in its adoption of the value-neutral, instrumental, and maximizational conception of rationality generally assumed in the theory of rational choice. They are the justification for contractarian consensus, non-altruistic clear choice motivation, the possibility of contractarian consensus in the circumstances of pluralism or relativism of individual autonomous values, and a neutral Archimedean criterion for assessing the justice of a society. However, as I developed them in the subsequent Chapters II, III, IV, the theory of rational choice could not guarantee these four foundations in view of four corresponding predicaments.

The predicaments are the dilemma of moral irrelevancy or circularity held between rationality and morality, indeterminacy between various rational choice models, incompetent assessment of the contents of individual values as well as insufficient political sensibility of prevalent conflicts of individual goods (let alone Marxist class conflict), and non-neutrality resulting from the futility of the flight from liberal historical cultures. Basically I sustain my critical views on these four predicaments. However, in view of our detailed discussions, I will articulate below several qualifications to my initial views.

This concluding chapter consists of three sections. Section A deals with the first two predicaments, viz., the contractarian dilemma and trilemma. Section B treats the last two predicaments, viz., incompetence and insufficiency, and non-neutrality. In other words, two sections correspond to the above mentioned two aspects of contractarian liberal ethics (i.e., the methodological aspect of rational foundationalism and the substantial aspect of liberalism). Section C suggests what my point of view is in connection with the agenda for the future of ethics.

Even though I have treated the two aspects, internal problems and external criticisms, and four predicaments of contractarian ethics as distinct, I do not mean that they are separate. How, then, are the predicaments related to one another? The circularity of prior moral assumptions is directly related to non-neutrality. Even the conception of instrumental rationality is circular in the sense that instrumental rationality underlies the modern, Western, liberal, individualistic *homo economicus* of the free market. Indeterminacy is applied not only to the various rational choice models but also to the various prior moral assumptions. Moral irrelevancy relates to the incompetent assessment of the contents of individual values.

In this Section A, I focus my attention on the contractarian dilemma and trilemma. I think the *modus operandi* of this study sufficiently demonstrated the dilemma and trilemma. Hobbes' ethics represents the first horn of the moral irrelevancy of rationality. Rawls' ethics represents the second horn of circular moral assumptions prior to rationality. Thus it is understandable that Rawls confines his theoretical linkage to Locke, Rousseau, and Kant. Hobbes' contractarian ethics of rational foundationalism fails since it cannot guarantee a fair agreement in the non-moral rational initial choice situation. Nor can it guarantee voluntary rational compliance to the agreed upon contractarian moral principles. In contrast, Rawls' assumption of rationality *cum* fairness in the original position under the thick veil of ignorance and his Kantian deontological assumption of the strict compliance in the well-ordered society show well the other horn. Furthermore, in view of the debate between Rawls and Harsanyi, Rawls does not show the unique rationality of the maximin strategic derivation of the two principles of justice. In turn, Nozick criticizes Rawls that his veil of ignorance reveals asymmetrical favoritism to the least advantaged persons.

Gauthier attempts to go beyond the dilemma and trilemma through the alleged unique rationality of narrow compliance with the Lockean proviso *cum* MRC/MRB. But, on the one hand, his idealization of the bargaining process is actually a version of the Rawlsian veil. And also his CM dispositional narrow compliance presupposes a preestablished moral community. Thus it has the same effect as with Rawlsian strict compliance. On the other hand, his Lockean proviso strongly reveals the rationality of Nozickean libertarian persons. His narrow compliance theory relies upon Hobbesian punishment, viz., the exclusion of SMs from cooperative enterprise. Therefore Gauthier is still torn between the Hobbesian and Rawlsian horns of the dilemma. Furthermore, Gauthier cannot solve the indeterminacy between Rawls, Nozick, and Harsanyi within the framework of liberal rationality (let alone the tension between liberalism and socialism in view of our discussions on Marx's possible criticisms of Gauthier, and on Macpherson's charge of contractarianism as possessive individualism).

Overall Gauthier's world-historical radical contractarian rational foundationalism fails heroically.

Some might claim that if rational foundationalism fails, the indeterminacy of rational choice models can be solved through a proper concept of rights. However, as we have seen, the situation is not so easy. Nozick and Gauthier propose the classical liberal natural property rights (in case of Gauthier, he does so in the sense that the Lockean proviso for rights is not an object of bargaining). Utilitarian liberal welfare economists suggest welfare rights, whereas Rawls and other left liberals claim revisionist human rights. The situation is the same with various precepts of distributive justice (viz., moral merit, contribution, need, effort, equality, etc.). Regardless of contract, rationality, rights, and precepts, there is no single guide to practice. If this is the case, "the irreducible plurality of moral criteria" seems unavoidable.[4]

Does, then, "universal abandon" or anti-theory *tout court* follow from this observation on the dilemma and trilemma?[5] The failure of the rational deduction project of morality triggers various skeptical and relativistic challenges to the foundational justificatory use of rational choice theory.[6] I agree with the basic spirit of the challenges. However, I do not agree with "universal abandon" of rationality and rational choice theory as used in moral inquiries. I think this is too heretical in view of our discussions in Chapter II on the historical development of the soul of modern economic man.

Chapter II dealt with the basic structure of rational choice theory and the paradoxes the theory generates. Maybe "[p]aradoxes are fun. In most cases, they are easy to state and immediately provoke one into trying to 'solve' them."[7] However, I have shown how the paradoxes of rationality are difficult to deal with. Without a capacity for coping with them, any kind of moral or political philosophy would be in vain. As far as moral theories take account of motivational problems, rationality and rational choice theory cannot be totally eradicated.

Throughout the history of Western philosophy (from Plato to Marx) many philosophers with different philosophic backgrounds have pointed to "a cleavage [which] exists between the particular and the common interest."[8] Moral philosophers still can use theory as a very helpful analytic and heuristic device (cf. TJ, pp.121,152). In turn, rational choice theory can be influenced by ethical theories, as when normative welfare economics was influenced by utilitarianism. Arrow's and Harsanyi's normative social choice theories are often called "ethification of decision theories."[9] As we have seen in Chapters II,III,IV, both Rawls and Gauthier are not merely passive adopters of rational choice theory.

At any rate, Elster, who is among the leading scholars of rational choice theory, admits that "rational choice theory yields indeterminate prescriptions and predictions in more cases than most social scientists and decision makers would like to think."[10] Therefore I conclude that the contractarian dilemma and trilemma have no solutions, and are, if anything, more serious than might be supposed.

At this moment of conviction that rational foundationalism of contractarian liberal ethics fails, the following question is crucial. "With what, then, are we left on this account of things?"[11] John Gray (in a section of his book *Liberalisms*, titled "After Liberalism: Pyrrhonism in Politics") answers that "We are left with the historic inheritance of liberal civil society."[12] In this post-Pyrrhonian age of liberalism, philosophers must be humble and give up foundational hubris. "In short, some knowledge has been gained here both about the worth and the limitations of the philosopher. These may not be unimportant things to know."[13] Then it seems that there is no other way than that moral and political philosophies demand a pragmatic capacity to adjust to historical experience in their efforts to coordinate social affairs intelligently.[14]

B. Human Nature, Rationality, Morality, and Ideology

As Nietzsche points out, for moral philosophers pursuing a rational foundation for morality, morality itself is accepted as given.[15] Then what is needed is historical philosophizing. It is not surprising that all non- or anti-foundationalistic philosophies or anti-philosophies (communitarianism, postmodernism, genealogical post-structuralism, deconstruction, and hermeneutics) become historical.[16] In this connection, Martin Schwab points out that there is no meaning in the distinction between "an original contract and a given social situation."[17] However, to figure out what is the historical givenness is always in dispute.

It has been often pointed out that abstract contractarian ethics presupposes a mistaken belief of natural man separated from historical community. As we have seen in Chapter IV, in providing for possessive individual rights, Gauthier definitely resorts to the fantasy of Robinson Crusoe as "natural man" (MA,pp.310-12). However, individualistic liberalism has a historical ground. Rawls has no need of using the thick veil. In turn, Gauthier has no need to claim the natural man.

The last two predicaments, to which I now move, are actually historical boundedness of contractarian ethics. The third predicament pointed to the incompetent assessment of the contents of individual values as well as the insufficient political sensibility to the prevalent conflicts of individual goods. The fourth predicament is non-neutrality resulting from the futility of the flight from liberal historical cultures. We can link up these two predicaments with the corresponding ones of individualism and liberalism. At a glance, there is an inconsistency here. Contractarian ethics is ahistorical as well as historical. But this inconsistency is resolved when we properly understand the exact meaning of the fourth predicament. Rawls and Gauthier do indeed attempt to provide an ahistorical neutral Archimedean point for assessing the justness of a society. But the avowed neutrality is heavily contaminated by liberal historical givenness.

In dealing with these two predicaments, I eventually suggest what is the relationship between human nature, rationality, morality, and ideology. The third predicament consists of two parts. The first is incompetent assessment of the contents of individual values. Basically the instrumental maximizational concept of rationality generates this problem. This problem is in a sense the unavoidable result of the contractarian concept of human goodness. As we have seen in Chapter II, Rawls and Gauthier do not accept the revealed preference theory. Rawls and Gauthier provide a regulation against unlimited individual preferences with the agreed contractarian principles.

But, in order to obtain the regulation, they do not embrace an intrinsic or perfectionistic fixation of human goodness. For them, if objective, perfectionist, and communitarian human goodness or virtues regulate the justness of society, there are many problems. They are the anti-democratic social pressures and their resultant breach of individual autonomy (breach of Arrow's condition D), the impossibility of criticizing a given community, and the indoctrination or inculcation problem.[18]

In this sense, communitarianism is a moral conservatism.[19] My sympathy with individual liberalism does not imply that all and every social arrangement can be questioned or criticized at once. Rather there are some parts to be corrected in the course of time. Perhaps MacIntyre's following charge against individual liberalism is right. He says that "[t]he rational and rationally justifiable autonomous moral subject ... is a fiction, an illusion."[20] However, MacIntyre does not treat the possible vices of his own communitarianism properly. It might be the case that MacIntyre's Aristotelian fixation of human nature is ahistorical. MacIntyre wants to provide us with "essential human purposes or functions" or "man-as-he-could-be-if-he-realized-his-essential-nature."[21]

Here we must be careful about "taking human nature as the basis of morality."[22] Even though individualism has many problems, the remedy cannot be found in a simple reversal and its replacement by a monolithic communitarianism dependent upon a spurious concept of human essence.[23] What we really need is to reconstruct individualism not just develop a yearning for its return.[24]. The reconstruction of individualism might have a form of individualism generated from the historical and social world inherited from the modern age in the contemporary world. Is it not the case that the loss of a virtue-oriented-community is a modern historical phenomenon? We witness the lonely crowd of Riesman, the fall of public man of Sennett, and additionally the closing of the American mind of Allan Bloom.[25]

John Dunn summarizes eloquently this kind of observation in his "The Future of Political Philosophy in the West." He says: "The instrumental assessment of human practices and the incessant reckoning of consequences is part of the way in which we have learnt to live and whatever the validity of idyllic representations of the unsullied holism of human societies in the distant past [indeed MacIntyre's Aristotelian past], there is no way back from the warily strategic and tactical consciousness of modern human beings."[26] I do not know whether the following point of view makes sense or not. Because of the historical loss of community or the eclipse of community, the quest for community is historically more urgent.[27]

In a sense, the all-or-nothing dichotomy between "bring man back in" and "bring society or community back in" is meaningless. I think what we need is a third ontology of the individual as a social individual, not as an abstract individual.[28]

None of these historical considerations implies that Rawls and Gauthier are right as they are now. Rawls claims that his recent "political conception of justice express[es] ways in which a political society can itself be an intrinsic good."[29] However, he must provide a more convincing argument for how the intrinsic good of political liberal community or society can be derived from individual instrumental values. By the same token, Gauthier maintains that contractarian morality is not of "purely instrumental value to us," and that "recognizing the need for community, the individual human being, women and men, embraces morals by agreement," (MA,pp.339,355). He also has to show how the non-instrumental value of the community of liberal individuals can be derived from the instrumental conception of rationality.

I agree with Rawls' and Gauthier's criticisms of MacIntyre's use of Aristotelian human essence. However, there arises a question whether their use of contractarian rationality also presupposes a fixation of human essence, as exemplified in their affinity with homo economicus. In this regard, I have argued that contractarian ethics has a liberal ideological boundedness. Others label it with a narrower and localizing mark of "English-speaking justice," or still narrower of "damagingly and parochially American" justice, or even of "Justice and Equality: Here and Now."[30]

However, as pointed out at the beginning of this section, there is always a debate about the historical givenness. That is, it can be questioned whether contractarian liberalism is the unique representation of America. Rather is it not Protestant moral majority? Libertarianism? Conservative capitalism? Pragmatism? Emersonian or Jeffersonian tradition? Classical or civic republicanism? The New Frontier? Civil rights movement? Furthermore concerning 'here' where is here? The north where Yankees are living? The south where "Dixies" are living? New York? Atlanta?

Now let us move to the remaining portion of the third predicament (insufficient political sensibility of prevalent conflicts of individual goods) and the fourth and final predicament (non-neutrality resulting from the futility of the flight from liberal historical cultures).   In dealing with these, I summarize a confrontation between contractarian liberal ethics and Marxism, which I dealt with in Chapter IV.

The remaining portion of the third predicament comes from the fact that regardless of consensus (Rawls) or bargaining (Gauthier) model, contractarian liberal ethics gives credit to the possibility of unanimous agreement.   For Marxists, contractarian political insensitivity has a deeper root.   It is not just an insensitivity but a cajolery for camouflaging class conflicts.   I do not think that this is all true. Rawls' use of maximin strategy makes representations to the least advantaged.   In this sense, Rawls might be a maximal Marx working within the confines of capitalistic liberal social arrangements.   In this connection, it is not surprising that Rawls himself definitely mentions that his maximin strategy has a strong affinity with Marx's famous slogan in *Critique of the Gotha Program*, viz., "From each according to his ability, to each according to his needs!"[31]

Gauthier presupposes a conflict of interest to share cooperative surplus.   Here an important thing to note is that that ideological charge is to be ascribed not only to contractarian liberal rational foundationalism, but also to Marxism itself.   In other words, Marxism itself as ideology (viz., its historical materialistic foundationalism, and obnoxiously and inexorably narrow vision of human society and of the representative role of the proletariat or communist party dictatorship) is also to be deconstructed.   In this connection, Gauthier's model might be a maximal Marxist strategy for collective bargaining on behalf of the labor union movement in the age of post-Marxism.[32]   Indeed, Gauthier regrets to find that collective bargaining is usually (if not always) dependent upon various threat advantages, which he rejects in his bargaining model.

If moral and political philosophy should take account of historical facts of human society, the recent Eastern European crisis has provided good material.   As I mentioned several times, there is always a controversy on what is the true(?) interpretation of the historical givenness.   On the one hand, communists themselves interpret it as a struggle for returning to socialism with a human face.   On the other hand, Fukuyama interprets it as the end of history.   He says: "What we may be witnessing ... is the end of history as such: that is, the end point of mankind's ideological evolution and the universalization of Western liberal democracy as the final form of human government."[33] He adds that "[i]n the post-historical period there will be neither art nor philosophy, just the perpetual caretaking of the museum of human history."[34] It seems that he is at least partially right. But Fukuyama goes too far in view of our discussion on the debates between various forms of liberalism or liberal democracy. "Liberalism in Search of Its Self" has not been accomplished yet.[35] Fukuyama reminds us of the Bell debate. That was the debate between "the end of ideology" and "the end of the end of ideology."[36]

I insert McLellan's observation here as an important qualification to my previous discussion concerning the ideological implications of contractarian ethics. He says the following:[37]

> Any examination of ideology makes it difficult to avoid the rueful conclusion that all views about ideology are themselves ideological. But avoided it must be — or at least modified by saying that some views are more ideological than others. For the simple thought that all views are ideological encounters two difficulties: first, that it borders on the vacuous, since it is so all-embracing as to be almost meaningless; secondly, and more damagingly, it contains the same logical absurdity as the declaration of Epimenides the Cretan who declared that all Cretans were liars.

Indeed, at this moment, I think that liberalism is less ideological and more neutral than non-liberalism. I know there is still a seeming paradox. How can liberalism be neutral, but yet the best?[38] Recently, Rawls has paid special attention to this paradox.[39]

Returning to the third predicament, if there is no agreement which can satisfy every member or class of society (as we saw in our discussion of indeterminacy), contractarian liberal ethics is idealistic. Contractarian ethics has to pay more attention to the "patterns of moral complexity," "hard choices," and "tragic choices."[40] At any rate, the idealistic character of the third predicament is naturally connected with the fourth and final predicament of non-neutrality. Our discussion of Marx and Macpherson clearly reveals the non-neutrality. Marx thinks that morality itself is an ideological oppressive device related to class conflicts. He says: "Morality, religion, metaphysics, all the rest of ideology and their corresponding forms of consciousness, thus no longer retain the semblance of independence."[41] Furthermore, Marx claims that the end of philosophy is involved here. He says: When reality is depicted, philosophy as an independent branch of activity loses its

medium of existence."[42] However, in recent times, many philosophers (Kai Nielsen, Allen Buchanan, Steven Lukes, Elliot Pruzan,
Norman Geras, R.G. Peffer — including analytical Marxists,
Richard Miller, John Roemer, Jon Elster, G.A. Cohen and others)
have actively engaged in the debate concerning the possibility of
Marx's moral philosophy. It might be the case that someday Marxism will become a major moral philosophy.

I do not intend here to treat the controversial issue of the end of
philosophy in general. Rather I confine my attention to providing
a vantage point for assessing whether the end of contractarian
liberal ethics, which is the theme of Section C, is a real possibility.
I pointed out in Chapter II that contractarian liberalism and the
theory of rational choice share an isomorphic structure of the
modern economic man. In this regard, it is pertinent to investigate
homo economicus as a view of human nature.

As we have seen in Chapter II, human nature has more than a
Janus-faced character to it. It might have a thousand faces.[43] I
mentioned first the distinction between homo totus and homo
partialis. Then I named several forms of homo partialis: homo
economicus, homo sociologicus, homo faber, and various psychological men.[44] Perhaps, among them, there is no unique representation of human essence. This observation does not imply that
there is, instead, the undissected holistic human essence. From the
Platonic educational scenario via Marx's concept of free individual
development in the communist society to conservative educational
philosophy, homo totus has been persistent. Quite apart from
recent technological specializations, one of Marx's serious errors is
exposed to us in the following yearning for homo totus along with
his concept of a species-being elsewhere[45]:

> ... [I]n communist society, where nobody has one exclusive sphere of activity
> but each can become accomplished in any branch he wishes, society regulates
> the general production and thus makes it possible for me to do one thing
> today and another tomorrow, to hunt in the morning, fish in the afternoon,
> rear cattle in the evening, criticize after dinner, just as I have a mind, without
> ever becoming hunter, fisherman, shepherd, or critic.

I do not think that Marx is yearning just for an all-round dilettante
here. Rather he is seeking for homo totus.

Returning to homo partialis, is it not the case that the
Hobbesian market self has a vantage point in the domain of

distributive justice in our times or possibly all times? In this regard, Gauthier claims that "[u]tility maximization is ... one of the core constituents in our sense of self. And this is not a contingent matter, although whether one lives in circumstances that facilitate or even permit the development of a clear sense of self is entirely contingent."[46]

The concept of self has been (especially since Hume) and is now on the front line of philosophy in connection with postmodernist deconstruction of modern self (Cartesian epistemic self, and Hobbesian or Kantian rational moral self): Death of man, death of the author, and the dissolution of the subject.[47] In Chapter II, we investigated Elster's multiple self and Parfit's mild Buddhist-like-no-self theory.

In this connection, it should be pointed out that Gauthier does not miss Foucault's observation concerning the modern self (MA,p.353). As is well-known, for Foucault, the modern self is a recent invention and its end is near. He says: "[M]an would be erased, like a face drawn in sand at the edge of the sea."[48] However, Foucault brings back the moral subject in his ethical turn (taken in his late years of life).[49] In the same vein, Derrida's position is to be made clear here. He says: "The subject is absolutely indispensable. I don't destroy the subject; I situate it. That is to say, I believe that at a certain level both of experience and of philosophical and scientific discourse one cannot get along without the notion of subject. It is a question of knowing where it comes from and how it functions."[50]

If major proponents of post-structuralism and deconstructionism did not really discard the modern self, Rawls' and Gauthier's affinity with homo economicus can be pardoned with a proper historicizing of it. In this sense, Rawls' deontological self and Gauthier's constrained maximizing self might be interpreted as a contractarian liberal project of how the historical modern market self can be transformed into a moral self. If this can be done in a more convincing manner, Sandel's and MacIntyre's communitarianism may lose its validity. In this regard, Rawls and Gauthier should pay attention to the historical and social formation of "the liberal mind" or to "the modern liberal theory of man."[51]

For some it is still problematic that contractarianism is hypothetical. I interpret the hypothetical contract not as an ahistorical but as an example of the exercise of the historical moral imagination. This kind of moral imagination is necessary if we are not to be merely acquiescing in de facto status quo or believing in ex post facto naive pragmatism. This historical moral imagination need not be fixed. It may be changed according to its capacity as an hyper-pragmatic experimental working hypothesis for solving social and historical conflicts. Choosing among various alternatives of social experiment requires, to a certain degree, an expectation of the practical results of them. This expectation can be determined by a hypothetical contractarian ethics. Apart from the hypothetical aspect, the historical practices of contract have been persistent in the Western life. In this connection, it is not surprising that, in the domain of economics, laws, and politics, contractarian liberal ethics still can recruit new proponents.[52]

In Chapter II, I connected the image of moral self as rational self with the three schools of rationality, viz., the neo-classical standard, the imperfect, and the extended schools. There I tried to make a partial linkage between them. Perhaps the unification of the three schools is a sort of forlorn dream of logical positivism. In this connection, I suggest that there might be a loose (not clearly separate) division of labor of different historical emphases. If it is true that America is engaging in a war on drugs, we have to pay special attention to the imperfect school's concept of irrationality. In an underdeveloped society, standard neo-classical rationality might be primary. In an advanced society, extended rationality might be a first concern. Indeed, there are overlapping places of the division of labor.

C. After Contractarian Liberal Ethics: End or Transformation?

Contractarian ethics is not uniquely for liberalism as we saw in the case of the Hobbesian absolute state. Jan Narveson recently used a contractarian method to derive libertarianism.[53] Even though Nozick dissociates himself from the social contract tradition (AST,p.132), the terms of Nozick's criticism of Rawls (as we saw in Chapter III. B.3) might suggest that the basis for his argument is some kind of contractarianism.[54] Danielson criticizes Gauthier that contractarianism may generate a moderate socialism.[55] Mueller calls Harsanyi's and Buchanan's positions utilitarian contracts.[56]   Thus, contractarianism is not uniquely for liberal ethics. In this connection, we have to think about a possible absurdity. If contractarianism produces everything, then it produces nothing. Needless to say, in the case of rational choice theory, the situation is the same. We see here another aspect of indeterminacy. From the logical point of view, this means that a tautology (true in every case) can be always derived from inconsistent propositions. Is contractarianism internally inconsistent?

There might be two interpretations of this indeterminacy. On the one hand, Diggs interprets it that "[c]ontractarianism in moral philosophy is a kind of ethical formalism; as such, it is theoretically compatible with a number of other views."[57] On the other hand, Hamlin reads it as a vantage point. He says: "A hallmark of the contract process is its indeterminacy. Some may see this as a fatal weakness, but, if the contractarian strategy is seen primarily as a means of examining alternative normative claims, this flexibility is a major strength. The contractarian strategy does not provide a simple test for the ideal polity, but it can provide a fundamentally liberal method for distinguishing the good polity from the bad."[58]

I agree with Hamlin (on the condition of my previous reformation of contractarian ethics from an Archimedean device into an hyper-pragmatic moral imaginative working hypothesis). In other words, the indeterminacy of contractarianism does not mean indeterminacy in the sense that if anything goes, nothing can be determined. I think even Heisenberg's indeterminacy or uncertainty principle does not imply sheer indeterminacy in this sense. If there is something like "Plank's constant" (which marks the threshold point between indeterminacy and determinacy) in moral and political philosophy, that might be something like the following.[59] There is a minimum requirement (which is not unimportant) for uncruelty, a non-fascist life after Auschwitz, and a liberal social individualistic (motivational) shield against totalitarian and authoritarian politico-economic temptation, and also a minimum requirement against stubborn and callous libertarian disinterestedness toward the ongoing sufferings of others.[60]

If we relate this observation to Arrow's theorem (viz., another theme of indeterminacy—the most controversial issue in the domain of social or public choice theory, as we saw in Chapter II. B.3), it is not surprising that many economists look to contractarian method as a way out of the theorem. For example, Pazner and Schmeidler say: "Regarding the theory of social choice pioneered by Arrow, the unanimous agreed upon social contract ('constitution') emerging from the present analysis may be an indication that the contractarian approach might offer a way out of some of the disturbing difficulties raised by Arrow's inquiry."[61]

Contractarian ethics can have a different theoretical starting point than the theory of rational choice as we saw Rawls' recent reinterpretation of the origin and subsequent transformation of his philosophy. Thus for Rawls the transformation of contractarian ethics has already happened. However, we must note that Rawls does not totally discard the concept of rationality and rational choice theory. As we have seen in Chapters I and III, his later position still keeps the concept of the rational under the regulation of the reasonable. Rawls says that "the Reasonable presupposes and subordinates the Rational."[62] The reason for this is clear. Rawls says:[63]

> The Reasonable presupposes the Rational, because, without conceptions of the good that move members of the group, there is no point to social cooperation nor to notions of right and justice, even though such cooperation realizes values that go beyond what conceptions of the good specify taken alone. The Reasonable subordinates the Rational because its principles limit, and in a Kantian doctrine limit absolutely, the final ends that can be pursued.

There are many labels attached to Rawls' later position. For example, pragmatic or Deweyian, Hegelian, postmodernist, political, descriptive, or even perfectionist.[64] Especially in view of the postmodernist interpretation of Rawls' recent transformation of contractarianism into a political liberalism (Rawls no longer wants to be a moral philosopher[65]), the following question about Gauthier also is very interesting. Is Gauthier still lingering on the edge of modernity? The following passage is revealing (MA,p.269, n.4):[66]

> 'I believe one should trust problems over solutions, intuitions over arguments, and pluralistic discord over systematic harmony. Simplicity and elegance are never reasons to think that a philosophical theory is true: On the contrary, they are usually grounds for thinking it false.' But why should philosophy differ so from science? Nevertheless, there is no better account of the view contrary to that underlying *Morals By Agreement*.

Fortunately, elsewhere in *Morals By Agreement* and in a recent article, he seems to make an entry onto the postmodern stage. He admits that his liberal individualistic market self does not emerge *ex nihilo* (MA,p.349). In this connection, he seems to give up his rational theoretical hubris. He says: "Although I have no doubt that, for significant areas of human interaction, the market would indeed be chosen, the formal apparatus of moral theory does not suffice to answer the question [whether or how far the market would be chosen]."[67]

If both Rawls and Gauthier take a postmodernistic (i.e., non-rational and non-foundationalistic) turn, the following question is the most important in this concluding chapter of this study. Is it the case that the four predicaments (the backbone of this study), which are generated by the old contractarian rational foundation-alism, naturally dissolve? In other words, at this stage, is this study to be burnt or be thrown away like the Humean metaphysical books in *Treatise* or a Wittgensteinian ladder in *Tractatus*? I do not think so, as I will now explain, because there are some good reasons for not burning still one more book.

First, Rawls posits a vantage point in his recent stance on politi-cal liberalism, which he thinks enables him to escape from two strands of the dilemma of liberalism. He says:[68]

> I conclude by commenting briefly on what I have called political liberalism. We have seen that this view steers a course between the Hobbesian strand in liberalism—liberalism as a *modus vivendi* secured by a convergence of self- and group-interests as coordinated and balanced by well-designed constitu-tional arrangements—and a liberalism founded on a comprehensive moral doctrine such as that of Kant or Mill. By itself, the former cannot secure an enduring social unity, the latter cannot gain sufficient agreement.

In view of this passage, Rawls no longer regards Kant as his original predecessor. Anyhow, we have seen that Rawls has been criticized by many because of his inability to escape from the dilemma. On the one hand, his political liberalism seems to make political philosophy a handmaiden of politics in the bad sense. What is his politics? Is it not the case that the so-called pluralistic democracy of political liberalism is just a balance between different interest groups? One the other hand, his political liberalism still contains historical and thus substantial liberal value concepts. In other words, the alleged neutrality of his position is not guaranteed. This means that the fourth (old) predicament revives again. Thus it is not surprising that Rawls has to make a very painful apology for his dilemmatic situation in a recent article.[69]

Since Rawls discards rational choice theory as a foundational justificatory device, the other device (viz., the reflective equilibrium) has become a focal point. Daniels, Nielsen, Rorty and others have developed it into the so-called wide reflective equilibrium.[70] Daniels wants to use it for sustaining the Rawlsian conclusion. However, Kai Nielsen takes it as a device for radical egalitarianism, whereas Rorty uses it as a Quinean web of belief or solidarity for his postmodern bourgeois liberalism. Interestingly enough, Nielsen interprets it as a hermeneutical circle.[71] However, Gadamer thinks that the circle is in the dilemma between distance and involvement, or between transcendence and immanence.[72] Needless to say, the recent fracas concerning Heidegger's involvement with Nazism shows well how difficult it is to keep the circle, which he proposed in *Being and Time*, from turning vicious.[73]

What is, then, Gauthier's position? He criticizes Rawls that even his recent transformation cannot give him a capacity to overcome the contractarian dilemma. While reviewing Grant's two books, *English-speaking Justice* and *Technology and Justice*, Gauthier explicitly indicates Rawls' dilemmatic situation as follows:[74]

> Grant would seem to have Rawls on the horns of a dilemma. Grant reads Rawls as arguing that justice is derived from general calculations about self-interest. On this reading Rawls treats the rational agreement of self-interested calculators as foundational. But, Grant insists, such a foundation does not yield the superstructure of assured liberty and equality. Rawls rejects the reading. The rational agreement of self-interested calculators is to be subordinated to the intuitive idea of a fair system of cooperation among free and equal persons. But this idea is a relic of our earlier understanding of the world in terms of a substantive good which Rawls explicitly rejects.

Does, then, Gauthier solve the dilemma? No. His recent position is just an acceptance of the limitation of the rational choice theory. He is still torn between Hobbesian self-interest and Lockean natural rights. Then, at this moment, should we declare the end of contractarian liberal ethics?

Before doing this, we have to look briefly into the major alternatives to contractarian ethics. In the case of libertarianism and utilitarianism, the situation is the same with contractarian liberal ethics, as we have seen in Chapters III and IV in connection with their debates concerning liberal (in the broad sense) rationality. How about Marx and Macpherson? In Chapter IV, I showed why their position is a victim to the second horn of the contractarian dilemma (viz., in the sense of efficiency, their position is irrational).

Then, can communitarians solve the dilemma? No. If communitarians see Unger's following diagram of communitarian dilemmas, they will be thwarted (some regard Unger himself as a communitarian):[75]

Table 13. The Dilemmas of Communitarian Politics

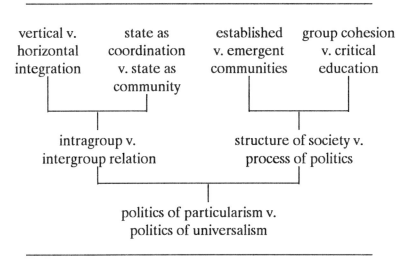

| vertical v. horizontal integration | state as coordination v. state as community | established v. emergent communities | group cohesion v. critical education |

intragroup v. intergroup relation   structure of society v. process of politics

politics of particularism v. politics of universalism

Anyhow, do communitarians themselves have anything to say about the contractarian dilemma and trilemma? MacIntyre claims that the impossibility of rational foundationalism comes from its indeterminacy between various forms of rational foundationalism. And he regards this as *"prima facie* evidence that their project has failed, even before we have examined their particular contentions and conclusions."[76] Even before! According to MacIntyre, then, this study represents nothing more than a fool's errand! In turn, Richard Rorty (some regard him as a communitarian) indicates how the indeterminacy between various communitarian models is deep. He says:[77]

> Unger ends *Knowledge and Politics* with an appeal to a *Deus absconditus*. MacIntyre ends *After Virtue* by saying that we "are waiting not for a Godot, but for another — doubtless very different — St. Benedict." Sandel ends his book by saying that liberalism "forgets the possibility that when politics goes well, we can know a good in common that we cannot know alone," but he does not suggest a candidate for this common good.

I think MacIntyre tries to answer this kind of charge in his most recent book, *Whose Justice? Which Rationality?* However, he does not show us clearly why and how his version of communitarianism must be uniquely chosen according to moral, rational, or whatever reasons (maybe he needs another book—see Bibliography for his new book). Furthermore, he seems to admit a circularity and indeterminacy involved in his enterprise. He says:[78]

> Fundamental disagreements about the character of rationality are bound to be peculiarly difficult to resolve. For already in initially proceeding in one way rather than another to approach the disputed questions, those who so proceed will have had to assume that these particular procedures are the ones which it is rational to follow. A certain degree of circularity is ineliminable.

Then, what is the case for various forms of anti-foundationalism, viz., postmodernism, deconstruction, hermeneutics, poststructuralism, and critical theory? As Rosen correctly points out, "Every hermeneutical program is at the same time itself a political manifesto or the corollary of a political manifesto."[79] Evan Simpson eloquently indicates various manifestoes of anti-foundationalism. He says:[80]

> On this view moral convictions are inherently ethnocentric, always expressing the traditions of a local community rather than fulfilling the universal aspirations of moral philosophy. In its anti-rationalism the view rejects revolutionary optimism and accommodates a range of views which include Alasdair MacIntyre's neo-Aristotelianism, Roger Scruton's Toryism, Richard Rorty's Whiggish "postmodernist bourgeois liberalism," and Michael Walzer's communitarian socialism. The boundaries of this intriguing political diversity are evidently very generous.

In turn, Habermas criticizes Foucault, Derrida, and Rorty as neo-conservatives.[81] Also, in turn, Gould thinks that Habermas' communicative ethics is victim to a circularity since its undistorted procedure of transcendental intersubjectivity already embraces a moral consensus of equality or emancipation, which he attempts to prove as the conclusion.[82]

Am I here wielding merely a *tu quoque* [you too] argument in order to demonstrate that the end of contractarian ethics is premature? Or am I jettisoning all kinds of philosophy? Or am I making an enumeration of meaningless and disconnected dilemmas and indeterminacies? Originally I thought that when contractarian liberal ethics discarded rational foundationalism, the four predicaments would dissolve. This kind of thought is well exemplified by Gray who says: "For the political Pyrrhonist, by contrast with the liberal, there are few universal political dilemmas and no universal solutions."[83] I agree with him that there are no universal solutions.

However, is it not the case that there are universal dilemmas and trilemmas? Is it not the case that because of these ubiquitous dilemmas, even though Hobbes rejects the Aristotelian *summum bonum* (as we saw in Chapter III. A), he has to resort to the doctrine of the *summum malum* (the Hobbesian fear of death or of social instability)?[84] By the same token, is it not a sort of common sense that comedy needs an inter-cultural translation but tragedy does not need it? For example, Koreans cannot enjoy the Johnny Carson show. But they can vividly feel the sorrows of the American homeless.

How can this mass chaos of contemporary philosophy be explained? Many scholars are talking about various methodological pluralisms, but it all seems more like anarchy. Some (Feyeraband) can say, anarchy just fine! But not in the domain of normative moral and political philosophy! Many scholars (Kuhn and others) are talking about incommensurability. However, is it not rather that there are many commensurable dilemmas? At this moment, we have to take seriously Paul Ricoeur's agenda, "Irrationality and the Plurality of Philosophical systems."[85]

Returning to contractarian ethics, the Gray problem, which I just mentioned above, might be solved in terms of what we have done. Is it not the case that when Rawls and Gauthier adopt Humean circumstances of justice, they are correct in regarding it as a permanent condition of mankind, which generates the four predicaments? If we do not like the expression "permanent," is it not at least a modern condition?[86] If this is the case, the various types of postmodernism might be hallucinatory. Perhaps, Habermas is right in his claim that modernity is an incomplete project.[87]

I think John Dunn's following observation is quite suggestive. He says: "the self-consciousness of modernity is not in reality a historical predicament but simply a historical consciousness of a condition inherent in a human nature and human society as such."[88] Do we, then, have to bring back some kind of foundationalism of human nature and society? It seems to be too reactionary in the vortex of anti-foundationalism.

While pondering the contractarian dilemma, I feel I am really stuck at a dilemma, too. Maybe the best way is to follow Rawls' guidance. He says in "Justice as Fairness: Political not Metaphysical" (p.223):

> I shall first discuss what I regard as the task of political philosophy at the present time and then briefly survey how the basic intuitive ideas drawn upon in justice as fairness are combined into a political conception of justice for a constitutional democracy. Doing this will bring out how and why this conception of justice avoids certain philosophical and metaphysical claims. Briefly, the idea is that in a constitutional democracy the public conception of justice should be, so far as possible, independent of controversial philosophical and religious doctrines. Thus, to formulate such a conception, we apply the principle of toleration to philosophy itself: the public conception of justice is to be political, not metaphysical. Hence the title.

What Rawls says here is that we need not know the philosophical causes of disease. All we need is to have a political therapeutic (*ad hoc*?) device. It sounds like a Wittgensteinian message. I see clearly here the case of the end of philosophy. I feel that, for all students of philosophy including the author of this study, it is very difficult to have self-referential toleration. At the end of his *A Theory of Justice*, doesn't Rawls give the following message to philosophers? It reads: "Purity of heart, if one could attain it [in this case, indeed, the self-toleration], would be to see clearly and to act with grace and self-command from this point of view [the end of philosophy]" (TJ,p.587).

In turn, does Gauthier have any message to philosophers? Maybe he has. At the end of *Morals By Agreement*, he says: "this mastery over himself [indeed, in this case, a philosopher's self-toleration] also necessarily gives him mastery over circumstances [the end of philosophy]" (MA,p.355). At this age of the end of philosophy, "we have a hope of a happier ending, and we shall conclude ... with a sketch of the liberal individual who ... enjoys the free affectivity that a society based on purely rational constraints allows" (MA,p.104).

But when shall the happier ending come? Another millennium? How long should the liberal individuals' odyssey for moral life continue? Can they generate or agree on morality without a thick veil of self-oblivion? Are they still thinking of themselves as castaways who make adventure fantasias of Robinson Crusoe? Do they have a navigation map to help them to treat their schizophrenia which is torn between efficiency and equality? Conservative capitalism or liberal socialism? Autonomy or control? Freedom or equality? Property rights or welfare rights? Liberalism or democracy? Growth or stability? Self-indulgence or envy? Consumption or saving? Are they so brave to steer between Scylla and Charybdis of rationality and morality? Are they not thinking just 'the big trade-off' as a real and permanent solution? Are they not finally acquiescent in 'living with contradiction' or in 'cultural contradictions of capitalism'?[89]

Such are some of the questions which press upon me when I contemplate the signs of our times. I wonder whether liberal individuals can understand and answer these questions properly without any kind of philosophizing (quite apart from Rorty's meaning of P as the foundational philosophy). Still do they not need contractarian liberal ethics as a social imaginative power (not as an abstract natural man's imagination)?

I conclude that the agenda for the future of contractarian liberal moral and political philosophy (and also for the future of non-contractarian philosophy, and philosophy in general) is to describe and prescribe the predicaments more properly: especially PD-structured human relations or interactions whether it is held between individuals, groups, societies, or beyond borders — e.g., free riders, parasites, antagonistic societies, technical or economic imperialism, and mutual-destruction game (which is more fatal than zero-sum game) with nuclear weapons, environmental contamination, and exhaustion of resources.

Perhaps, the future of mankind will depend upon its competence to cope with the dilemmatic, trilemmatic, and tetralemmatic predicaments which it generates.   At this moment, we can meaningfully raise a series of questions.   For example, "Does [Contractarian liberal] Moral Philosophy Rest on a Mistake?" "Does Liberalism Rest on a Mistake?"[90] Even though, as we have seen, Rawls and Gauthier admit their theoretical mistakes and limitations, the blame is not only ascribed to them. The failure of contractarian ethics here and now gives a great impetus to understanding the depth of the predicaments we have here and now, and to a radical transformation of contractarian liberal ethics with a better armor. Contractarian liberal ethics has a vantage point. For it knows what kinds of predicaments it has. In a sense, contractarian ethics is the unique and true(?) representation—*Ecce Homo* crowned with thorns—of the modern predicament. In this conclusion, unfortunately, I have only adumbrated a possible radical transformation of contractarian liberal ethics.

The competence of mankind's struggle against the predicaments might be invigorated by the radically transformed contractarian liberal moral and political philosophy. If this radical transformation will appeal to everyone in the near future, contractarian liberal and moral philosophy will be praised for its contribution (negatively as an ethics of survival or a doctor of modernity, whereas positively it will be praised as an ethics of human flourishing far beyond the postmodern age) to the relatively long survival of the otherwise ephemeral human species on this tiny and fragile planetary earth in the infinite time and vast space of the universe.

Notes

1   In a sense, contractarian liberal ethics is an ethics of post-existentialism or - emotivism. I mean that Rawls' (at one time) and Gauthier's use of instrumental rationality as the foundation for their contractarian liberal ethics still partially keeps the individualistic existential or emotivistic skeptical flavor concerning human essence or objective good. Contractarian liberal ethics, then, is nothing but seeking for a possible "overlapping or minimum objective consensus" or for a bargaining agreement among subjective and relative individuals (consensus on the normative criterion for social justice through the instrumental rationality in the milieu of the post-existentialism or - emotivism). For the term, "minimum objective" see Rawls' article, "The Domain of the Political and Overlapping Consensus," p.241. As we have seen in Chapter IV. A.2., Gauthier proposes subjectivistic and relativistic value theory. MacIntyre's view on this observation in *After Virtue* is brilliant. See especially chs.3,4 of the book.

2   Jeffrey Stout, *Ethics after Babel: The Language of Morals and Their Discontents* (Boston: Beacon Press, 1988).

3   Kai Nielsen, "Searching for an Emancipatory Perspective: Wide Reflective Equilibrium and the Hermeneutical Circle," in *Anti-Foundationalism and Practical Reasoning*, p.144. For this book, See n.28 of Chapter I.

4   James Gouinlock, "Dewey," in Robert J. Cavalier, James Gouinlock, and James P. Sterba, eds., *Ethics in the History of Western Philosophy* (New York: St. Martin's Press, 1989), p.316.

5   Andrew Ross, ed., *Universal Abandon?: The Politics of Postmodernism* (Minneapolis: University of Minnesota Press, 1988). Stanley G. Clarke and Evan Simpson, eds., *Anti-Theory in Ethics and Moral Conservatism* (Albany: State University Press of New York, 1989). Cf. Chapter IV. n.32.

6   See John Kekes, "The Sceptical Challenge to Rationality," *Meta Philosophy*, 2 (1971), pp.121-136. Cf. his *A Justification of Rationality* (Albany: State University of New York Press, 1976). Also see Martin Hollis and Steven Lukes, eds., *Rationality and Relativism* (Cambridge: The MIT Press, 1982); J. Margolis, M. Krausz, and R.M. Burian, eds., *Rationality, Relativism and The Human Sciences* (Dordrecht: Martinus Nijhoff Publishers, 1986).

7   R. M. Sainsbury, *Paradoxes* (Cambridge: Cambridge University Press, 1988), p.1.

8   Marx, *The German Ideology*, in *Marx and Engels: Basic Writings on Politics and Philosophy*, p.254.

9   Hans W. Gottinger and Werner Leinfeller, eds., *Decision Theory and Social Ethics*, p.vii.

10 Jon Elster, *Cement of Society*, p.viii.

11 John Gray, *Liberalisms: Essays in Political Philosophy* (London: Routledge, 1989), p.262.

12 Ibid. Gray here makes a note that he is indebted to Livingston for the conception of post-Pyrrhonism. See Donald Livingston, *Hume's Philosophy of Common Life* (Chicago: The University of Chicago Press, 1984), Ch.I. "Post-Pyrrhonian Philosophy." Now Livingston's theme is popular. See David R. Hiley, *Philosophy in Question: Essays on a Pyrrhonian Theme* (Chicago: The University Press of Chicago, 1988).

13 Nicholas Fotion, *Moral Situations* (Yellow Springs, Ohio: The Antioch Press, 1968), p.115.

14 Indeed, the concept of social intelligence is Dewey's. For a comprehensive discussion on this concept, see Gouinlock, *Excellence in Public Discourse: John Stuart Mill, John Dewey, and Social Intelligence* (New York: Teachers College Press, 1985). Also see his *John Dewey's Philosophy of Value* (New York: Humanities Press, 1972); *The Moral Writings of John Dewey* (New York: Hafner Press, 1976).

15 Friedrich Nietzsche, *Beyond Good and Evil*, trans. Walter Kaufmann (New York: Vintage Books, 1966), p.97.

16 Cf. Richard Rorty, J.B. Schneewind, and Quentin Skinner, eds., *Philosophy in History: Essays on the Historiography of Philosophy* (Cambridge: Cambridge University Press, 1989).

17 Martin Schwab, "Foreword," in Manfred Frank, *What is Neostructuralism?* trans. Sabine Wilke and Richard Gray (Minneapolis: University of Minnesota Press, 1989), p.xvi.

18 Robert B. Louden, "Some Vices of Virtue Ethics," *American Philosophical Quarterly*, 21 (1984), pp.227-236. As far as I know, the most comprehensive treatment of communitarianism is Peter A. French, ed., *Ethical Theory: Character and Virtue*, vol.xiii. *Midwest Studies in Philosophy* (Notre Dame: University Press of Notre Dame, 1988). There are many commentaries on the confrontation between liberalism and communitarianism. For a very helpful critical and bibliographic treatment, see one volume special issue "Universalism and Communitarianism: Contemporary Debates in Ethics." *Philosophy and Social Criticism*, 14 (1988).

19 See Evan Simpson, "Moral Conservatism," *Review of Politics*, 49 (1987), pp.29-57. Robert Nisbet, *Conservatism* (Minneapolis: University of Minnesota Press, 1986).

20 MacIntyre, *After Virtue*, p.114.

21 Ibid., pp.59, 52.

22 Kai Nielsen, "On Taking Human Nature as the Basis of Morality," *Social Research*, 29 (1962), pp.157-176. In connection with the debate between individualism and communitarianism, see Christopher J. Berry, *Human Nature* (Atlantic Highlands: Humanities Press International. Inc., 1986).

23 Fred R. Dallmayr, ed., *From Contract to Community: Political Theory at the Crossroads* (New York: Marcel Dekker, Inc., 1978), p.9.

24 See Thomas C. Heller, Morton Sosna, and David E. Wellbery, eds., *Reconstructing Individualism: Autonomy, Individuality, and the Self in Western Thought* (Stanford: Stanford University Press, 1986). Also see John Kekes, *Moral Tradition and Individuality* (Princeton: Princeton University Press, 1989). Herbert J. Gans, *Middle American Individualism: The Future of Liberal Democracy* (New York: The Free Press, 1988).

25 David Riesman with Nathan Glazer and Reuel Denney, *The Lonely Crowd: A Study of the Changing American Character* (New Haven: Yale University Press, 1961; abridged ed. with 1969 preface). Richard Sennett, *The Fall of Public Man: On the Social Psychology of Capitalism* (New York: Vintage Books:1978). Cf. Allan Bloom, *The Closing of the American Mind* (New York: A Touchstone Book, 1987).

26 John Dunn, *Rethinking Modern Political Theory* (Cambridge: Cambridge University Press, 1985), Ch.10, p177. Also see his *Western Political Theory in the Face of the Future* (Cambridge: Cambridge University Press, 1979).

27 See, for example, Robert Nisbet, *The Quest for Community* (New York: Oxford University Press, 1953); Maurice R. Stein, *The Eclipse of Community* (Princeton: Princeton University Press, 1960). For a helpful comment on these books, see Dennis H. Wrong, *Skeptical Sociology* (New York: Columbia University Press, 1976), Ch.4. The Idea of Community: A Critique.

28 I am in debt to Gould, *Rethinking Democracy*, p.105. Cf. Chapter IV. n.32. Gould originally initiated this idea in *Marx's Social Ontology: Individuality and Community in Marx's Theory of Social Reality* (Cambridge: The MIT Press, 1980).

29 Rawls, "The Priority of Right and Ideas of the Good," *Philosophy & Public Affairs*, 17 (1988), p.273.

30 George Parkin Grant, *English-speaking Justice* (Notre Dame: University of Notre Dame Press, 1974). Dunn, *Rethinking Modern Political Theory*, p.161.

Frank S. Lucash, ed., *Justice and Equality: Here and Now* (Ithaca: Cornell University Press, 1986).

31 Rawls, "Some Reasons for the Maximin Criterion," *The American Economic Review*, 64 (1974), p.145. For Marx's slogan, see *Critique of the Gotha Program* in *Basic Writings*, p.119. This slogan is often called "Louis Blanc's Principle." See Charles E. Larmore, *Patterns of Moral Complexity* (Cambridge: Cambridge University Press, 1987), p.116.

32 See Michael Burway, *Manufacturing Consent: Changes in Labor Process under Monopoly Capitalism* (Chicago: University of Chicago Press, 1979); Michael Ryan, *Marxism and Deconstruction: A Critical Articulation* (Baltimore: The Johns Hopkins University Press, 1982); Fredric Jameson, "Marxism and Postmodernism," *New Left Review*, 176 (1989), pp.331-45; Norman Geras, "Post-Marxism," *New Left Review*, 163 (1987), pp.40-82.

33 Francis Fukuyama, "The End of History," *The National Interest*, Summer 1989, p.4.

34 Ibid., p.18. Also see "A Reply to My Critique," *National Interest*, winter 1989/90. One who has interest in this debate should follow many critical articles in *The National Interest* and *National Review*.

35 Dennis Auerbach, "Liberalism in Search of Its Self," *Critical Review,*" 1 (1987), pp.7-29.

36 Daniel Bell, *The End of Ideology* (Cambridge: Harvard University Press, 1960; with a new Afterword, 1988); Chaim I. Waxman, *The End of Ideology Debate* (New York: Funk & Wagnalls, 1968).

37 David McLellan, *Ideology* (Minneapolis: University of Minnesota Press, 1986), p.2.

38 See David Lloyd-Thomas, *In Defense of Liberalism* (New York: Basil Blackwell, 1988).

39 Especially see "The Priority of Right and Ideas of The Good." Cf. Robert B. Thigpen, "Liberalism and Neutrality Principle, "*Political Theory*, pp.585-600.

40 Isaac Levi, *Hard Choices: Decision Making under Unresolved Conflict* (Cambridge: Cambridge University Press, 1986). For the other two, see n.31 of this section and n.139 of Chapter IV.

41 Marx, *German Ideology*, in *Basic Writings*, p.247.

42 Ibid., p.248.

43 Cf. Joseph Campbell, *The Hero with a Thousand Faces* (Princeton: Princeton University Press,1972; rev. ed.,1988).

44 The list of homo partialis is endless. For example, zoon politikon, zoon logos ekon (political or rational animal; Aristotle), metaphysical animal

(Schopenhauer), irrational man (Barrett), homo hierarchicus (Dumont), ecce homo (John/ Nietzsche), homo academicus (Bourdieu), homo politicus (Lasswell), homo ludens (Huizinga), homo viator (Marcel), homo symbolicus (Cassirer), homo significans (Barthes), psychological man (Rieff/Lasch), ecclesial man (Farley), homo religiosus, homo sapiens, homo habilis, homo creator (Mühlman), homo dionysiacus, homo ecologicus, the planetary man (Desan), homo cosmopolitan, homo erectus (Black), homo aequalis (Dumont), homo loquens (Hernandez), homo necans (Burcket), homo uniformis (Aldias), and even homo soveticus (Zinovive /Janson). In connection with homo economicus it is very interesting to note that, in the soviet bloc, Nove proves the existence of homo economicus soveticus. For a good discussion, see Hans van Den Doel, *Democracy and Welfare Economics*, pp.124f. For homo partialis in general, see Calvin O. Schrag, *Radical Reflection and the Origin of the Human Sciences* (West Lafayette, Indiana: Purdue University Press, 1980); Antony Flew, *A Rational Animal and Other Philosophical Essays on the Nature of Man* (Oxford: Clarendon Press, 1978).

45 Marx, *German Ideology*, p.254. Marx mentions species-being at the section of "Alienated Labor" in *The Economic and Philosophical Manuscripts* in *Early Writings*.

46 Gauthier, "Morality, Rational Choice, and Semantic Representation," p.220.

47 For a good comment on this issue, see Madan Sarup, *An Introductory Guide to Post-Structuralism and Postmodernism* (Athens: The University of Georgia Press, 1989), p.167; Calvin O. Schrag, *Communicative Praxis and the Space of Subjectivity* (Bloomington: Indiana University Press, 1989), p.213.

48 Michel Foucault, *The Order of Things: An Archaeology of the Human Sciences* (New York: Vintage Books, 1970), p.387.

49 Foucault, "On the Genealogy of Ethics: An Overview of Work in Process," in Hubert L. Dreyfus and Paul Rainbow, *Michel Foucault: Beyond Structuralism and Hermeneutics* (Chicago: The University of Chicago Press, 1982; 2nd. ed., with an Afterword and an Interview by Michel Foucault, 1983), pp.229-252. Foucault promised to write six volumes on *The History of Sexuality*. But he published only three volumes and did not complete the fourth one. The third volume, *The Care of the Self*, trans. Robert Hurley (New York: Vintage Books, 1988), is very relevant here. One of the best introductory books on Foucault's ethics so far is Jeffrey Minson, *Genealogies of Morals. Nietzsche, Foucault, Donzelot and the Eccentricity of Ethics* (New York: St. Martin's Press, 1985).

50 Jacques Derrida, "Structure, Sign, and Play in the Discourse of the Human Sciences," in *The Languages of Criticism and the Sciences of Man: The Structuralist Controversy*, eds. Richard Macksey and Eugenio Donato (Baltimore: Johns Hopkins University Press, 1970), p.271. I am in debt to G.B. Madison, "Postmodern Philosophy," *Critical Review*, 2 (1988), pp.166-82.

51 K.R. Minogue, *The Liberal Mind* (London: Methuen & Co. Ltd., 1963). Gerald F. Gaus, *The Modern Liberal Theory of Man* (London: Croom Helm, 1983).

52 See, for example, Oliver E. Williamson, *The Economic Institutions of Capitalism: Firms, Markets, Relational Contracting* (New York: The Free Press, 1985), Ch.2. Contractual Man.

53 Jan Narveson, *The Libertarian Idea* (Philadelphia: Temple University Press, 1988). There are several new approaches. For example, Ron Replogle uses "widely acknowledged norms of competence" in *Recovering the Social Contract* (Totowa, NJ: Roman & Littlefield, 1989). In turn, Thomas W. Pogge tries to expand Rawls' theory into a broad perspective, including international relations in his *Realizing Rawls* (Ithaca: Cornell University Press, 1989). Rex Martin links Rawls' theory mainly with the doctrine of rights in his *Rawls and Rights* (Lawrence: University Press of Kansas, 1985). Fishkin reconstructs social contract theory according to a concept of self-reflective political culture. See his "Bargaining, Justice, and Justification: Towards Reconstruction," in *The New Social Contract: Essays on Gauthier*, pp.46-64. Also see his "Liberal Theory: Strategies of Reconstruction," in *Liberals on Liberalism*, pp.54-64. But Gauthier points out that "Fishkin's — and Habermas's — attempt to provide a transcendental deduction is a mistake." See Gauthier, "Morality, Rational Choice, and Semantic Representation," p.196.

54 See Lessnoff, *Social Contract*, p.149.

55 Danielson, "The Visible Hand of Morality," p.372. See n.66 of Chapter IV.

56 Mueller, *Public Choice*. See n.82 of Chapter III.

57 B.J. Diggs, "Utilitarianism and Contractarianism," in *The Limits of Utilitarianism*, Harlan B. Miller and William H. Williams, eds. (Minneapolis: University of Minnesota Press, 1982), p.101.

58 Hamlin, "Liberty, Contract and the State," in *The Good Polity*, p.100. See n.1 of Chapter III.

59 There are many highly technical commentaries on the uncertainty principle and Plank's constant. I recommend a plain explanation. See Stephen W. Hawking, *A Brief History of Time* (Toronto: Bantam Books, 1988), Ch.5. The Uncertainty Principle.

60 Cf. Jean-Francois Revel, *The Totalitarian Temptation* (New York: Penguin Books, 1978).

61 Elisha A. Pazner and David Schmeidler, "Social Contract Theory and Ordinal Distributive Equality," in Leonid Hurwicz, David Schmeidler, and Hugo Sonnenschein, eds., *Social Goals and Social Organization* (Cambridge: Cambridge University Press, 1985), p.312.

62 Rawls, "Kantian Constructivism in Moral Theory," p.530.

63 Ibid.

64 Andrew Altman, "Rawls' Pragmatic Turn," *Journal of Social Philosophy*, 14 (1983), pp.8-12; William A. Galston, "Moral Personality and Liberal Theory," *Political Theory*, 10 (1982), p.512; Charles Altieri, "Judgment and Justice under Postmodern Conditions; or, How Lyotard Helps us Read Rawls as a Postmodern Thinker," in Reed Way Dasenbrock, ed., *Redrawing the Lines: Analytic Philosophy, Deconstruction, and Literary Theory* (Minneapolis: University of Minnesota Press, 1989), pp.61-91; Joseph Raz, "Facing Diversity: The Case of Epistemic Abstinence," *Philosophy & Public Affairs*, 19 (1990), pp.3-46; Richard Dien Winfield, *Reason and Justice* (Albany: State University of New York Press, 1988), pp.11-14; Galston, p.498.

65 Rawls, "Justice as Fairness: Political not Metaphysical," p.224. n.2. "Whether constructivism is reasonable for moral philosophy is a separate and more general question."

66 Inside quotation is from T. Nagel, *Mortal Questions* (New York: Cambridge University Press, 1979), p.x.

67 Gauthier, "Moral Artifice," p.413.

68 Rawls, "The Idea of An Overlapping Consensus," pp.23-4.

69 Rawls, "The Domain of the Political and Overlapping Consensus," pp.233-55.

70 For Rawls' original reflective equilibrium, See Chapter III, B.1. According to Daniels, narrow equilibrium is "an ordered pair of (a) a set of considered moral judgments acceptable to a given person P at a given time, and (b) a set of moral principles that economically systemizes (a)." "On Some Methods of Ethics and Linguistics," *Philosophical Studies*, 37 (1980), p.22. In contrast, "[t]he method of wide reflective equilibrium is an attempt to produce coherence in an ordered triple of sets of belief held by a particular person, namely, (a) a set of considered judgments, (b) a set of moral principles, (c) a set of relevant background theories." "Wide Reflective Equilibrium and Theory Acceptance in Ethics," *The Journal of Philosophy*, 76 (1979), p.256; Richard Rorty, "The Priority of Democracy to Philosophy," in Merrill D. Peterson and Robert C. Vaughan, eds., *The Virginia Statue of Religious Freedom* (Cambridge: Cambridge University Press, 1987), p.271; "Postmodernist Bourgeois Liberalism," *The Journal of Philosophy*, 80 (1983), p.586.

71 See n.3 of this chapter.

72 Gadamer, "Über die Möglichkeit einer Philosophischen Ethik," in *Keine Schriften I: Philosophie Hermeneutik* (Tübingen: J.C.B. Mohr, 1967), p.181. For a very helpful discussion on the circle, see John Llewelyn, *Beyond*

Metaphysics: *The Hermeneutic Circle in Contemporary Continental Philosophy* (Atlantic Highlands: Humanities Press, 1985). Also see one volume special issue "Hermeneutics in Ethics and Social Theory," in *The Philosophical Forum*, 21 (1989-90).

73 Victor Farias, *Heidegger and Nazism* (Philadelphia: Temple University Press, 1989). From a logical point of view in general, see Douglas N. Walton, "Are Circular Arguments Necessarily Vicious?" *American Philosophical Quarterly*, 22 (1985), pp.263-274.

74 Gauthier, "George Grant's Justice," pp.126-27. See Chapter IV. n.174.

75 Roberto Mangabeira Unger, *Knowledge and Politics* (New York: The Free Press, 1975), p.289.

76 MacIntyre, *After Virtue*, p.21.

77 Rorty, "The Priority of Democracy to Philosophy," p.272.

78 MacIntyre, *Whose Justice? Which Rationality?*, p.4.

79 Stanley Rosen, *Hermeneutics as Politics* (New York: Oxford University Press, 1987), p.138.

80 Evan Simpson, "Conservatism, Radicalism, and Democratic Practice, " *Praxis International*, 9 (1989), p.273.

81 Jürgen Habermas, *The New Conservatism*, trans. S.W. Nicholsen (Cambridge: The MIT Press, 1989).

82 Gould, *Rethinking Democracy*, p.127.

83 Gray, *Liberalisms*, p.264.

84 Cf. William Galston, "Defending Liberalism," *The American Political Science Review*, 76 (1982), p.626.

85 Paul Ricoeur, "Irrationality and the Plurality of Philosophical Systems," *Dialectica*, 39 (1985), pp.297-319.

86 Cf. Lawrence E. Cahoone, *The Dilemma of Modernity: Philosophy, Culture, and Anti-Culture* (Albany: The State University of New York Press, 1988).

87 Jürgen Habermas, "Modernity—An Incomplete Project," in *The Anti-Aesthetic: Essays on Postmodern Culture*, Hal Foster, ed. (Port Townsend, Washington: Bay Press, 1983), pp.3-15. Also see Suzi Gablik, *Has Modernism Failed?* (New York: Theme & Hudson, 1984).

88 Dunn, *Rethinking Modern Political Theory*, p.177.

89 Aside from Marx's laws of motion (contradictions) of capitalism (see Chapter IV. n.176), there are many observations which regard present socio-politico-

economic and cultural situations of liberal (and/or non-liberal) society as in a dilemma. See, for example, Daniel Bell, *The Cultural Contradictions of Capitalism* (New York: Basic Books, 1976); Robert A. Dahl, *Dilemmas of Pluralistic Democracy: Autonomy vs. Control* (New Haven: Yale University Press, 1982); Arthur M. Okun, *Equality and Efficiency: The Big Tradeoff* (Washington, D.C.: The Brookings Institutions, 1975); Abigail Solomon-Godeau, "Living with Contradictions: Critical Practices in the Age of Supply-Side Aesthetics," in *Universal Abandon?*, pp.191-213; Raymond Plant, "Hirsh, Hayek, and Habermas: Dilemmas of Distribution?," in *Dilemmas of Liberal Democracies* (London: Tavistock Publications, 1988); William Leiss, *C.B. Macpherson: Dilemmas of Liberalism and Socialism* (New York: St. Martin's Press, 1988). Gilles Deleuze and Felix Guatari, *A Thousand Plateaus: Capitalism & Schizophrenia*, trans. Brian Massumi (Minneapolis: University of Minnesota Press, 1988). For two more schizophrenias (psychological and cultural — Anti-Oedipus), see Chapter II. n.89. Finally in ethics, Michael Stocker, "The Schizophrenia of Modern Ethical Theories," *Journal of Philosophy*, 73 (1976), pp.453-466. I think the following book, which is edited by Nancy Rosenbaum, should receive special attention by all who are interested in the above dilemmas. *Liberalism and Moral Life* (Cambridge: Harvard University Press, 1989). At any rate, maybe, for Fukuyama, all the above dilemmas are pseudo, and they are already solved (if not absolutely, they are relatively solved compared to non-capitalistic social arrangements). It is not surprising that we can find many who think like Fukuyama. Cf. Robert Heilbroner, "The Triumph of Capitalism," *The New Yorker*, Jan. (1989), pp.98-109. Jefferey Friedman says that "One of the empirical assumptions long made by participants in that debate has been that capitalism trades economic equality for greater productivity, while socialism provides equality at the express of prosperity. Harmon Zeigler and Thomas Dye challenge this assumption in their important review of Barrington Moore's most recent work." See "Liberalism and Post-Liberalism," *Critical Review*, 2 (1988), p.11. For the review article, see their "Freedom vs. Equality?," in the same volume, pp.189-201. Also see Barrington Moore, Jr. *Authority and Inequality under Capitalism and Socialism: USA, USSR, and CHINA* (Oxford: Clarendon Press, 1987). Then, is it the case that "The only decisive answers to these questions are of course the answers the history itself will eventually provide us with." See G.B. Madison, "Postmodern Philosophy?" *Critical Review*, 2 (1988), p.175. In contrast, what is the meaning of Marx's following observation? He says: "The materialist doctrine that men are products of circumstances and upbringing, and that, therefore, changed men are products of other circumstances and changed upbringing, forgets that it is men that change circumstances, and that the educator himself needs educating." *Theses on Feuerbach* in *Basic Writings*, p.244. Then, once again, we are in the dilemma and indeterminacy. Are we, mankind, a passive waiting-for-Godot or a homo creator?

90 H.A. Prichard," Does Moral Philosophy Rest on a Mistake?" *Mind*, 21 (1921). Rpt. in Wilfrid Sellars and John Hospers, eds., *Readings in Ethical Theory*, 2nd. ed. (Englewood Cliffs: Prentice Hall, 1970), pp.86-105. Richard A. Rodewald, "Does Liberalism Rest on a Mistake?," *Canadian Journal of Philosophy*, 15 (1985), pp.231-51.

Bibliography

I. Contractarian Moral and Political Philosophy

A. Traditional

1. *Primary sources*

Barker, Ernest, ed. with Introduction. *Social Contract: Essays by Locke, Hume, and Rousseau.* London: Oxford University Press, 1947.

Hobbes, Thomas. *Leviathan.* ed. with Introduction. C.B. Macpherson. Harmondsworth: Penguin Books, 1986.

_____. *De Cive: The English Version; Philosophical Rudiments Concerning Government And Society.* ed. Howard Warrender. Oxford: Clarendon Press, 1983.

_____. *Elements of Law Natural and Politic.* Tönnies edn. Cambridge: Cambridge University Press, 1989.

Kant, Immanuel. *Foundations of the Metaphysics of Morals.* trans. Lewis White Beck. Indianapolis: Bobbs-Merrill Educational Publishing, 1959.

_____. *Critique of Practical Reason.* trans. Lewis White Beck. Indianapolis: Bobbs-Merrill Educational Publishing, 1956.

Locke, John. *The Second Treatise of Government* in *Two Treatises of Government.* ed. Peter Laslett. New York: A Mentor Book, 1963.

Rousseau, Jean-Jacques. *Of The Social Contract.* trans. Charles M. Sherover. New York: Harper & Row, 1984.

_____. *Discourse on the Origin and the Foundations of Inequality among Men* in *Jean-Jacques Rousseau: The First and Second Discourses.* trans. Victor Gourevitch. New York: Haper & Row, 1987.

2. Secondary sources

a. Books

Arblaster, Anthony. *The Rise and Decline of Western Liberalism.* Oxford: Basil Blackwell, 1984.

Baumin, Bernard. *Hobbes' Leviathan: Interpretation and Criticism.* Belmont: Wadsworth, 1969.

Brown, K.R., ed. *Hobbes Studies.* Oxford: Basil Blackwell, 1965.

Gough, J.W. *The Social Contract.* Oxford: Clarendon Press, 1936.

Gray, John. *Liberalism.* Minneapolis: University of Minnesota Press, 1986.

_____. *Liberalisms: Essays in Political Philosophy.* London: Routledge, 1989.

Hampton, Jean. *Hobbes and Social Contract.* Cambridge: Cambridge University Press, 1986.

Herzog, Don. *Without Foundations: Justification in Political Theory.* Ithaca: Cornell University Press, 1985.

Johnston, David. *The Rhetoric of Leviathan: Thomas Hobbes and Cultural Transformation.* Princeton: Princeton University Press, 1986.

Kavka, Gregory S. *Hobbesian Moral and Political Theory.* Princeton: Princeton University Press, 1986.

Lessnoff, Michael. *Social Contract.* Atlantic Highlands, N.J.: Humanities Press, 1986.

Levine, Andrew. *Liberal Democracy: A Critique of Its Theory*. New York: Columbia University Press, 1981.

Myers, Milton L. *The Soul of Modern Economic Man: Ideas of Self-Interest; Thomas Hobbes to Adam Smith*. Chicago: University of Chicago Press, 1983.

McCormick, Peter J. *Social Contract and Political Obligation: A Critique and Reappraisal*. New York: Garland Publishing, Inc., 1987.

Pateman, Carol. *The Problem of Political Obligation: A Critique of Liberal Theory*. Cambridge: Polity Press, 1985.

Rapaczynski, Andrzej. *Nature and Politics: Liberalism in the Philosophies of Hobbes, Locke, and Rousseau*. Ithaca: Cornell University Press, 1987.

Rogers, G.A.J. and Alan Ryan, eds. *Perspectives on Thomas Hobbes*. Oxford: Clarendon Press, 1988.

Rosenbaum, Alan S. *Coercion and Autonomy: Philosophical Foundations, Issues, and Practices*. New York: Greenwood Press, 1986.

Seidler, Victor J. *Kant, Respect and Injustice: The Limits of Liberal Moral Theory*. London: Routledge & Kegan Paul, 1986.

Shapiro, Ian. *The Evolution of Rights in Liberal Theory*. Cambridge: Cambridge University Press, 1986.

Sorell, Tom. *Hobbes*. London: Routledge & Kegan Paul, 1986.

b. Articles

Auerbach, Dennis. "Liberalism in Search of Its Self." *Critical Review*, 1 (1987), 7-29.

Berry, C.J. "From Hume to Hegel: the Case of the Social Contract." *Journal of the History of Ideas*, 34 (1977), 691-90.

Bogart, J.H. "Lockean Provisos and State of Nature Theories." *Ethics*, 95 (1985), 828-36.

Braybrooke, D. "The Insoluble Problem of the Social Contract." *Dialogue*, 15 (1976), 3-37.

Browne, D.E. "The Contract Theory of Justice." *Philosophical Papers*, 5 (1976), 1-10.

Chroust, Anton-Hermann. "The Origin and Meaning of the Social Compact Doctrine." *Ethics*, 57 (1946), 38-56.

Evers, Williamson. "Social Contract: A Critique." *The Journal of Libertarian Studies*, 1 (1977), 185-94.

Farrell, Daniel M. "Taming Leviathan: Reflections on Some Recent Works on Hobbes." *Ethics*, 98 (1988), 793-805.

George, Rolf. "The Liberal Tradition: Kant, and the Pox." *Dialogue*, 27 (1988), 195-206.

Kavka, Gregory S. "Hobbes's War of All Against All." *Ethics*, 93 (1983), 291-310.

Laslett, Peter. "Social Contract." in Paul Edwards, ed. *The Encyclopedia of Philosophy*.

Paul, Ellen Frankel. "Of the Social Contract within the Natural Rights Theory." *The Personalist*, 59 (1978), 9-21.

Plamenatz, John. "On le forcere d'être," in *Hobbes and Rousseau: A Collection of Critical Essays*. eds. M. Cranston and R.S. Peters. New York: Anchor Books, 1972., 318-32.

Rempel, Henry David. "On Forcing People to be Free." *Ethics*, 87 (1976), 18-34.

Rotenstreich, Nathan. "Faces of the Social Contract." *Revue Internationale de Philosophie*, 33 (1979), 484-505.

Ripstein, Arthur. "Foundationalism in Political Theory." *Philosophy & Public Affairs*, 16 (1987), 116-37.

Runciman, W.G. and A.K. Sen. "Games, Justice and the General Will." *Mind*, 79 (1965), 554-62.

Sarkar, Husain. "Lockean Proviso." *Canadian Journal of Philosophy*, 12 (1982), 47-59.

Simmons, A. John. "Locke's State of Nature." *Political Theory*, 17 (1989), 449-70.

Zaitchik, A. "Hobbes's Reply to the Fool: The Problem of Consent and Obligation." *Political Theory*, 10 (1982), 245-266.

B. John Rawls

1. *Primary sources*

a. Book

A Theory of Justice. Cambridge: The Belknap Press of Harvard University Press, 1971.

b. Articles

"Outline of a Decision Procedure of Ethics." *The Philosophical Review*, 60 (1951), 177-97.

"Review of *An Examination of the Place of Reason in Ethics* by Stephen Toulmin." *The Philosophical Review*, 60 (1951), 572-80.

"Two Concepts of Rules." *The Philosophical Review*, 67 (1955), 3-32.

"Justice as Fairness." *The Journal of Philosophy*, 54 (1957), 653-70.

"Justice as Fairness." *The Philosophical Review*, 67 (1958), 164-69.

"Constitutional Liberty and the Concept of Justice." in *Justice: Nomos* VI, eds. Carl J. Friedrich and John W. Chapman. New York: Atherton Press, 1963., 98-125.

"The Sense of Justice." *The Philosophical Review*, 72 (1963), 281-305.

"Legal Obligation and the Duty of Fair Play." in *Law and Philosophy.* ed. Sidney Hook. New York: New York University Press, 1964., 3-18.

"Distributive Justice." in *Philosophy, Politics, and Society.* Third Series, eds. Peter Laslett and W.G. Runciman. London: Basil Blackwell, 1967., 58-82.

"Distributive Justice: Some Addenda." *Natural Law Forum*, 13 (1968), 51-71.

"The Justification of Civil Disobedience." in *Civil Disobedience: Theory and Practice.* ed. Hugo A. Bedau. New York: Pegasus Books, 1969., 240-55.

"Justice as Reciprocity." in *Utilitarianism: John Stuart Mill With Critical Essays.* ed. Samuel Gorovitz. New York: Bobbs-Merrill Co., 1971., 242-68.

"Reply to Lyons and Titleman." *The Journal of Philosophy*, 69 (1972), 556-57.

"Distributive Justice." in *Economic Justice.* ed. Edmund S. Phelps. London: Penguin Books, 1973., 319-62.

"Some Reasons for the Maximin Criterion." *The American Economic Review*, 64 (1974), 141-46.

"Reply to Alexsander and Musgrave." *The Quarterly Journal of Economics*, 88 (1974), 633-55.

"A Kantian Conception of Equality." *The Cambridge Review*, 96 (1975), 94-99.

"The Independence of Moral Theory." *Proceedings and Addresses of the American Philosophical Association*, 48 (1974-75), 5-22.

"Fairness to Goodness." *The Philosophical Review*, 84 (1975), 536-54.

"The Basic Structure as Subject." *American Philosophical Quarterly*, 14 (1977), 159-65.

"The Basic Structure as Subject." in *Values and Morals*. eds. A.I. Goldman and Jaegwon Kim. Dordrecht: D. Reidel Publishing Co., 1978., 47-71.

"A Well-Ordered Society." in *Philosophy, Politics, and Society*. 5th Series. eds. Peter Laslett and James Fishkin. New Haven: Yale University Press, 1979., 94-99.

"The Kantian Constructivism in Moral Theory." *The Journal of Philosophy*, 77 (1980), 515-72.

"Social Unity and Primary Goods." in *Utilitarianism and Beyond*, eds. A.K. Sen and Bernard Williams. Cambridge: Cambridge University Press, 1982., 159-85.

"Justice as Fairness: Political not Metaphysical." *Philosophy & Public Affairs*, 14 (1985), 223-51.

"The Basic Liberties and Their Priority." in *Liberty, Equality and Law*. ed. Sterling M. McMurrin. Salt Lake City: University of Utah Press, 1987., 1-87.

"The Idea of Overlapping Consensus." *Oxford Journal of Legal Studies*, 7 (1987), 1-25.

"The Priority of Right and Ideas of the Good." *Philosophy & Public Affairs*, 17 (1988), 251-76.

"The Domain of the Political and Overlapping Consensus." *New York University Law Review*, 64 (1989), 233-55.

"Themes in Kant's Moral Philosophy." in *Kant's Transcendental Deductions: The Three Critiques and the Opus Postumum*. ed. Eckart Förster. Stanford: Stanford University Press, 1989., 81-113.

2. Secondary Sources

a. Books

Barry, Brian. *The Liberal Theory of Justice*. Oxford: Clarendon Press, 1973.

Blocker, H. Gene and Elizabeth H. Smith, eds. *John Rawls' Theory of Social Justice*. Athens: Ohio University Press, 1980.

Daniels, Norman., ed. *Reading Rawls: Critical Studies on Rawls' 'A Theory of Justice.'* Oxford: Basil Blackwell, 1975. With a New Preface. Stanford, California: Stanford University Press, 1989.

Elfstrom, Gerard. *The Import of Moral Being in John Rawls' Theory of Justice*. Ph.D. Dissertation. Atlanta: Emory University, 1975.

Hardin, Russell., ed. *Symposium on Rawlsian Theory of Justice: Recent Developments. Ethics*, 99 (1989).

Martin, Rex. *Rawls and Rights*. Lawrence: University Press of Kansas, 1986.

Miller, David. *Social Justice*. Oxford: Clarendon Press, 1976.

Nielsen, Kai and Roger A. Shiner, eds. *New Essays on Contract Theory. Canadian Journal of Philosophy*. suppl. 3 (1977).

Pettit, Philip and Chandran Kukathas. *Rawls: 'A Theory of Justice' and Its Critique*. Stanford: Stanford University Press, 1990.

Pogge, Thomas W. *Realizing Rawls*. Ithaca: Cornell University Press, 1989.

Schaefer, David Lewis. *Justice or Tyranny?*: *A Critique of John Rawls's Theory of Justice*. Port Washington, N.Y.: Kennikat Press, 1979.

Wellbank, J.H., Denis Snook, and David T. Mason. *John Rawls and His Critics*: *An Annotated Bibliography*. New York: Garland Publishing, 1982.

Wolff, Robert Paul. *Understanding Rawls*. Princeton: Princeton University Press, 1977.

b. Articles

Altieri, Charles. "Judgment and Justice under Postmodern Conditions; or How Lyotard Helps us Read Rawls as a Postmodern Thinker?" in *Redrawing the Lines: Analytic Philosophy, Deconstruction, and Literary Theory*. ed. Reed Way Dasenbrock. Minneapolis: The University of Minnesota Press, 1989., 61-91.

Altman, Andrew. "Rawls' Pragmatic Turn." *Journal of Social Philosophy*, 14 (1983), 8-12.

Care, Norman S. "Contractualism and Moral Criticism." *The Review of Metaphysics*, 23 (1969), 85-101.

Cooper, W.E. "The Perfectly Just Society." *Philosophy and Phenomenological Research*, 38 (1977-8), 46-55.

Daniels, Norman. "Wide Reflective Equilibrium and Theory Acceptance in Ethics." *The Journal of Philosophy*, 76 (1979), 256-82.

Feinberg, Joel. "Justice, Fairness and Rationality." *Yale Law Journal*, 81 (1972), 1004-31.

Fishkin, James. "Justice and Rationality." *The American Political Science Review*, 69 (1975), 615-29.

Frankel, Charles. "Justice and Rationality." in *Philosophy, Science, and Method*. eds. Sidney Morgenbesser, Patrick Suppes, and Morton White. New York: St. Martin Press, 1969., 400-14.

Galston, William A. "Moral Personality and Liberal Theory: John Rawls' 'Dewey Lectures.'" *Political Theory*, 10 (1982), 492-519.

Gibson, Mary. "Rationality." *Philosophy & Public Affairs*, 6 (1977), 193-225.

Gordon, Scott. "The New Contractarians." *Journal of Political Economy*. 84 (1976), 141-67.

Howe, R. E. and J. E. Roemer. "Rawlsian Justice as the Core of a Game." *American Economic Review*, 71 (1981), 880-95.

Kultgen, John. "Rational Contractors." *Journal of Value Inquiry*, 21 (1987), 185-98.

Keyt, David. "The Social Contract as an Analytic, Justificatory, and Polemical Device." *Canadian Journal of Philosophy*, 4 (1974), 241-252.

Machan, Tibor R. "Social Contract as a Basis of Norms: A Critique." *The Journal of Libertarian Studies*, 7 (1983), 141-46.

Macpherson, C.B. "Rawls's Models of Man and Society." *Philosophy of the Social Sciences*, 3 (1973), 341-47.

Mouffe, Chantal. "Rawls: Political Philosophy without Politics." *Philosophy and Social Criticism*, 13 (1987), 105-23.

Neal, Patrick. "A Liberal Theory of the Good?" *Canadian Journal of Philosophy*, 17 (1987), 567-82.

Nelson, William. "The Very Idea of Pure Procedural Justice." *Ethics*, 90 (1980), 502-11.

Nielsen, Kai. "A Note On Rationality." *The Journal of Critical Analysis*, 9 (1972), 16-9.

_____. "Rawls and Classical Amoralism." *Mind*, 86 (1977), 19-30.

_____. "Rawls' Defense of Morality, Amoralism, and the Problem of Congruence." *The Personalist*, 59 (1978), 93-100.

Pollock, Lansing. "A Dilemma for Rawls?" *Philosophical Studies*, 22 (1971), 37-43.

Porebski, Czeslaw. "The Moral Point of View and the Rational Choice Theory." in *The Tasks of Contemporary Philosophy*. eds. Werner Leinfeller and Franz M. Wukeits. Vienna: Hölder-Pichler Tempsky, 1986., 880-95.

Sadurski, Wojciech. "Contractarianism and Intuition: On the Role of Social Contract Arguments in Theories of Justice." *Australasian Journal of Philosophy*, 61 (1983), 321-47.

Schaefer, David. "'Moral Theory' Versus Political Philosophy: Two Approaches to Justice," *Review of Politics*, 39 (1977), 192-219.

Schwartz, Adina. "Moral Neutrality and Primary Goods." *Ethics*, 83 (1983), 294-397.

C. David Gauthier

1. *Primary Sources*

a. Books

Practical Reasoning: The Structure and Foundations of Prudential and Moral Arguments and Their Exemplification in Discourse. Oxford: Clarendon Press, 1963.

The Logic of Leviathan: The Moral and Political Theory of Thomas Hobbes. Oxford: Clarendon Press, 1969.

ed. *Morality and Rational Self-interest*. Englewood Cliffs: Prentice Hall, 1970.

Morals By Agreement. Oxford: Clarendon Press, 1986.

Moral Dealing: Contract, Ethics, and Reason. Ithaca: Cornell University Press, 1990.

2. *Articles*

"Rule-utilitarianism and Randomization." *Analysis*, 25 (1965), 68-9.

"Progress and Happiness." *Ethics*, 78 (1967), 77-82.

"Morality and Advantage." *The Philosophical Review*, 76 (1967), 460-75.

"Moore's Naturalistic Fallacy." *American Philosophical Quarterly*, 4 (1967), 315-20.

"How Decisions are Caused." *The Journal of Philosophy*, 65 (1967), 147-51.

"How Decisions are Caused But not Predicted." *The Journal of Philosophy*, 65 (1968), 170-71.

"Yet Another Hobbes." *Inquiry*, 12 (1969), 449-65.

"Brandt on Egoism." *The Journal of Philosophy*, 69 (1972), 697-98.

"Rational Cooperation." *Nôus*, 8 (1974), 53-63.

"The Impossibility of Rational Egoism." *The Journal of Philosophy*, 71 (1974), 439-456.

"Reason and Maximization." *Canadian Journal of Philosophy*, 4 (1975), 411-433.

"Justice and Natural Endowment: Toward A Critique of Rawls' Ideological Framework." *Social Theory and Practice*, 3 (1974), 3-26.

"Coordination." *Dialogue*, 14 (1975), 195-221.

"Critical Notices of Stephan Körner: *Practical Reason.*" *Dialogue*, 3 (1977), 510-18.

"The Social Contract as Ideology." *Philosophy & Public Affairs*, 6 (1977), 130-64.

"Social Choice and Distributive Justice." *Philosophia*, 7 (1978), 239-253.

"Critical Notice of Harsanyi's *Essays on Ethics, Social Behavior and Scientific Explanation.*" *Dialogue*, 17 (1978), 696-706.

"Economic Rationality and Moral Constraints." in *Midwest Studies in Philosophy*: Vol. iii. *Studies in Ethical Theory.* eds. Peter A French, Theodore E. Uehling, Jr., and Howard K. Wettstein. Minneapolis: University of Minnesota Press, 1978., 75-96.

"Thomas Hobbes: Moral Theorist." *The Journal of Philosophy*, 76 (1979), 547-559.

"David Hume, Contractarian." *The Philosophical Review*, 88 (1979), 3-38.

"Bargaining Our Way into Morality." *Philosophic Exchange*, 2 (1979), 14-27.

"The Politics of Redemption." in *Trent Rousseau Papers.* eds. Jim Macadam, Michael Neuman, and Guy Lafrance. Ottawa: University of Ottawa Press, 1980., 71-98.

"The Irrationality of Choosing Egoism." *Canadian Journal of Philosophy*, 10 (1980), 179-88.

"On the Refutation of Utilitarianism." in *The Limits of Utilitarianism*. eds. Harlan B. Miller and William H. Williams. Minneapolis: University of Minnesota Press, 1982., 144-63.

"Three Against Justice: The Fool, the Sensible knave, and the Lydian Shepherd." in *Midwest Studies in Philosophy*. vol. vii. *Social and Political Philosophy*. eds. Peter French, Theodore E. Uehling, Jr., and Howard K. Wettstein. Minneapolis: University of Minnesota Press, 1982., 11-29.

"No Need for Morality: The Case of the Competitive Market." *Philosophic Exchange*, 3 (1982), 41-56.

"Justified Inequality?" *Dialogue*, 21 (1982), 431-43.

"Critical Notice: Jon Elster, *Ulysses and the Sirens*: *Studies in Rationality and Irrationality. Canadian Journal of Philosophy*, 13 (1983), 133-40.

"Deterrence, Maximization, and Rationality." *Ethics*, 94 (1984), 474-495. Rpt. in *The Security Gamble*: *Deterrence Dilemma in the Nuclear Age*. Maryland Studies in Public Philosophy. ed. Douglas MacLean. Totowa, NJ.: Rowan & Allanheld, 1984.

"Justice as Social Choice." in *Morality, Reason and Truth*. ed. David Copp. Totowa: Rowan & Allanheld, 1984., 251-69.

"The Incompleat Egoist." in *The Tanner Lectures on Human Values*. vol.i. Salt Lake City: The University of Utah Press, 1984.

"Maximization Constrained: The Rationality of Cooperation." in *Paradoxes of Rationality and Cooperation*: *Prisoner's Dilemma and Newcomb's Problem*. eds. Richmond Campbell and Lanning Sowden. Vancouver: The University of British Columbia Press, 1985., 75-93.

"Bargaining and Justice." in *Ethics and Economics*. *Social Philosophy and Policy*, 2 (1985), 29-47.

"The Unity of Reason: A Subversive Reinterpretation of Kant." *Ethics*, 96 (1985), 74-88.

"Reason to be Moral?" *Synthesis*, 72 (1987), 5-27.

"Taming Leviathan." *Philosophy & Public Affairs*, 16 (1987), 280-298.

"Reply to Wolfram." *Philosophical Books*, 28 (1987), 134-9.

"Hobbes's Social Contract." in *Perspectives on Thomas Hobbes*. eds. G.A.J. Rogers and Alan Ryan. Oxford: Clarendon Press, 1988., 125-52.

"Hobbes's Social Contract." *Nôus*, 22 (1988), 71-82.

"Moral Artifice: A Reply." *Canadian Journal of Philosophy*, 18 (1988), 385-418.

"Morality, Rational Choice, and Semantic Representation: A Reply to My Critics." in *The New Social Contract: Essays on Gauthier*. eds. Ellen Frankel Paul et al. Oxford: Basil Blackwell, 1988., 173-221.

"Critical Notices: George Grant's Justice." *Dialogue*, 27 (1988), 121-34.

2. Secondary Sources

a. Books

Baier, Annette C. et al. *Symposium on David Gauthier: Morals by Agreement. Canadian Journal of Philosophy*, 18 (1988).

Barry, Brian and Russell Hardin, eds. *Rational Man and Irrational Society*. Beverly Hills: Sage Publications, 1982.

_____. *Theories of Justice*. Berkely: University of California Press, 1989.

Darwall, Stephen L. *Impartial Reason*. Ithaca: Cornell University Press, 1983.

Goldman, Alan H. *Moral Knowledge*. London: Routledge, 1988.

Paul, Ellen Frankel et al., eds. *The New Social Contract: Essays on Gauthier*. Oxford: Basil Blackwell, 1988.

Russell, Hardin., ed. *Symposium on David Gauthier's Morals by Agreement*. *Ethics*, 97 (1987).

Ullmann-Margalit, Edna. *The Emergence of Norms*. Oxford: The Clarendon Press, 1977.

Vallentyne, Peter., ed. *Contractarianism and Rational Choice*: *Essays on David Gauthier's Morals by Agreement*. New York: Cambridge University Press, 1990.

b. Articles

Arneson, Richard J. "Locke Versus Hobbes in Gauthier's Ethics." *Inquiry*, 30 (1987), 295-316.

Baier, Annette C. "Pligrim's Progress." *Canadian Journal of Philosophy*, 18 (1988), 315-30.

Bales, R. Eugene. "Act-Utilitarianism: Account of Right-Making Characteristics or Decision-Making Procedure?" *American Philosophical Quarterly*, 8 (1971), 257-65.

Barnett, Philip M. "Rational Behavior in Bargaining Situations." *Nôus*, 17 (1983), 621-36.

Betram, Morris. "Gauthier on Hobbes' Moral and Political Philosophy." *Philosophy and Phenomenological Research*, 33 (1973), 387-92.

Braybrooke, David. "Social Contract Theory's Fanciest Flight." in *Symposium on David Gauthier's Morals by Agreement*. *Ethics*, 97 (1987), 750-764.

Bovens, Luc. "Review of 'Morals by Agreement.'" *Theory and Decision*, 24 (1988), 289-93.

Buchanan, Allen. "Justice as Reciprocity versus Subject-centered Justice." *Philosophy & Public Affairs*, 19 (1990), 227-52.

Campbell, Richmond. "Moral Justification and Freedom." *The Journal of Philosophy*, 85 (1988), 192-213.

_____. "Critical Study: Gauthier's Theory of Morals by Agreement." *The Philosophical Quarterly*, 38 (1989), 343-64.

Copp, David. "Review of 'Morals by Agreement.'" *The Philosophical Review*, 98 (1989), 411-14.

Danielson, Peter. "The Visible Hand of Morality." *Canadian Journal of Philosophy*, 18 (1988), 357-84.

Darwall, Stephen L. "Rational Agent, Rational Act." *Philosophical Topics*, 14 (1986), 33-57.

Dayton, Eric. "Utility Maximizers and Cooperative Understandings." *Ethics*, 90 (1970), 130-41.

Freeman, Samuel. "Reason and Agreement in Social Contract Views." *Philosophy & Public Affairs*, 19 (1990), 122-57.

Griffin, Nicholsa. "Aboriginal Rights: Gauthier's Arguments for Despoliation." *Dialogue*, 20 (1981), 690-96.

Hampton, Jean. "Can We Agree On Morals?" *Canadian Journal of Philosophy*, 18 (1988), 331-56.

Hannaford, R.V. "Gauthier, Hobbes and Hobbesians." *International Journal of Moral and Social Sciences*, 3 (1988), 239-54.

Hausman, Daniel M. "Are Markets Morally Free Zones?" *Philosophy & Public Affairs*, 18 (1989), 317-333.

Hubin, Donald C. and Mark B. Lambeth. "Providing for Rights." *Dialogue* 27 (1988), 489-502.

Jolley, Nicholas. "Hobbes's Dagger in the Heart." *Canadian Journal of Philosophy*, 17 (1987), 855-74.

Kavka, Gregory. "Review of Gauthier's *Morals by Agreement*." *Mind*, 96 (1987), 117-21.

Kraus Jody S. and Coleman, Jules L. "Morality and the Theory of Rational Choice." in *Symposium on Gauthier's Morals by Agreement'*. *Ethics*, 97 (1987), 715-40.

Lomasky, Loren E. "Agreeable Morality?" *Critical Review*, 2 (1988), 36-49.

MacIntosh, Duncan. "Libertarian Agency and Rational Morality: Action-Theoretic Objections to Gauthier's Dispositional Solution of the Compliance Problem." *The Southern Journal of Philosophy*, 26 (1988), 499-525.

_____. "Two Gauthiers?" *Dialogue*, 28 (1989), 43-61.

McMachan, Christopher. "Promising and Coordination." *American Philosophical Quarterly*, 26 (1989), 239-247.

Mendola, Joseph. "Gauthier's *Morals by Agreement* and Two Kinds of Rationality." in *Symposium on Gauthier's 'Morals by Agreement'*. *Ethics*, 97 (1987), 765-774.

Narveson, Jan. "Review of Gauthier's *Morals by Agreement*." *International Philosophical Quarterly*, 27 (1987), 336-38.

_____. "McDonald and McDogal, Pride and Gain, and Justice: Comment on a Criticism of Gauthier." *Dialogue*, 27 (1989), 503-6.

Nelson, Alan. "Economic Rationality and Morality." *Philosophy & Public Affairs*, 17 (1988), 149-66.

Nelson, William N. "Justice and Rational Cooperation." *Southern Journal of Philosophy*, 14 (1976), 303-12.

Perkins, Michael and Donald C. Hubin. "Self-Subverting Principles of Choice." *Canadian Journal of Philosophy*, 16 (1986), 1-10.

Provis, C. "Gauthier on Coordination." *Dialogue*," 16 (1977), 507-09.

Ripstein, Arthur. "Gauthier's Liberal Individual." *Dialogue*, 28 (1989), 63-76.

Sobel, Jordan Howard. "Maximizing, Optimizing, and Prospering." *Dialogue*, 27 (1988), 233-62.

Summer, L.W. "Justice Contracted." *Dialogue*, 16 (1987), 523-548.

Vallentyne, Peter. "Critical Notice: Gauthier on Rationality and Morality." *Eidos*, 1 (1986), 79-95.

Weirich, Paul. "Hierarchical Maximization of Two Kinds of Expected Utility." *Philosophy of Science*, 55 (1988), 560-82.

Wolfram, Sybil. "Review of Gauthier's *Morals by Agreement*." *Philosophical Books*, 28 (1987), 129-34.

II. Rationality and The Theory of Rational Choice

A. Books

Agassi, Joseph and Ian Charles Jarvie, eds. *Rationality: The Critical View*. Dordrecht: Martinus Nijhoff Publishers, 1987.

Arrow, Kenneth J. *Social Choice and Individual Values*. 2nd edn. New Haven: Yale University Press: 1951.

Axelrod, Robert. *The Evolution of Cooperation*. Oxford: Oxford University Press, 1984.

Basu, Kaushik. *Revealed Preference of Government.* Cambridge: Cambridge University Press, 1980.

Bell, David., and Howard Raiffa, and Amos Tversky, eds. *Decision Making: Descriptive, Normative, and Prescriptive Interactions.* Cambridge: Cambridge University Press, 1988.

Benn, S.I. and G.W. Mortimore, eds. *Rationality and the Social Sciences: Contributions to the Philosophy and Methodology of the Social Sciences.* London: Routledge & Kegan Paul, 1976.

Bennett, Jonathan. *Rationality.* London: Routledge & Kegan Paul, 1964.

Biderman, Shlomo., and Ben-Ami Scharfstein, eds. *Rationality in Question: On Eastern and Western Views of Rationality.* Leiden: E.J. Brill, 1989.

Bonner, John. *Introduction to the Theory of Social Choice.* Baltimore: The Johns Hopkins University Press, 1986.

Brown, Harold I. *Rationality.* New York: Routledge, 1988.

Brubaker, Rogers. *The Limits of Rationality: An Essay on the Social and Moral and Thought of Max Weber.* London: George Allen & Unwin, 1984.

Buchanan, James. *The Limits of Liberty: Between Anarchy and Leviathan.* Chicago: The University of Chicago Press, 1975.

_____. and G. Tullock. *The Calculus of Consent: Logical Foundations of Constitutional Democracy.* Ann Arbor: University of Michigan Press, 1962.

_____. *Freedom in Constitutional Contract.* College Station and London: Texas A&M University Press, 1977.

_____. *What Should Economist Do?* Indianapolis: Liberty Press, 1979.

_____. and Robert D. Tollison. eds. *The Theory of Public Choice II*. Ann Arbor: The University of Michigan Press, 1984.

_____. *Economics: Between Predictive Science and Moral Philosophy*. Texas A&M University Press, College Station, 1987.

_____. *Explorations into Constitutional Economics*. Austin: Texas A&M University Press, 1989.

Calabresi, Guido and Philip Bobbitt. *Tragic Choice: The Conflicts Society Confronts in the Allocation of Tragically Scarce Resources*. New York: W.W. Norton & Co., 1978.

Campbell, Richmond and Lanning Sowden, eds. *Paradoxes of Rationality and Cooperation: Prisoner's Dilemma and Newcomb's Problem*. Vancouver: The University of British Columbia Press, 1985.

Cherniak, Christopher. *Minimal Rationality*. Cambridge: MIT Press, 1986.

Colman, Andrew M. *Game Theory and Experimental Games: A Study of Strategic Interaction*. Oxford: Pergamon Press, 1982.

Downs, A. *An Economic Theory of Democracy*. New York: Haper, 1957.

Dyke, C. *Philosophy of Economics*. Englewood Cliffs: Prentice-Hall, 1981.

Elster, Jon. *Ulysses and the Sirens: Studies in Rationality and Irrationality*. Cambridge: Cambridge University Press, 1979.

_____. *Sour Grapes: Studies in the Subversion of Rationality*. Cambridge: Cambridge University Press, 1983.

_____., ed. *The Multiple Self*. Cambridge: Cambridge University Press, 1986.

_____., ed. *Rational Choice*. New York: New York University Press, 1986.

_____. *Cement of Society: A Study of Social Order*. Cambridge: Cambridge University Press, 1989.

Etzioni, Amitai. *The Moral Dimension: Toward a New Economics*. New York: The Free Press, 1988.

Friedrich, Carl J., ed. *Rational Decision: Nomos* VII. New York: Atherton Press, 1964.

Frohock, Fred M. *Rational Association*. Syracuse: Syracuse University Press, 1987.

Gärdenfors, Peter and Nils-Eric Sahlin, eds. *Decision, Probability, and Utility*. Cambridge: Cambridge University Press, 1988.

Geraets, Theodore F., ed. *Rationality To-Day*. Ottawa: The University of Ottawa Press, 1979.

Godelier, Maurice. *Rationality and Irrationality in Economics*. trans. Brian Pearce. New York: Monthly Review Press, 1972.

Goodin, Robert E. *The Politics of Rational Man*. London: John Wiley & Sons, 1976.

Gottinger, Hans and Werner Leinfeller, eds. *Decision Theory and Social Ethics: Issues in Social Choice*. Dordrecht: D. Reidel Publishing Company, 1978.

Hahn, Frank and Martin Hollis, eds. *Philosophy and Economic Philosophy*. Oxford: Oxford University Press, 1979.

Hamlin, Alan P. *Ethics, Economics and the State*. New York: St. Martin's Press, 1986.

Hardin, Russell. *Collective Action*. Baltimore: Johns Hopkins University, 1982.

_____., ed. *Symposium on Rationality and Morality. Ethics,* 96 (1985).

Harsanyi, John C. *Essays on Ethics, Social Behavior, and Scientific Explanation.* Dordrecht: D. Reidel Publishing Company, 1976.

_____. *Rational Behavior and Bargaining Equilibrium in Games and Social Situations.* Cambridge: Cambridge University Press, 1977.

Hausman, Daniel M., ed. *The Philosophy of Economics.* Cambridge: Cambridge University Press, 1984.

Heath, Anthony. *Rational Choice and Social Exchange.* Cambridge: Cambridge University Press, 1976.

Hilpinen, Risto., ed. *Rationality in Science: Studies in the Foundations of Science and Ethics.* Dordrecht: D. Reidel Publishing Company, 1980.

Hindess, Barry. *Choice, Rationality, and Social Theory.* London: Unwin Hyman, 1988.

Hollis, Martin., and Edward J. Nell. *Rational Economic Man: A Philosophical Critique of Neo-Classical Economics.* London: Cambridge University Press, 1975.

_____. and Steven Lukes, eds. *Rationality and Relativism.* Cambridge: The MIT Press, 1982.

Hogarth, Robin M, and Melvin W. Reder, eds. *Rational Choice: The Contrast between Economics and Psychology.* Chicago: University of Chicago Press, 1986.

Hooker, C.A. et al. eds. *Foundations and Applications of Decision Theory.* 2 vols. Dordrecht: D. Reidel Publishing Company, 1978.

Kelly, J.S. *Arrow's Impossibility Theorem.* New York: Academic Press, 1978.

Kekes, John. *A Justification of Rationality.* Albany: State University of New York Press, 1976.

Lea, Stephene., Roger Tarpy, and Paul Webley. *The Individual in the Economy: A Survey of Economic Psychology.* Cambridge: Cambridge University Press, 1987.

Leibenstein, Harvey. *Beyond Economic Man: A New Foundation for Microeconomics.* Cambridge: Harvard University Press, 1976.

Levi, Isaac. *Hard Choices: Decision Making Under Unresolved Conflict.* Cambridge: Cambridge University Press, 1987.

Luce, R.D. and H. Raiffa. *Games and Decisions.* New York: Wiley, 1957.

Machlup, Fritz. *Methodology of Economics and Other Social Sciences.* New York: Academic Press, 1978.

Mackay, Alfred. *Arrow's Theorem: The Paradox of Choice; A Case Study in the Philosophy of Economics.* New Haven: Yale University Press, 1980.

Margolis, Howard. *Selfishness, Altruism, and Rationality: A Theory of Social Choice.* Cambridge: Cambridge University Press, 1982.

Margolis, J., M. Krauz, and R.M. Burian. *Rationality, Relativism, and the Human Sciences.* Dordrecht: Martinus Nijhoff, 1986.

Marsden, David. *The End of Economic Man* (Brighton, Sussex: Wheat Sheat, 1986).

McClennen, Edward F. *Rationality and Dynamic Choice: Foundational Explorations.* New York: Cambridge University Press, 1990.

Mele, Alfred R. *Irrationality: An Essay on Akrasia, Self-Deception and Self-Control*. New York: Oxford University Press, 1987.

Moser, Paul K., ed. *Rationality in Action: Contemporary Approaches*. New York: Cambridge University Press, 1990.

Mueller, D.C. *Public Choice*. Cambridge: Cambridge University Press, 1979.

Nathanson, Stephen. *The Ideal of Rationality*. Atlantic Highlands: Humanities Press, 1985.

Norman, Richard. *Reasons For Actions: A Critique of Utilitarian Rationality*. New York; Barnes & Nobel, 1971.

Olson, Mancur. *The Logic of Collective Action*. Cambridge: Cambridge University Press, 1965.

Ordeshook, Peter C. *Game Theory and Political Theory*. Cambridge: Cambridge University Press, 1986.

Pears, David. *Motivated Irrationality*. New York: Oxford University Press, 1984.

Rescher, Nicholas. *Rationality: A Philosophical Inquiry into the Nature and the Rationale of Reason*. Oxford: Clarendon Press, 1988.

Resnik, Michael D. *Choices: An Introduction to Decision Theory*. Minneapolis: University of Minnesota Press, 1987.

Robinson, Joan. *Economic Philosophy*. Chicago: Alding Publishing Co., 1962.

Roemer, John., ed. *Analytical Marxism*. Cambridge: Cambridge University Press, 1986.

Rosenberg, Alexander. *Microeconomic Laws: A Philosophical Analysis*. Pittsburgh: University of Pittsburgh Press, 1976.

Roth, Paul A. *Meaning and Method in the Social Sciences*. Ithaca: Cornell University Press, 1987.

Rowley, C. and A. Peacock. *Welfare Economics: A Liberal Restatement*. London: Martin Robertson, 1975.

Schick, Frederic. *Having Reasons: An Essay on Rationality and Society*. Princeton: Princeton University Press, 1984.

Schotter, Andrew. *Free Market Economics: A Critical Appraisal*. New York: St. Martin's Press, 1985.

Sen, Amartya. *Collective Choice and Social Welfare*. San Francisco: Holden-Day, Inc., 1970.

_____. *Choice, Welfare and Measurement*. Oxford: Blackwell, 1982.

_____. *On Ethics and Economics*. Oxford: Basil Blackwell, 1987.

Simon, Hebert A. *Models of Man: Social and Rational*. New York: John Wiley & Sons, 1957.

_____. *Models of Bounded Rationality*. vol.I. *Economic Analysis and Public Policy*. Cambridge: Cambridge University Press, 1982.

Skyrms, Brian. *The Dynamics of Rational Deliberation*. Cambridge: Harvard University Press, 1990.

Slote, Michael. *Beyond Optimizing: A Study of Rational Choice*. Cambridge: Harvard University Press, 1989.

Tammy, Martin and K. D. Irani, eds. *Rationality in Thought and Action*. New York: Greenwood Press, 1986.

Van Den Doel, Hans. *Democracy and Welfare Economics*. trans. Brigid Biggins. Cambridge: Cambridge University Press, 1979.

Von Neuman, J. and O. Morgenstern. *Theory of Games and Economic Behavior*. Princeton: Princeton University Press, 1944.

Wilson, Brayan., ed. *Rationality*. Evanston: Haper & Row, 1970.

B. Articles

Arrow, K.J. "Values and Collective Decision-Making." in *Philosophy, Politics, and Society*. 3rd ser. Oxford: Basil Blackwell, 1967., 215-32.

_____. and L. Hurwicz. "An Optimality Criterion for Decision-Making." in *Uncertainty and Expectations in Economics*. eds. C.F. Carter and J.L. Ford. Oxford: Oxford University Press, 1972.

_____. "Some Ordinalist-Utilitarian Notes on Rawls' Theory of Justice." *The Journal of Philosophy*, 70 (1973), 245-63.

_____. "Current Developments in the Theory of Social Choice." *Social Research*, 44 (1977), 607-22.

_____. "Formal Theories of Social Welfare." in *Dictionary of the History of Ideas*. ed. P. Wiener. New York: Charles Scribner's Sons, 1973.

_____. "Extended Sympathy ands the Possibility of Social Choice." *Philosophia*, 7 (1978), 223-37.

_____. "Rawls' Principle of Just Saving." in *Collected Works of Kenneth J. Arrow*. vol.I. *Social Choice and Justice*. Cambridge: The Belknap Press of Harvard University Press, 1983., 133-46.

Ball, Stephen W. "Choosing Between Choice Models of Ethics." *Theory and Decision*, 22 (1987), 209-24.

Benneth, Kenneth D. "Contemporary Irrationalism and the Idea of Rationality." *Studies in Philosophy and Education*, 6 (1967-68), 317-40.

Buchanan, Allen. "Revolutionary Motivation and Rationality." *Philosophy and Public Affairs*, 9 (1979), 59-82.

Buchanan, James and Loren E. Lomasky. "The Matrix of Contractarian Justice." in *Liberty and Equality*. eds. Ellen Frankel Paul et al. Oxford: Oxford University Press, 1985., 12-32.

Coleman, Jules L. "Market Contractarianism and the Unanimity Rule." in *Ethics and Economics*. eds. Ellen Frankel Paul et al. Oxford: Oxford University Press, 1985., 69-114.

Dahrendorf, Ralf. "Homo Sociologicus." in *Essays on the Theory of Society*. London: Routledge & Kegan Paul, 1968.

Diesing, Paul. "The Nature and Limitations of Economic Rationality." *Ethics*, 61 (1950), 12-26.

Edwards, W. "The Theory of Decision Making." in *Decision Making*. eds. Ward Edwards and Amos Tversky. Baltimore: Penguin Books, 1967., 13-64.

Friedman, Milton. "The Methodology of Positive Economics." in *Essays in Positive Sciences*. Chicago: University of Chicago Press, 1953.

Hamlin, Alan. "Liberty, Contract and the State." in *Good Polity*: *Normative Analysis of the State*. eds. Alan Hamlin and Philip Pettit. Oxford: Basil Blackwell, 1989.

Hardin, Russell. "Difficulties in the Notion of Economic Rationality." *Social Science Information*, 23 (1984), 453-467.

Harsanyi, John C. "Can the Maximin Principle Serve as a Basis for Morality?" *The American Political Science Review*, 69 (1975), 594-606.

_____. "Morality and the Theory of Rational Behavior." in *Utilitarianism and Beyond*. eds. A. Sen and B. Williams. Cambridge: Cambridge University Press, 1982., 39-62.

_____. "Basic Moral Decisions and Alternative Concepts of Rationality." *Social Theory and Practice*, 9 (1983), 231-44.

_____. "Does Reason Tell Us What Moral Code to Follow and, Indeed, to Follow Any Moral Code at All?" *Ethics*, 96 (1985), 42-55.

_____. "Review of Gauthier's *Morals by Agreement.*" *Economics and Philosophy*, 3 (1987), 339-351.

Lippke, Richard L. "The Rationality of the Egoist' Half-Way House." *The Southern Journal of Philosophy*, 25 (1987), 515-28.

Luke, Timothy W. "Reason and Rationality in Rational Choice Theory." *Social Research*, 52 (1985), 65-98.

_____. "Methodological Individualism: The Essential Ellipsis of Rational Choice Theory." *Philosophy of the Social Sciences*, 17 (1987), 341-55.

Machina, Mark J. "Rational Decision Making versus Rational Decision Modelling?" *Journal of the Mathematical Psychology*, 24 (1981), 163-175.

McClennen, Edward F. "Rational Choice and Public Policy: A Critical Essays." *Social Theory and Practice*, 9 (1983), 335-379.

Mueller, D.C., R.D. Tollison, and T.D. Willett. "The Utilitarian Contract: A Generalization of Rawls' Theory of Justice." *Theory and Decision*, 4 (1974), 345-67.

Pettit, Philip. "Rational Man Theory." in *Actions & Interpretation*: *Studies in the Philosophy of the Social Sciences*. eds. Christopher Hookway and Philip Pettit. Cambridge: Cambridge University Press, 1978., 43-63.

Ploit, Charles R. "Axiomatic Social Choice Theory: An Overview and Interpretation." *Journal of Political Sciences*, 20 (1976), 511-96.

Rae, Douglas W. "The Limits of Consensual Decision." *The American Political Science Review*, 69 (1975), 1270-98.

Roemer, John. "The Mismarriage of Bargaining Theory and Distributive Justice." *Ethics*, 97 (1986), 88-110.

Seabright, Paul. "Social Choice and Social Theories." *Philosophy and Public Affairs*, 18 (1984), 365-387.

Schelling, Thomas. "Game Theory and the Study of Ethical Systems." *Journal of Conflict Resolution*, 12 (1968), 34-44.

_____. "Some Thoughts on the Relevance of Game Theory to the Analysis of Ethical System." in *Game Theory in the Behavioral Sciences*. eds. Ira R. Buchler and Hugo G.Nutini. Pittsburgh: University of Pittsburgh Press, 1969., 53-60.

Schwartz, Thomas. "Rationality and the Myth of Maximum." *Nôus*, 6 (1972), 97-117.

Sen, Amartya. "Impossibility of A Paretian Liberal." *The Journal of Political Economy*, 78 (1970), 152-7.

_____. "Choice, Orderings and Morality." in *Practical Reasoning*. ed. Stephan Körner. New Haven: Yale University Press, 1974., 54-82.

_____. "Rational Fools: A Critique of the Behavioral Foundations of Economic Theory." *Philosophy & Public Affairs*, 6 (1976-7), 317-44.

_____. "Rationality and Uncertainty." *Theory and Decision*, 18 (1985), 109-27.

_____. "Foundations of Social Choice Theory: An Epilogue." in *Foundations of Social Choice Theory*. eds. Jon Elster and Aanund Hylland. Cambridge: Cambridge University Press, 1986., 213-248.

Schutz, Alfred. "The Problems of Rationality in the Social World." *Econometrica*, 10 (1943). Rpt. Dorothy Emmet and Alasdair MacIntyre, eds. *Sociological Theory and Philosophical Analysis*. New York: The Macmillan, 1970., 89-114.

Shue, Henry. "The Current Fashions: Trickle-Downs by Arrow and Close-Knits by Rawls." *The Journal of Philosophy*, 71 (1974), 319-27.

Strasnick, Steven. "The Problems of Social Choice: From Arrow to Rawls." *Philosophy and Public Affairs*, 5 (1975), 793-804.

Suppes, Patrick. "Decision Theory." in *The Encyclopedia of Philosophy*. ed. Paul Edwards. New York: The Macmillan Company & Free Press, 1967.

Tuck, Richard. "Is There a Free-rider Problem, and If So, What is it?" in *Rational Action*. ed. Ross Harrison. Cambridge: Cambridge University Press, 1979., 147-156.

Weber, Max. "The Meaning of 'Ethical Neutrality' in Sociology and Economics." in *The Methodology of Social Sciences*. eds. and trans. E.A. Shils and H.A. Finch. Glenco: The Free Press, 1949.

III. Critiques of Contractarian Liberal Ethics and Other Works Cited.

A. Books

Aristotle. *Nicomachean Ethics*. trans. Terence Irwin. Indianapolis: Hackett Publishing Company, 1985.

Baier, Kurt. *The Moral Point of View: A Rational Basis of Ethics*. Ithaca, NY: Cornell University Press, 1958.

Bell, Daniels. *The End of Ideology*. Cambridge: Harvard University Press, 1960; with new Afterword, 1988.

Bentham, Jeremy. *An Introduction to the Principle of Morals and Legislation*. Oxford: Blackwell, 1948.

Braithwaite, R.B. *Theory of Games as a Tool for the Moral Philosopher*. Cambridge: Cambridge University Press, 1955.

Brittan, Samuel. *A Restatement of Economic Liberalism*. Atlantic Highlands: Humanities Press, 1988.

Blanshard, Brand. *Reason and Goodness*. London: G. Allen, 1961.

Cahoone, Lawrence E. *The Dilemma of Modernity: Philosophy, Culture, and Anti-Culture*. Albany: The State University of New York Press, 1988.

Clarke, S.G. and Evan Simpson, eds. *Anti-Theory and Moral Conservatism*. Albany: State University of New York Press, 1989.

Cohen, Ronald L. *Justice: Views from the Social Science*. New York: Plenum Press, 1986.

Dallmayr, Fred R., ed. *From Contract to Community: Political Theory at the Crossroads*. New York: Marcel Dekker, 1978.

Damico, Alfonso., ed. *Liberals on Liberalism*. Totowa: Rowman & Littlefield, 1986.

De Jasay, Anthony. *Social Contract, Free Ride: A Study of the Public Goods Problem*. Oxford: Oxford University Press, 1989.

Demarco, Joseph and Richard M. Fox, eds. *New Directions in Ethics*. London: Routledge & Kegan Paul, 1986.

Dewey, John. *Theory of Moral Life*. New Delhi: Wiley Eastern Private Limited., 1967.

Dunn, John. *Rethinking Modern Political Theory*. Cambridge: Cambridge University Press, 1985.

Dworkin, Gerald. et al. eds. *Markets and Morals*. Washington: Hemisphere Publishing Co., 1977.

Engels, Frederick. *The Origin of Family, Private Property, and the State*. New York: International Publishing Co., 1942.

Fallers, Lloyd A. *Inequality: Social Stratification Reconsidered*. Chicago: University of Chicago Press, 1973.

Foucault, Michel. *The Order of Things: An Archaeology of the Human Sciences*. New York: Vintage Books, 1970.

Fotion, Nicholas. *Moral Situations*. Yellow Springs: The Antioch Press, 1968.

French, Peter., ed. *Ethical Theory: Character and Virtue*. vol.xiii. *Midwest Studies in Philosophy*. Notre Dame: University Press of Notre Dame, 1988.

Friedman, Milton. *Capitalism and Freedom*. Chicago: University of Chicago Press, 1962.

Gablik, Suzi. *Has Modernism Failed?* New York: Theme & Hudson, 1984.

Gaus, Gerald F. *Modern Liberal Theory of Man*. London: Croom Helm, 1983.

Gert, Bernard. *The Moral Rules: A New Rational Foundation For Morality*. New York: Haper & Row Publishers, 1966.

Gewirth, Alan. *Reason and Morality*. Chicago: The University of Chicago Press, 1978.

Gillman, Joseph. *The Falling Rate of Profit: Marx's Law and Its Significance to Twentieth Century Capitalism*. New York: Cameron Associates, 1985.

Gordis, Robert. *Politics and Ethics*. Santa Barbara, California: Center for the Study of Democratic Institutions, 1961.

Gordon, David. *Critics of Marxism*. New Brunswick: Transaction Books, 1986.

Gordon Scott. *Welfare, Justice, and Freedom*. New York: Columbia University Press, 1980.

Gouinlock, James. *John Dewey's Philosophy of Value*. New York: Humanities Press, 1972.

_____. *The Moral Writings of John Dewey*. New York: Hafner Press, 1976.

_____. *Excellence in Public Discourse: John Stuart Mill, John Dewey, and Social Intelligence*. New York: Teacher's College Press, 1985.

Gould, Carol. C. *Rethinking Democracy*. Cambridge: Cambridge University Press, 1988.

Grant, George. *Technology and Empire*. Toronto: Anansi, 1969.

_____. *English-Speaking Justice*. Notre Dame: University of Notre Dame Press, 1985.

_____. *Technology & Justice*. Notre Dame: University of Notre Dame Press, 1986.

Grice, G. R. *The Grounds of Moral Judgment*. Cambridge: The University Press, 1967.

Habermas, Jürgen. *The Theory of Communicative Action*. vol.i. *Rationality and Rationalization*. trans. T. McCarthy. Boston: Beacon Press, 1984.

_____. *New Conservatism*. trans. S.W. Nicholsen. Cambridge: Cambridge University Press, 1989.

Haan, Norma et al. eds. *Social Science as Moral Inquiry*. New York: Columbia University Press, 1983.

Hare, R. M. *Freedom and Reason*. Oxford: Oxford University Press, 1963.

Hayek, Friedrich. *Law, Legislation, and Liberty*. 3 vols. Chicago: University of Chicago Press, 1973; 1976; 1979.

_____. *The Fatal Conceit: The Errors of Socialism*. Chicago: University of Chicago Press, 1989.

Herzog, Don. *Happy Slaves: A Critique of Consent Theory*. Chicago: University of Chicago Press, 1989.

Hofstadter, R. *Social Darwinism in American Thought*. Boston: Beacon Press, 1955.

Hume, David. *A Treatise of Human Nature*. ed. L.A. Selby-Bigge. 2nd edn. Oxford: Oxford University Press, 1978.

_____. *An Enquiry concerning the Principles of Morals* in L.A. Selby-Bigge., ed. *Enquiries concerning Human Understanding and concerning the Principles of Morals*, 3rd edn. Oxford: Oxford University Press, 1975.

Kekes, John. *Moral Tradition and Individuality*. Princeton: Princeton University Press, 1989.

Keynes, J.M. *Economic Consequences of the Peace*. London: Macmillan, 1919.

Körner, Stephan., ed. *Practical Reason*. New Haven: Yale University Press, 1974.

Krauz, M., ed. *Relativism: Interpretation and Confrontation*. Notre Dame: University of Notre Dame Press, 1989.

Larmore, E. Charles. *Patterns of Moral Complexity*. Cambridge: Cambridge University Press, 1987.

Lee, Keekok. *A New Basis of Moral Philosophy*. London: Routledge & Kegan Paul, 1985.

Leuiss, William. *C.B. Macpherson: Dilemmas of Liberalism and Socialism*. New York: St. Martin's Press, 1988.

Livingston, Donald. *Hume's Philosophy of Common Life*. Chicago: The University of Chicago Press, 1984.

Lucash, Frank S., ed. *Justice and Equality: Here and Now*. Ithaca: Cornell University Press, 1986.

MacIntyre, Alasdair. *After Virtue*. 2nd ed. Notre Dame: University of Notre Dame Press, 1984 (1st ed. 1981).

_____. *Whose Justice? Which Rationality?* Notre Dame, Indiana: University of Notre Dame Press, 1988.

_____. *Three Rival Versions of Moral Inquiry: Encyclopedia, Genealogy, and Tradition*. Notre Dame: University of Notre Dame Press, 1990.

Macpherson, C.B. *The Political Theory of Possessive Individualism: Hobbes to Locke*. Oxford: Oxford University Press, 1962.

_____. *Democratic Theory: Essays in Retrieval*. Oxford: Clarendon Press, 1973.

_____. *Rise and Fall of Economic Justice and Other Essays*. Oxford: Oxford University Press, 1985.

Marx, Karl. *Early Writings*. trans and ed. T.B. Bottomore. New York: McGraw Hill, 1963.

_____. *Karl Marx: Selected Writings*. ed. David McLellan. Oxford: Oxford University Press, 1977.

_____. and Engels. *Basic Writings on Politics & Philosophy*. ed. Lewis S. Feuer. Garden City: Anchor Books, 1959.

McLellan, David. *Ideology*. Minneapolis: University of Minnesota Press, 1986.

Mill, John Stuart. *Utilitarianism.* London: Collins, 1974.

Miller, Harlan B. and William H. Williams, eds. *The Limits of Utilitarianism,* Minneapolis: University of Minnesota Press, 1982.

Miles, Robert. *Capitalism and Unfree Labour: Anomaly or Necessity?* London: Tavistock Publications, 1987.

Morscher, E. and R. Stranzinger, eds. *Ethics: Foundations, Problems, and Applications.* Vienna: Hölder-Pichler-Tempsky, 1981.

Nagel, Thomas. *View from Nowhere.* Oxford: Oxford University Press, 1986.

Narveson, Jan. *Morality and Utility.* Baltimore: Johns Hopkins University Press, 1976.

_____. *The Libertarian Idea.* Philadelphia: Temple University Press, 1988.

Nietzsche, Friedrich. *Beyond Good and Evil.* trans. Walter Kaufmann. New York: Vintage Books, 1966.

Nozick, Robert. *Anarchy, State, And Utopia.* New York: Basic Books, 1974.

Olson, Robert G. *The Morality of Self-Interest.* New York: Harcourt Brace World, 1965.

Overing, Joanna. *Reason and Morality.* Tavistock: Tavistock Press, 1985.

Parfit, Derek. *Reasons and Persons.* Oxford: Oxford University Press, 1986.

Plato. *The Republic.* trans. G.M.A. Grube. Indianapolis: Hackett Publishing Company, 1974.

Raz, Joseph, ed. *Practical Reasoning*. Oxford: Oxford University Press, 1978.

_____. *Morality of Freedom*. Oxford: Clarendon Press, 1986.

Reeve, Andrew. *Property*. Atlantic Highlands: Humanities Press, 1986.

Replogle, Ron. *Recovering Social Contract*. Totowa: Roman & Littlefield, 1989.

Roemer, John E. *Free to Lose: An Introduction to Marxist Economic Philosophy*. Cambridge: Cambridge University Press, 1988.

Rorty, Richard. *Contingency, Irony, and Solidarity*. Cambridge: Cambridge University Press, 1989.

Ross, Andrew., ed. *Universal Abandon?: The Politics of Postmodernism*. Minneapolis: University of Minnesota Press, 1988.

Sandel, Michael J. *Liberalism and Limits of Justice*. Cambridge: Cambridge University Press, 1982.

_____., ed. *Liberalism and Its Critics*. New York: New York University Press, 1984.

Schwartz, Barry. *The Battle for Human Nature*. New York: W.W. Norton Co., 1986.

Seanor, Douglas and Nicholas Fotion. *Hare and Its Critics*. Oxford: Clarendon Press, 1988.

Sen, Amartya and Bernard Williams, eds. *Utilitarianism and Beyond*. Cambridge: Cambridge University Press, 1982.

Simpson, Evan., ed. *Anti-foundationalism and Practical Reasoning*. Edmonton: Academic Printing and Publishing, 1987.

Smith, Adam. *An Enquiry into the Nature and Causes of the Wealth of Nations*. ed. Edwin Cannan. Chicago: University of Chicago Press, 1976.

Sprigge, T.L.S. *The Rational Foundations of Ethics*. London: Routledge & Kegan Paul, 1988.

Stevenson, Leslie. *Seven Theories of Human Nature*. 2nd. edn. Oxford: Oxford University Press, 1974.

Stout, Jeffrey. *Ethics after Babel: The Language of Morals and their Discontents*. Boston: Beacon Press, 1988.

Summer, L.W. *The Moral Foundation of Rights*. Oxford: The Clarendon Press, 1987).

Taylor, Richard. *Good And Evil: A New Direction; A Forceful Attack on the Rationalistic Tradition in Ethics*. Buffalo: Prometheus Books, 1984.

Toulmin, Stephen. *An Examination of the Place of Reason in Ethics*. Cambridge: Cambridge University Press, 1950.

Unger, Robert M. *Knowledge and Politics*. New York: The Free Press, 1975.

Veatch, Henry. *Human Rights: Fact or Fancy?* Baton Rouge: Louisiana, 1985.

Waxman, Chaim. *The End of Ideology Debate*. New York: Funk & Wagnalls, 1968.

Weber, Max. *The Protestant Ethics and the Spirit of Capitalism*. trans. Talcott Parsons. London: Unwin Paperbacks, 1985.

_____. *General Economic Theory*. Brunswick: Transaction Books, 1982.

Williams, Bernard. *Ethics and Limits of Philosophy*. Cambridge: Massachusetts, Harvard University Press, 1985.

Winfield, Richard Dien. *Reason and Justice*. New York: State University of New York Press, 1988.

B. Articles

Althusser, Louis. "Ideology and Ideological State Apparatuses." in *Lenin and Philosophy and Other Essays*. trans. Ben Brewster. London: Monthly Review Press, 1971., 127-86.

Apel, Karl-Otto. "Normative Ethics and Strategical Rationality: The Philosophical Problem of a Political Ethics." *Graduate Faculty Philosophy Journal*, 9 (1982), 81-109.

Baier, Kurt. "The Conceptual Link between Morality and Rationality." *Nôus*, 16 (1982), 78-88.

_____. "Rationality and Morality." *Erkenntnis*, 11 (1977), 197-223.

Batens, Diderik. "Rationality and Ethical Rationality." *Philosophica*, 22 (1978), 23-43.

Brandt, Richard B. "Rational Desires." *Proceedings of the American Philosophical Association*, 43 (1969-70), 43-64.

_____. "Rationality, Egoism and Morality." *The Journal of Philosophy*, 69 (1972), 681-97.

Breiner, Peter. "Democratic Autonomy, Political Ethics, and Moral Luck." *Political Theory*, 17 (1989), 530-74.

Conee, Earl. "Utilitarianism and Rationality." *Analysis*, 42 (1982), 55-59.

Derrida, Jacques. "Structure, Sign, and Play in the Discourse of the Human Sciences." in *The Languages of Criticism and the Sciences of Man: The Structuralist Controversy*. eds. Richard Macksey and Eugenio Donato. Baltimore: Johns Hopkins University Press, 1970.

DiaQuattro, Arthur. "Market and Liberal Values." *Political Theory*, 8 (1990), 183-222.

Diggs, B. J. "Utilitarianism and Contractarianism." in *The Limits of Utilitarianism*. eds. Harlan B. Miller and William H. Williams. Minneapolis: University of Minnesota Press, 1982., 101-43.

Donagan, Alan. "Moral Rationalism and Variable Social Institutions." in *Midwest Studies in Philosophy*. Vol.7. eds. Peter A French, Theodore E. Uehling, Jr., and Howard K. Wettstein. Minneapolis: University of Minnesota Press, 1982., 3-10.

Elster, Jon. "Rationality, Morality, and Collective Action." *Ethics*, 96 (1985), 136-56.

Frankena, William K. "Concepts of Rational Action in the History of Ethics. *Social Theory and Practice*, 9 (1983), 165-98.

Galston, William. "Defending Liberalism." *The American Political Science Review*, 76 (1982), 621-29.

Gewirth, Alan. "The Future of Ethics: The Moral Powers of Reason." *Nôus*, 15 (1981), 15-40.

Gibson, Mary. "A Practical Link Between Morality and Rationality." *Nôus*, 16 (1982), 89-90.

Gouinlock, James. "Dewey." in *Ethics in the History of Western Philosophy*. eds. Robert J. Cavalier, James Gouinlock, and James P. Sterba. New York: St. Martin's Press, 1989., 306-228.

Habermas, Jürgen. "Modernity—An Incomplete Project." in *The Anti-Aesthetic*: *Essays on Postmodern Culture*. ed. Hal Foster. Port Townsend: Bay Press, 1983., 3-15.

_____. "Über Moralität und Sittlichkeit." in *Rationalität*. ed. H. Schnädelbach. Frankfurt: Suhrkamp, 1984., 218-35.

Hardwig, John. "The Achievement of Moral Rationality." *Philosophy and Rhetoric*, 6 (1973), 171-85.

Harrison, Bernard. "Morality and Interest." *Philosophy*, 64 (1989), 303-322.

Held, Virginia. "Non-Contractual Society." in *Science, Morality, and Feminist Theory*. eds. Marsh Hanen and Kai Nielsen. *Canadian Journal of Philosophy*, 13. suppl. (1987), 111-38.

Herring, Frances W. "What has Reason to do with Morality?" *The Journal of Philosophy*, 50 (1953), 688-97.

Kekes, John. "The Sceptical Challenge to Rationality." *Meta Philosophy*, 2 (1971), 121-136.

Kirzner, Israel. "Some Ethical Implications for Capitalism of the Socialist Calculational Debate." in *Capitalism*. eds. Ellen Frankel Paul et al. Oxford: Basil Blackwell, 1989., 165-82.

Loudon, Robert B. "Some Vices of Virtue Ethics." *American Philosophical Quarterly*, 21 (1984), 227-236.

Mandel, Ernest. "The Myth of Market Socialism." *New Left Review*, 169 (1988), 108-120.

Margolis, Joseph. "Moral and Rational." *The Journal of Value Inquiry*, 6 (1972), 286-93.

Miller, David. "Marx, Communism, and Market." *Political Theory*, 15 (1987), 182-204.

Mouffe, Chantel. "American Liberalism and Its Critics: Rawls, Taylor, Sandel, Walzer." *Praxis International*, 8 (1988), 193-205.

Mueller, D.C., R.D. Tollison and T.D. Willett. "The Utilitarian Contract: a Generalization of Rawls' Theory of Justice." *Theory and Decision*, 4 (1973-4), 350-62.

Nielsen, Kai. "Searching for an Emancipatory Perspective: Wide Reflective Equilibrium and the Hermeneutical Circle." in *Anti-Foundationalism*. ed. Evan Simpson., 143-63.

Perry, Charner M. "Bases, Arbitrary and Otherwise, For Morality: A Critique Criticized; the Arbitrary as a Basis For Rational Morality." *International Journal of Ethics*, 43 (1933), 127-166.

Prichard, H. A. "Does Moral Philosophy Rest on a Mistake?" *Mind*, 21 (1921). Rpt. in *Readings in Ethical Theory*. eds. Wilfrid Sellars and John Hospers. Englewood Cliffs: Prentice Hall, 1970., 86-105.

Ralls, Anthony. "Rational Morality for Empirical Man." *Philosophy*, 44 (1969), 205-216.

Rodewald, Richard A. "Does Liberalism Rest on a Mistake?" *Canadian Journal of Philosophy*, 15 (1985), 231-51.

Rorty, Richard. "Postmodernist Bourgeois Liberalism." *The Journal of Philosophy*, 80 (1983), 583-89.

_____. "The Priority of Democracy to Philosophy." in *The Virginia Statute for Religious Freedom*. eds. Merrill D. Peterson and Robert C. Vaughan. Cambridge: Cambridge University Press, 1988., 257-81.

Scanlon, T.M. "Liberty, Contract, and Contribution." in *Markets and Morals*. eds. Gerald Dworkin et al., 43-68.

_____. "Contractualism and Utilitarianism." in *Utilitarianism and Beyond*. eds. Amartya Sen and Bernard Williams. Cambridge: Cambridge University Press, 1982., 103-28.

Singer, Marcus George. "The Ideal of a Rational Morality." *Proceedings and Addresses of the American Philosophical Association*, 60 (1986), 15-38.

Sowden, Lanning and Sheldon Wein. "Justice and Rationality: Doubts about the Contractarian and Utilitarian Approaches." *Philosophia*, 17 (1987), 127-40.

Sterba, James P.   "A Marxist Dilemma For Social Contract Theory." *American Philosophical Quarterly*, 19 (1982), 51-60.

Veatch, Henry B. "The Rational Justification of Moral Principles: Can There Be Such a Thing?" *The Review of Metaphysics*, 29 (1975), 217-38.

Wild, John. "Ethics as A Rational Discipline and the Priority of the Good." *The Journal of Philosophy*, 51 (1954), 776-87.

Wolff, Robert Paul. "Reflections on Game Theory and the Nature of Value." *Ethics*, 72 (1962), 171-79.

Xenos, Nicholas.   "Liberalism and the Postulate of Scarcity." *Political Theory*, 15 (1987), 225-243.

Index